DEVELOPMENT COOPERATION *in a* FRACTURED GLOBAL ORDER

An ARDUOUS TRANSITION

FRANCISCO SAGASTI AND GONZALO ALCALDE

INTERNATIONAL DEVELOPMENT RESEARCH CENTRE

Published by the International Development Research Centre
PO Box 8500, Ottawa, ON, Canada K1G 3H9

Legal deposit: 2nd quarter 1999
National Library of Canada
ISBN 0-88936-889-9

The catalogue of IDRC Books may be consulted online at
http://www.idrc.ca/index_e.html

This book may be consulted online at http://www.idrc.ca/books/focus.html

CONTENTS

PREFACE

The international context for development efforts has undergone fundamental transformations during the last two decades. As a consequence, it is necessary to renew the repertoire of concepts to apprehend the realities of development finance and international cooperation. This essay aims at contributing some ideas to the debate on the future of development assistance. It traces the evolution of the institutional arrangements for development cooperation during the last five decades, examines the emergence of a fractured global order during the 1980s and 1990s, analyzes the frameworks that have been proposed to interpret these changes, and explores their implications for development finance and international cooperation.

Two rather different but complementary activities converged in the preparation of this work. In 1993, with support from the Carnegie Corporation of New York, I embarked on a major intellectual exercise to reinterpret the concepts of development and progress from the perspective of knowledge generation and use. Although the final report is still in preparation, the material gathered in this project provided most of the background information for Chapters 2, 3, and 4 of this book. At the same time, I was asked by the President of the Canadian International Development Research Centre (IDRC) to help in the design of strategies to cope with the changing context for development cooperation. Our interactions provided much of the material for Chapters 5 and 6. To complement these international engagements, my work as Director of the AGENDA: Perú program on development strategies and democratic governance provided a firm developing-country anchor for my international flights of fancy.

Along the way, I had the opportunity to prepare reports at the request of the Administrator, the Director of Policy and Planning, and the Head of Strategic Planning of the United Nations Development Programme (UNDP), the Chair of the United Nations Committee on Science and Technology for Development, the Secretary of the Development Committee of the World Bank, IDRC, and the Director the Carnegie Commission on Preventing Deadly Conflict. This allowed me to test some of my ideas and to learn from the experiences of these organizations. In addition, my participation in events organized by the Carnegie Corporation of New York, IDRC, the American Association for the Advancement of Science, the

Carter Center, UNDP, the International University Menéndez Pelayo and the Pablo Iglesias Foundation in Spain, the Inter-American Development Bank, the Latin American Economic System, the South American Peace Commission, and the Peruvian Diplomatic Academy, among other institutions, exposed me to the views of many experts on international development issues.

I would like to thank Patricia Rosenfield and Akin Adubifa from the Carnegie Corporation of New York for their continuous support and Pierre Beemans from IDRC for his encouragement and wise counsel. I also benefited greatly from many discussions and conversations with Silvia Charpentier, Geoffrey Oldham, John Hardy, David Hopper, Ruth Zagorin, James Gustav Speth, Elena Martínez, Sharon Capeling-Alakija, Carlos Lopes, Janet Donnelly, Uner Kirdar, Gus Edgren, Anders Vijkman, Felipe Gómez-Pallete, Pilar Cuevas, Alexander Shakow, Carl Dahlman, John Stremlau, Esther Brimmer, Colin Bradford, Michael Colby, Louis Emmerij, Manuel Castells, Carlos Contreras, Claudio Herzka, Allan Wagner, Jorge Valdez, Fernando Guillén, Max Hernández, Pepi Patrón, Helan Jaworski, Antonio Gonzáles Norris, and Mariano Valderrama. Eliana Chrem and Patricia Alcocer provided research assistance and administrative support, and Gonzalo Alcalde worked closely with me in the preparation of this essay and made many significant contributions to it.

Last, but not least, I want to express my appreciation and recognition to Keith Bezanson and David Hamburg for their unwavering support, encouragement, and friendship. Keith and David not only know about the fractures in the global order but are also doing something to bridge them. I dedicate this book to both of them.

Francisco Sagasti
Lima, Peru
April 1999

CHAPTER 1

INTRODUCTION

A new and as yet fluid world order is in the making as we begin the transition to the 21st century. Profound changes in all aspects of human activity are challenging established habits of thought and forcing a reinterpretation of what is meant by progress and development. As a consequence, the concept and practice of international cooperation for development are under close scrutiny and are undergoing major transformations.

Our times are the product of a particular set of historical processes that have unfolded over the last four centuries, which have witnessed the rise and worldwide spread of Western civilization. With the benefit of hindsight, it is possible to argue that what gave this period of human history its unique character was the articulation and implementation of what may be called the Baconian program, whose main architect was the philosopher Sir Francis Bacon, Lord Chancellor of the British Crown. Whereas the specific methodological and scientific contributions of Bacon have been the subject of debate, he was, during the early 17th century, the first to put forward a coherent view of how the power of modern science could be used to improve the human condition (Sagasti 1997b).

The Baconian program has been defined in the following terms: "to aim knowledge at power over nature, and to utilize power over nature for the improvement of the human lot" (Jonas 1984, p. 140). Three key features distinguish this program from other views of the production and use of knowledge current in Bacon's time: an awareness of the importance of appropriate research methods (scientific methodology), a clear vision of the purpose of the scientific enterprise (improving the human condition), and a practical understanding of the arrangements needed to put the program into practice (scientific institutions and state support). In later times, and particularly during the Enlightenment, the idea of indefinite, linear, and cumulative human progress would become the driving force of the Baconian program and give it a powerful and unique character that would allow it to withstand the test of time and endure until our days. Through the application of this idea, the human condition has improved in ways that Bacon and his contemporaries could hardly have imagined.

The main engine that made the Baconian program run was a belief in the unending, linear, and steady advance of humanity — the idea of progress — which mobilized human energies during the 18th and 19th centuries. Beginning with the Hellenistic and Roman notions that knowledge can be acquired step by step through experience and through trial and error, the idea of progress has evolved over the whole history of Western civilization. Cyclic conceptions of the universe in which events repeat themselves over the course of a "great year" had to be overcome before embracing a belief in the open-ended and cumulative character of advances in human history (Bury 1960; Jaki 1974; Nisbet 1980). Faith in a divine design for the cosmos played a major role in the evolution of the idea of progress during the Middle Ages. The Renaissance added a revaluation of the individual and of human actions as a means to improve the human condition while the scientific and geographical discoveries of the 16th and 17th centuries laid the ground for a belief in the inevitability of progress through the accumulation of knowledge (Heller 1981).

With the emergence and subsequent triumph of rationalism during the 17th, 18th, and 19th centuries, the idea of progress gradually lost its religious underpinnings. During the Enlightenment, it became a thoroughly secular idea, in which divine providence played a marginal role, if any. Progress acquired a distinctively social character and was seen as the almost inevitable result of human actions. Through the early 20th century, the general idea of progress would remain ingrained in Western minds as a positive driving force for improvements in the human condition, as the engine that made the Baconian program run.

However, the events that took place during the first 40 years of what Eric Hobsbawm has called the "Short Twentieth Century" challenged our beliefs in any notion of continuous and indefinite human progress. "The decades from the outbreak of the First World War to the aftermath of the Second, was an Age of Catastrophe for [Western] society. For forty years it stumbled from one calamity to another." This period stands in stark contrast to Hobsbawm's "Long Nineteenth Century" (from the 1780s to 1914), "which seemed, and actually was, a period of almost unbroken material, intellectual *and moral* progress." (Hobsbawm 1994, pp. 7, 13, his emphasis).

The decades that saw the carnage of World War I, the emergence of communism, the rise of fascism, the Great Depression, the Holocaust, World War II, and the atomic bombing of Hiroshima and Nagasaki could hardly be considered conducive to harbouring and nurturing the idea of progress. With the waning belief in the inevitability of progress, the achievements of the Baconian age also began to be seen as suspect.

Yet, the end of World War II changed the mood of gloom and despair of the "Age of Catastrophe." The triumph of the Allied forces over the Axis brought to the victors a new sense of optimism, satisfaction, and euphoria. The belief that purposeful interventions could improve the human condition was thus reinstated, but with considerable help from the availability of new techniques for managing the economy, planning investments and production, and organizing large-scale enterprises. Wartime advances in science and technology also found many civilian uses and spilled over into the private sector. The Age of Catastrophe was left behind, and a renewed faith in human progress took hold.

The development-cooperation experiment

One key expression of the renewed belief in progress was the emergence of the concept of development, which can be considered the latest incarnation of the idea of progress within the framework of the Baconian program. The notion of development implicit in the various definitions offered at that time could be summarized in the following terms: to achieve in the span of one generation the material standards of living that the industrialized West achieved in three generations or more, but without incurring in the heavy social costs the West had to pay or inflict on others. Development was also supposed to guarantee a minimum level of material comfort to all human beings.

Faith in the possibility of development was sustained and reinforced by the economic successes of the postwar decades. During the period from the late 1940s to the early 1970s, the world economy grew practically everywhere at an unprecedented pace. Jump-started by the financial resources, capital, consumer goods, and technical assistance offered under the Marshall Plan, European economies recovered and grew at nearly 5% a year. Led by Japan, the economies of Asia registered an average annual growth rate of 6%, and Eastern Europe grew at 4.7% a year; Latin America, at 5.3%; and even Africa, at 4.4%. As Angus Maddison put it,

> The years 1950 to 1973 were a golden age of unparalleled prosperity. World per capita GDP [gross domestic product] grew by 2.9 percent a year — more than three times as fast as in 1913–1950. World GDP rose 4.9 percent a year, and world exports 7 percent. The dynamism could be observed in all regions. In all of them, GDP per capita grew faster than in any other [period]. The acceleration was greatest in Europe and Asia.
>
> (Maddison 1995, p. 73)

This "Golden Age" of world economic growth was also a period of considerable international generosity. Added to a variety of other motivations, linked to economic and political interests, this generosity helped to expand international cooperation. Following the success of the Marshall Plan to support the postwar economic recovery of Europe, the United States launched the Point IV Program to expand bilateral aid to developing countries in 1949 and created the Technical Cooperation Administration to implement the Point IV Program (CCSTG 1992; Foreign Affairs 1997). The development-cooperation experiment was launched, and for the next two and one-half decades resources to assist poor countries increased continuously, which led to the creation of a large array of bilateral and multilateral institutions to channel and administer these resources.

However, right from the beginning, the onset of the Cold War hijacked the concept of development and the development-cooperation experiment, making them hostage to East–West rivalries. Two alternative ways of achieving development were put forward: one based on market economies and liberal democracy and the other based on central planning and a single-party system. In the decades that followed, each trumpeted its successes and sought to enlist the poor countries, many of which were emerging from decades or centuries of colonial rule in their camp. Developing countries became contested ground for trying one or another set of recipes to promote economic growth and improve living standards. Moreover, the East–West struggle became the lens through which practically all political, economic, and social events would be filtered and seen.

The Golden Age came to an end in the early 1970s, and the world entered into what Hobsbawm called the "Crisis Decades," which extended (although not uniformly) into the early 1990s: "The history of the twenty years after 1973 is that of a world which lost its bearings and slid into instability and crisis. And yet, until the 1980s it was not clear how irretrievably the foundations of the Golden Age had crumbled" (Hobsbawm 1994, p. 403). The sharp reductions in economic growth of the early and mid-1970s led to average rates of growth during the period of 1973–92 that, with the exception of the average growth rate in Asia, were substantively below those of the Golden Age. The slowdown was most noticeable in Eastern Europe and Africa, where the average rate of growth of gross domestic product (GDP) per capita was negative (−0.1% in each), and in Latin America, where the rate of economic growth barely exceeded that of population increases. The world average growth rate of GDP per capita during this period was 1.2%, in comparison with 2.9% for 1950–73.

During the early 1980s, the debt crisis in a large number of developing countries threatened the international financial system, and in advanced economies, both unemployment and social discontent increased significantly. The reversal of the socioeconomic gains of the previous 25 years made the 1980s a "Lost Decade" for most developing regions, with the notable exception of Southeast Asia. The major upheavals experienced by the Soviet Union and Eastern Europe during the second half of the 1980s and the early 1990s led to precipitous declines in living standards in these countries, and in Western Europe the economic recovery of the late 1980s and early 1990s did not manage to reduce unemployment rates. Following a prolonged period of economic stagnation in the early 1990s, Japan was seriously affected by the collapse of East Asian currencies and stock markets in 1997. Income inequalities worsened everywhere (with the exception of some East Asian countries), and for the first time since the Great Depression, poor and homeless people became highly visible in several cities in advanced industrial nations. The concept of "social exclusion" emerged, first in France and later in the European Union, to account for the reemergence of social problems that were thought to have been solved decades earlier (Rodgers et al. 1995).

The Crisis Decades that ended the Short Twentieth Century witnessed profound changes in all realms of human activity. We have seen the end of the Cold War, the spread of ethnic and religious violence, and the emergence of new international security concerns; the globalization of production and finance, the restructuring of international trade, and the transformation of productive and service activities; the disappearance of centrally planned economies and the worldwide expansion of capitalism (in many cases into areas that lack the supporting institutions for a functioning capitalist economy); and a host of social transformations, which include the demographic changes experienced by both rich and poor countries, the explosion of social demands in the developing regions, and the emergence of serious unemployment problems in both rich and poor nations.

To these transformations, it is necessary to add the extraordinary advances in scientific research and the accelerating pace of technological innovation; the renewed interest in ethical and spiritual matters; the growing role played by religious concerns, ethnic allegiances, and cultural identity in domestic and international politics; the prominence acquired by concerns for the environment and the sustainable use of natural resources; and the challenges posed by the need to renew governance structures at all levels, from the local to the global.

Such a bewildering and turbulent combination of changes and transformations, crystallizing in the emerging "fractured global order" (Sagasti 1989a,b), has created deep unease and uncertainty, which Hobsbawm described:

> The Short Twentieth Century ended in problems, for which nobody had,
> or even claimed to have, solutions. As citizens of the fin-de-siècle tapped

their way through the global fog that surrounded them, into the third
millennium, all they knew for certain was that an era of history had
ended. They knew very little else.

... The century ended in a global disorder whose nature was unclear,
and without an obvious mechanism for either ending it or keeping it
under control.

The reasons for this impotence lay not only in the genuine profundity
and complexity of the world's crisis, but also in the apparent failure of
all programmes, old and new, for managing or improving the affairs of
the human race.

(Hobsbawm, 1994, pp., 558–559, 562, 563)

The turbulence we are experiencing in the transition to a new century and
a new millennium signals more than just the end of a Golden Age, of the Cold
War, or of the Short Twentieth Century. It is an indication of the exhaustion of
the Baconian program that organized and mobilized human endeavours for nearly
four centuries and of the need to reassess the idea of progress that became its
driving force. In this light, the concept of development can be seen as the latest,
and possibly the last, attempt to reinterpret the idea of progress within the framework of the Baconian program. We are now beginning a transition to the post-
Baconian age, whose main features cannot as yet be discerned.

Because of the lags involved in reflecting on our experience and in trans-
mitting what we learn to the next generation of leaders and policymakers, we run
the risk of confronting the problems of the 21st century with the outmoded mind-
sets of the Short Twentieth Century. Most political authorities, business leaders,
and policymakers acquired their knowledge and experience during the Cold War,
some of them during the Golden Age of prosperity, and still others during the
Crisis Decades. The Cold War disappeared with surprising swiftness; the Golden
Age is long past; the Crisis Decades still bewilder us; and we are beginning a long
and uncertain journey into the post-Baconian age. If we are to enter the 21st century with a minimum of surety and aplomb, we must assimilate the lessons of
experience while unlearning the habits of thought that constrain our perceptions
and limit our capacity to apprehend the new realities.

Against this background, it can be seen that the development-cooperation
experiment of the past 50 years took place at a very special time in history. It was
also designed, organized, and carried out in ways that suited the spirit of those
times, which are now gone. The Cold War provided a stark ideological backdrop
to the experiment and helped justify allocating resources to it. An unprecedented
period of world-trade growth and economic expansion made it easier to accommodate the development-assistance needs of the poor nations. The dominance of the

economic and technological position of the United States, amply demonstrated through the success of the Marshall Plan, made the spread of the "American Way of Life" one of the implicit objectives of Western development assistance in its first decades. A sense of moral certitude, optimism, and generosity ensured ample public support for aid, first in the United States, and later in Europe and Japan.

The Soviet Union and its allies also expanded development assistance, focusing on those developing countries closely aligned with their ideological point of view. Soviet aid was seen as another weapon in the fight against Western capitalism and took the form primarily of subsidized exports of oil and machinery, as well as purchases of primary commodities above world-market prices. In addition, massive fellowship programs were established in practically all academic fields for developing-country nationals within their sphere of influence. All of this was in addition to the extensive provision of military assistance, a practice also common in the West.

A changed context for development finance and international cooperation

Over time, the institutions, ideas, and practices of development cooperation evolved and experienced many transformations. However, as the 20th century draws to a close, a multiplicity of signals indicate that the development-cooperation experiment, as we knew it, is coming to an end. Western official development assistance (ODA) flows to developing countries, which are usually channeled through bilateral and multilateral development-assistance agencies, have lost ground in relation to direct foreign investment, portfolio flows to emerging stock markets, and commercial bank lending, even though these private flows concentrate mostly on a few countries. Private firms that rate the risks of investments in countries and corporations (Moody, Standard & Poor, Duff and Phelps) have acquired enormous influence in the economic affairs of developing countries, as their views steer the flow of private funds in one or another direction. With the end of the Cold War, development-assistance flows from the former Soviet Union and East European countries were abruptly cut, and developing countries that relied on Soviet aid found themselves in a very difficult situation. The problem was particularly acute for countries such as Cuba, which depended on the Soviet Union for subsidized oil to its supply energy needs.

Development-assistance budgets have been cut in practically all donor countries at the same time as new tasks demand a growing share of a diminishing pool of public funds for international cooperation. Postconflict reconstruction, humanitarian relief, and assistance to refugees now compete with the support of democratic institutions, improvement of governance structures, assistance to transition economies, and efforts to fight drug traffic and crime. This has been squeezing out resources allocated to fields that once were the main focus of development assistance: health and population, food and nutrition, education and training, small and medium-size enterprises, technical assistance, and balance-of-payments support. Moreover, the poorest countries of Africa and Asia, which have relied primarily on concessional flows, have been most affected by reductions in foreign assistance budgets.

By the mid-1990s, the United States had abdicated its traditional leading role in the field of development assistance. The US Congress refused to honour contribution pledges made by the Administration to the United Nations Development Programme (UNDP) and to the International Development Association (IDA) and also refused to pay its assessed contributions to the United Nations central and peacekeeping budgets. This made France, Japan, and other European countries the main contributors to development cooperation. However, after years of steady increases, at a time when other rich countries were slashing their cooperation budgets, Japan reduced its foreign aid by 10% in 1996. Even what were once called the "like-minded" countries, owing to their unwavering support for development assistance (Canada, Denmark, the Netherlands, Norway, and Sweden) have reduced the budgets they allocate for this purpose and have increased the conditions on access to these funds.

Despite the setbacks experienced during the last decade by traditional bilateral and multilateral mechanisms for development cooperation, new possibilities are opening up for rich and poor countries to collaborate in some specific fields, such as environmental sustainability, the prevention of weapons proliferation, and the fight against drug traffic and international crime. At the same time, private sources of funds are becoming more important in a few aspects of development cooperation, such as building policy-research capabilities in transition economies, helping to fight diseases in the developing world, and removing antipersonnel mines. Nongovernmental organizations (NGOs) have acquired greater prominence and are providing international leadership in some specific fields, particularly in environmental conservation, social conditions, and human rights.

In December 1997, the Parties to the United Nations Framework Convention on Climate Change approved the Kyoto Protocol, which seeks to limit, and even reduce, the emission of gases that contribute to global warming. The Kyoto Protocol establishes a "clean-development mechanism," which is designed to assist developing countries, and this mechanism could eventually lead to the transfer of hundreds of millions of dollars a year from rich to poor countries. Although a lot of ground still needs to be covered to make this mechanism operational, there are early indications that developing countries can reap substantive benefits from the sale of unused emission rights if their forests can absorb greenhouse gases in amounts above their emission limits. On other fronts, concerns about the proliferation of nuclear weapons in the post-Cold War period have prompted some highly industrialized nuclear powers, particularly the United States, to offer financial and other incentives to developing countries to renounce the use and development of nuclear weapons. Financial and trade rewards have also been offered to drug-producing countries that collaborate with US and European efforts to curb the international drug trade.

Private financial flows to developing countries, which include direct foreign investment and portfolio investments in emerging markets, have experienced major increases during the 1990s. They are now five times larger than official flows provided by government agencies and international organizations, in contrast to the situation prevailing in the mid-1980s, when they represented about 50% of total financial flows to developing countries. However, private financing is concentrated in a fairly small number of emerging and transition economies, while the vast majority of developing countries still depend on official aid for external financing. Grants provided by private foundations (Ford, Rockefeller, Pew, MacArthur, Carnegie Corporation, Tinker) remain a relatively small component of international development cooperation, but their impact is magnified because they focus on training, building local capabilities, and strengthening public and civil-society institutions.

During the last decade, a few wealthy individuals have joined the ranks of private philanthropy, once the province of well-established foundations and religious organizations that focused primarily on humanitarian relief. The three most visible examples of this new breed of philanthropist are George Soros, who has contributed hundreds of millions of dollars to humanitarian organizations, human-rights activists, and policy-research centres in Eastern Europe; Ted Turner, who in late 1997 pledged $1 billion (US dollars throughout) to support the United Nations; and Bill Gates, who has recently established two foundations to donate hundreds of millions of dollars annually. They have also been joined by internationally known musicians and media personalities. A series of rock concerts broadcast on television in the early 1990s, linked to a phone-in campaign soliciting pledges from viewers, raised more funds to combat AIDS in Africa than did formal-pledging conferences organized under United Nations auspices. Toward the end of 1997, and in just a few weeks royalties from a compact disc issued in memory of Lady Diana generated more than $100 million in just a few weeks for campaigns to remove antipersonnel mines in war-torn countries.

Countries until recently heralded as major successes of the development-cooperation experiment, such as the four Southeast Asian Tigers, experienced severe financial difficulties during 1997, which are likely to impair their growth prospects for several years. For example, 1 year after joining the rich-countries club of the Organisation for Economic Co-operation and Development (OECD), South Korea's currency and stock market plunged more than 40%. From being the 11th largest economy in the world, the country slipped to 20th place in just a few months. After about 8 weeks of preparation and in less than 1 hour of discussion in early December 1997, the World Bank approved up to $10 billion in emergency loans to South Korea, more than it had loaned to that country in the previous three decades and about half the total annual lending volume of this multilateral financial institution.

The economic and financial crises of 1997–99, which first hit several developing countries in East Asia, eventually affected economies in nearly all regions of the world, including the Russian Federation and Latin America. The overall crisis has had consequences that far transcend the world of financial markets; it has had a significant impact on the development efforts of countries such as Indonesia, where, in just a few weeks, the number of poor increased dramatically. Analysts initially explained the crisis on the basis of weaknesses in the financial systems and economic policies of individual developing countries like South Korea and Thailand, together with the close integration of global financial markets, as a result of which disturbances are rapidly transmitted beyond national borders. However, the serious global impact of the crisis has led a growing number of analysts to search beyond these factors for a systemic cause (Bezanson 1999). This in turn has shifted attention to the apparently inadequate role of multilateral institutions like the World Bank and the International Monetary Fund (IMF) in ensuring stability and promoting sustainable development (The South Letter 1998). Moreover, it has been observed that the East Asian crisis and its repercussions "have led to serious questioning of the relevance of the Washington Consensus as a standard development template and about whether a new development model or 'paradigm' is needed" (Bezanson 1999, p. 17).

All of these changes suggest that the international context, the channels, and the mechanisms for cooperation between rich and poor countries and the structure of financial flows to developing regions are changing fundamentally in the transition to a new century, and it cannot be expected that the institutional arrangements designed and put in place four or five decades ago will continue to be effective in this new situation. In this sense, the development-cooperation experiment — as we knew it — is coming to an end. Yet, both enduring motivations and new rationales will give rise to new forms of cooperation, policies, and institutions more in tune with the spirit of the times.

CHAPTER 2

THE EVOLUTION OF DEVELOPMENT COOPERATION

This chapter reviews the evolution of ideas since the late 1940s on how to bring about development and reviews how these ideas led to a rather complex set of institutional arrangements for development cooperation. The discussion focuses on development cooperation provided by the Western countries, primarily because the assistance provided by the former Soviet Union and its allies did not reach the level of institutional and conceptual elaboration that development cooperation attained in the West. In addition to providing military assistance and armaments (which were also provided by the West), East-block countries exchanged oil and manufactured goods at subsidized prices for primary commodities, such as sugar and minerals, as well as providing fellowships and arranging training programs for nationals of developing countries of strategic importance. Moreover, in a stunning reversal, countries once part of the former Soviet Union and its allies became recipients of Western development assistance during the 1990s.

The development experience: concepts and insights

Ideas on how to bring about development and how to organize development co-operation have changed and evolved during the last half century (Meier and Seers 1984; Montoliu-Muñoz 1990; Cowen and Shelton 1996). For example, at different times between the late 1940s and the early 1970s, development thinking and practice were based on concepts such as the need for a "big push" of investment and capital to initiate self-sustaining economic growth, as advocated by Paul Rosenstein-Rodin and Ragnar Nurkse; the priority of investments in human capital, whose main proponents were Theodore Schultz and Hans Singer; the importance of fostering import-substitution industrialization and exploiting backward and forward linkages, which were argued for by Raul Prebisch and Albert Hirschman, respectively; and Walt W. Rostow's imperative of advancing through a well-established sequence of stages that lead to a take-off into self-sustained growth (Rostow 1971).[1]

Over time, notions such as "unlimited supply of labour" (Arthur Lewis), "deterioration of the terms of trade" (Hans Singer, Raul Prebisch), "poles of development" (Francois Perroux), "development planning" (P. Mahalanobis, Jan Timbergen), "circular cumulative causation" (Gunnar Myrdal), "unbalanced growth" (Albert Hirschman), "dependency theory" (Fernando Henrique Cardoso, Osvaldo Sunkel), "structural underdevelopment" (Celso Furtado), "unequal exchange" (Aghiri Emmanuel), "redistribution with growth" (Hollis Chennery), "basic needs" (Hans Singer, Paul Streeten, Richard Jolly, Manfred Max Neef), "export-oriented industrialization" (Ann Kruger, T.N. Srinivasan), "small is beautiful" (E.F. Schumacher), "another development" (Marc Nerfin), "ecodevelopment" (Ignacy Sachs, Maurice Strong), among many others, were used to interpret the reality of developing countries and to offer policy recommendations.

In addition, some religious groups, most notably the Roman Catholic Church, had a significant influence in development thinking. For example, during the 1950s and 1960s, Father Louis-Joseph Lebret, a French priest who worked extensively with developing countries, put forward the idea of developing a "humane economy" based on the concept of solidarity, and this idea greatly influenced the development of Social Christian political thought. Similarly, during the 1960s and 1970s, the views put forward by Peruvian priest Gustavo Gutiérrez on "liberation theology" focused on the need to eradicate poverty and provided an ethical and moral underpinning to many grass-roots development efforts in Latin America and elsewhere in the developing world.

Several schools of thought emerged during the last five decades to organize these ideas. Even though these schools competed with each other, at any given time a dominant view of how to bring about development prevailed in most development-cooperation agencies and international financial institutions. The promotion of investment and project planning held sway in the 1950s; growth-oriented "trickle-down" and import-substitution strategies were prevalent in the 1960s; and basic needs and redistribution with growth became the key ideas of the 1970s. During the Crisis Decades, when structural adjustment policies dominated the scene, development thinking and practice appeared to be in disarray. This

---

[1]   There have been many accounts of the history of the idea of development. For reviews of the evolution of development thinking, see, among others, Van Nieuwenhuijze (1972), Hettne and Wallensteen (1978), UNESCO (1982), Meier and Seers (1984), Lewis and Kallab (1986), Arndt (1987), Coquery-Vidrovitch et al. (eds.) (1988), the special issue of *Daedalus* (Daedalus 1989), and Oman and Wignaraja (1991). In addition, three other articles provide an interesting perspective on development theory, written by Hirschman (1981), Sen (1983), and Krugman (1995).

prompted calls for a major overhaul and renewal of development theory and policies, as well as leading to spirited debates on the future of development economics
as a profession (Sen 1983).

One of the recurrent themes in the evolution of the idea of development
is the tension between the diversity of situations in developing countries and the
use of standard models and theories to interpret these situations and to give policy
advice. During the past two decades, the recognition of the growing heterogeneity
of the developing world — one of the main features of emerging global order —
has shifted the balance in the direction of paying more attention to diversity and
the variety of development experiences.

The preoccupation with diversity in development thinking and practice has
taken many forms over time and encompasses a wide range of contributions. For
example, Albert Hirschman has been one of the leading figures in the development
scene and has insisted on the diverse character of economic experience across
countries, across time, and even across individuals. This insight led him to resist
the temptation to apply reductionist theories and uniform prescriptions to developing countries (Rothschild 1995). Amartya Sen's inquiry into the meanings of
equality and inequality starts by acknowledging the empirical fact of pervasive
human diversity, and he proceeds to develop a framework with concepts such as
functionings, capabilities, and effective freedom that allows him to incorporate
ethical considerations when examining the different types of inequality embedded
in social arrangements (Sen 1992, p. xi).[2]

The concern about ignoring the diversity of specific situations and basing
policy prescriptions on the prevailing conventional wisdom was clearly articulated
by Jacques Lesourne nearly a decade ago in his concluding remarks at a symposium to celebrate the 25th Anniversary of the OECD Development Centre:

> We ... have to be wary of the latest fads in the development field. They
> are frequently transformed into simplistic and extremist ideologies which
> often cruelly mark the life of nations. The current welcome emphasis on
> markets is no reason for disregarding their shortcomings, and highlighting

---

[2]   Russell Ackoff, professor of system science at the Warthon School of the University
of Pennsylvania, commented on the difficulties of taking into account the diversity of development
experiences and on what he considers the futility of attempting to construct a theory of development. He has argued that "development is an exception and theories are not constructed to
account for exceptions" (R. Ackoff, University of Pennsylvania, Philadelphia, PA, personal communication, Apr 1982). Albert Hirschman has made a similar point: "When change turned out pretty
well it was often a one-time unrepeatable feat of social engineering, an outcome that only gives
confidence that a similar unique constellation of circumstances can occur again; but trying to repeat
the sequence of events formulaically in another context won't work" (Hirschman 1995, pp.
314–315).

> the weakness of the State as a producer must not lead us to overlook the contributions government policies have made to development in certain countries. Conversely, the failure of many attempts to foist doctrinaire socialism irrespective of realities on societies with their own long-standing structures must be acknowledged. There is not just one possible development model, although this does not mean that all models can work.
>
> (Lesourne 1989, p. 298)

At another level, the "case-by-case" and "country-focus" approaches adopted by international financial institutions during the second half of the 1980s, most notably the World Bank, can be seen as attempts to cope with diversity within the framework of their mandates. These approaches can also be considered a response to the criticism that international financial institutions and, to a lesser extent, bilateral cooperation agencies provide the same standardized policy advice to developing countries facing very different situations and impose an inflexible and rigid set of conditions on obtaining access to their resources and those of other financing agents. The policies advocated by the IMF to cope with the 1997–98 collapse of currencies and stock markets in several East Asian countries, which critics have considered inappropriate (Feldstein 1998), have revived the debates on the question of whether international financial institutions are oblivious to the differences between country situations and between the situation at different times in the same country.

Parallel to the development community's growing preoccupation with diversity, the search has continued for conceptual frameworks that can accommodate widely diverse situations while helping to identify common features and allowing us to learn from the mistakes and successes of others. As a consequence, during the last decade, a more eclectic and flexible set of ideas on how to bring about improvements in living standards has been gaining ground. For example, rather than viewing concepts such as state intervention and market forces as opposites or treating structural adjustment and human development as irreconcilable, these new ideas focus on how such concepts and approaches might complement each other, and these new ideas have led to such conceptions as "market-friendly strategies," put forward by the World Bank (1991), and "adjustment with a human face," advocated by the United Nations Children's Fund (UNICEF) (Cornia et al. 1987). Perhaps one of the best expressions of this synthesis of concepts and experience is the World Bank's *World Development Report 1991: The Challenge of Development*, prepared under the direction of Vinod Thomas and supervised by Stanley Fischer (World Bank 1991). This report was rather unusual for the World Bank series of annual reports on development because, instead of focusing on a single topic — such as health, poverty, infrastructure, environment, labour markets, or transition economies — it provided an overview of the development experience of several decades and outlined the challenges of the future. *World Development Report 1997*, which focused on the new role of the State in economic development, also argued for a more eclectic approach to designing development strategies and policies (World Bank, 1997d).

During the last 15 years, development thinking and practice have placed greater emphasis on the institutional and social aspects of development, including poverty reduction, building capable states, good governance, and conflict prevention and resolution. In particular, Ralph Dahrendorf's concept of "vital opportunities" (Dahrendorf 1983) and Amartya Sen's criticisms of utility theory, which led Sen to introduce the concepts of "functionings," "capabilities," and "entitlements" (Sen 1992, 1984; Nussbaum and Sen 1993), constitute the most promising avenues for the renewal of ideas about development and how to bring it about.

The concept of "sustainable human development," put forward by the UNDP, is a recent addition to the evolving set of ideas about development. It attempts to integrate economic growth, social development, and environmental sustainability within the same framework (Speth 1994). Sustainable human development aims at providing all individuals, both now and in the future, with equal opportunities to enlarge their human capabilities to the fullest possible extent and to put those capabilities to the best use in political, economic, social, environmental, and cultural fields. As such, it can be considered more as a statement of aspirations than an operational concept.

Considering such a rich and evolving array of concepts and ideas, what has been the result of five decades of attempts to promote development? Not surprisingly, the development efforts of the past five decades have been neither a great success nor a dismal failure. On the positive side, a handful of low-income countries, particularly in East Asia, have in one generation achieved the standards of living of the industrialized nations; life expectancy and educational levels have increased in most developing countries; and income per capita has doubled in countries like Brazil, China, South Korea, and Turkey in less than a third of the time it took to do so in the United Kingdom or the United States a century or more earlier.

On the negative side, poverty has increased throughout the world; income disparities between rich and poor nations and between the rich and the poor in both developed and developing countries have become more pronounced; the environment has been subjected to severe stress, both in developing countries that have remained poor and in those that industrialized rapidly; and social demands have grown many times over throughout the developing world (World Bank 1991; UNDP 1994b).

The extent to which development assistance — which includes grants, long-term loans at below-market rates, technical cooperation, and food donations — was responsible for the successes or contributed to the failures has been the subject of considerable debate (Bauer 1984; Hancock 1989; Cassen 1994; Griffin and McKinley 1994; DAC 1995b). Considering the high expectations of the late 1940s and 1950s (particularly after the resounding success of the Marshall Plan) and the actual results several decades later, it may be appropriate to state that the results of the development-cooperation experiment have been inconclusive. It worked in some places at some times (and in a few instances, where it was not expected to do so!), but it certainly did not lead to the worldwide levels of prosperity envisaged five decades ago.

Both successes and failures provide valuable insights on how to accelerate economic growth and improve social conditions (Bezanson and Sagasti 1995). We have learned, for example, that environmental considerations must be adequately integrated into the design of development strategies and policies so as to ensure that improvements in living standards achieved by the current generation do not limit the opportunities of future generations. Remedial actions have proven rather costly and often ineffective.

We have also learned that the capacity to acquire, generate, and use knowledge in all its forms — including the recovery and upgrading of traditional knowledge — has been one of the most important factors in the improvement of material standards of living. This is consistent with the view that development is a reinterpretation of progress within the framework of the Baconian program, which emphasizes the key role that scientific and technological knowledge plays in improving the human condition. The experience of the handful of developing countries whose incomes and living standards have reached those of the rich nations indicates that major investments in education, research, technology acquisition, and scientific and technological services — which allowed these developing countries to bridge the knowledge divide between rich and poor nations — have all played a crucial role in their success (Sagasti 1997a, b; World Bank 1998).

Perhaps one of the most important insights we have acquired during five decades of development efforts is the recognition of the importance of institutional factors. Institutions comprise patterns of behaviour, long-standing social relations, organizations, and formal rules and regulations, all of which give structure to the fabric of society, allow its members to develop shared purposes and commitments, provide the basis for more cooperative behaviour, and create the stability and predictability needed for effective human actions (North 1990; Putnam 1993; Stiglitz 1995; Eggertsson 1997). We have also found, especially since the fall of the Berlin Wall, that institutions stand a better chance of responding adequately to the growing and rapidly changing demands of the increasing interdependence of nations and economies in our times if the institutions are flexible, participatory, decentralized, pluralistic, and capable of accommodating a diversity of views and perspectives.

In the political realm, the institutions associated with democratic governance have proven most effective in channeling and processing a wide variety of social demands toward the centres of power, primarily through mediating institutions, such as political parties. A well-functioning democracy also allows for orderly changes in the exercise of political power, through periodic elections, and prevents the excessive concentration of power, by establishing checks and balances. These characteristics have also made democratic governance a powerful force for maintaining peace and preventing deadly conflicts (CCPDC 1997).

In the economic realm, the institutions associated with markets and competition have proven most effective in promoting economic growth and improving performance in many fields of human activity. However, societies that can strike a balance between competitive pressures, on the one hand, and considerations of trust and solidarity and concerns for the disadvantaged, on the other, are likely to be more effective in improving living standards and avoiding social exclusion. There is a strong interaction between effective governance, economic growth, and active networks of civic and social engagement, all of which combine to reduce the likelihood of the "nothing-left-to-lose" syndrome that may drive some social groups toward violent actions (Sagasti 1998).

At the same time, most of the serious problems and challenges that development now faces — for example, limiting environmental degradation, maintaining economic stability, reducing poverty, and preventing deadly conflicts — no longer have purely local or national solutions. Preserving peace, improving living standards, and creating of opportunities for all increasingly depend on cross-border exchanges of goods, services, knowledge, and information. This makes it necessary to focus more attention on the critical role that regional and international institutions of all types play in the development process.

During the last few years, particularly since the end of the Cold War, we have also realized that for most of the past five decades culture, religion, and ethnic allegiances were all but ignored in development thinking and practice. Yet, beyond meeting survival needs, most of humanity is driven by ethical and spiritual motives. Values and nonmaterial aspects of human activities play a most important role in development efforts, especially in the prevention of violent conflict. But cultural identities, ethnic loyalties, spiritual concerns, religious allegiances, and ethical principles may conflict with each other (Ryan 1995). This highlights the importance of tolerance as a precondition for the incorporation of other values and nonmaterial considerations into the idea of development. The paradoxical lesson is that in order to accept the diversity of value systems, it is essential to first recognize the primacy of certain universal values, such as tolerance, respect for the views of others, and freedom to express dissent.

These insights have focused our attention on the need for developing broader perspectives on the process of development and to acknowledge its inherent complexity. Economic, social, political, cultural, and psychological perspectives must all be considered and integrated in any attempt to improve the human condition, specifically in the attempt to prevent deadly conflict.

Four decades of institutional arrangements for development cooperation

As mentioned in the introductory chapter, the development-cooperation experiment of the past 50 years took place at a very special time in history. The first decades of the development-cooperation experiment, which covered the Golden Age of world economic growth, were characterized by efforts to "modernize" what were considered "backward" societies and coincided with a widespread belief in the effectiveness of government interventions and planning as ways to ensure the rational allocation of resources.[3] Modern science and technology were almost without exception seen positively as the means of improving living standards and the quality of life, whereas little or no attention was paid to the negative impact of economic growth on the environment. Traditional values and religious beliefs were largely seen as a hindrance to modernity and economic rationality. The development cooperation experiment was a thoroughly secular enterprise, notwithstanding the active participation of churches and religious organizations in some

---

[3] Some influential figures in the early stages of the development-cooperation experiment had a clearly unsympathetic attitude to non-Western cultures and values. For example, Eugene Staley proclaimed the superiority of Western modern culture: "In the Orient, until recently, the standard way to seek happiness has been to cut down on desires. The West in modern times has sought happiness by increasing possessions. There can be no doubt that the ascetic philosophy of the East is losing ground to the activist philosophy of the West. In many Eastern communities the most respected person was the man who withdrew from society, but abnegation is no longer held in such high esteem. The man who tries to better his community and himself is gaining respect" (Staley 1954, pp. 20–21).

of its aspects, such as offering views on the nature of development and organizing humanitarian relief and assistance to the poorest countries. The United Nations Universal Declaration of Human Rights, adopted in 1947, provided practically all the ethical guidance required.

The Marshall Plan was designed and carried out during the late 1940s and early 1950s to assist European countries in the reconstruction of their war-shattered economies. Its successful implementation inspired a belief in the effectiveness of foreign-aid programs and gave a major boost to the development-cooperation experiment. In a display of exceptionally enlightened self-interest (Jenkins 1997), the United States injected, between 1947 and 1951, the 1997 equivalent of $88 billion in balance-of-payments support, financial assistance, and soft loans to most countries in Western Europe, as well as providing technical assistance and access to US managerial and manufacturing know-how. Although the immediate objective of the plan was, as George C. Marshall stated in his famous 1947 Harvard address, to fight "hunger, poverty, desperation and chaos" (Marshall 1947), the longer term aim was to lay the foundations for financial recovery, economic growth, political stability, and military security in the face of a Soviet threat. The Marshall Plan, which Winston Churchill once referred to as "the most unsordid act in Western history," has also been linked to the subsequent surge in world trade during the 1950s and 1960s, to the drive toward European integration, and to global economic stability (Rostow 1997).

Fifty years after the Marshall Plan was launched, several of its key features still make it highly regarded as a model for development-assistance programs. These include the cooperative and multilateral nature of the plan, which involves both donor and recipients in its design and implementation; the incorporation of a training program for European businesspeople, which transfers valuable know-how to the private sector; and the clear link between the provision of balance-of-payments support, on the one hand, and monetary discipline and trade liberalization, on the other. The limited and temporary nature of the plan has also been highlighted as a desirable feature, as it has been considered "the model of what a foreign aid program ought to be. It ended ahead of schedule and under budget, the last significant program of its kind to do that" (Holt 1997, p. 7).

However, it is also clear that the Marshall Plan's success owed much to the specific historical and geographical context in which it was carried out, because it involved the industrial reconstruction of countries that had decades or even centuries of manufacturing experience, a well-educated labour force, the well-developed institutional structures needed to support a modern economy, and high living standards before World War II. The Marshall Plan was a historically unique experience and probably cannot be exactly replicated in developing regions today (Gordon 1977; Hoagland 1997). Indeed, the various calls during the last decades for "a Marshall Plan" to address a specific development problem can only be understood in the most general sense as appeals to the enlightened self-interest of rich countries, attempts to mobilize political will, and efforts to promote an allocation of resources commensurate with the task at hand.

Between the late 1940s and the early 1960s, development assistance was almost exclusively bilateral. In addition to helping European reconstruction through the Marshall Plan, the United States took the lead in promoting economic growth in developing countries through the Point IV Program, articulated by President Truman (CCSTG 1992). Strategic and security interests, linked to the containment of communism during the Cold War, provided the main motivation for engaging in international cooperation for development. The United States also had a reasonably strong capacity to design and implement reconstruction and development-assistance programs, particularly following the *Foreign Assistance Act* of 1961, which created the United States Agency for International Development (USAID). The United States accounted for more than 50% of total ODA during the 1950s and for about 45% in the early 1960s, out of which more than 85% was provided through bilateral channels, by USAID in particular.

A common practice of bilateral assistance, especially during the early years of the development-cooperation experiment, was to tie aid to the donor country's provision of goods and services. The reasoning was that tying aid would allow donor countries to build greater political support for development assistance while at the same time reducing their financial burden. However, tied purchases of goods and services usually led to the recipient country paying a higher price and thus to a reduction in the value of bilateral aid. Similar considerations apply to the provision of technical assistance and consultant services.

There were only four major multilateral institutions responsible for concessional aid through the early 1960s: IDA, attached to the World Bank and created in 1960; the Fund for Special Operations of the Inter-American Development Bank (IDB), which was established in 1959; the cooperation fund of the European Economic Community (EEC), created in 1959; and the UNDP, which was organized in 1965 through the merger of several United Nations financial facilities, including the Special Fund and the Expanded Program of Technical Assistance. The contribution of these four institutions to total ODA was less than 10%, and decision-making in most of these multilateral agencies was dominated by the United States. The concessional windows of international financial institutions complemented their regular lending programs and provided resources to borrowers at very low interests rates, with loans to be repaid over 30 to 40 years. Growth-oriented trickle-down conceptions of development prevailed in this period, and financial and technical assistance tended to concentrate on large physical-infrastructure projects that served the bilateral economic interests of major donors, generally through the involvement of private corporations in procurement.

The period from the mid-1960s to the mid-1970s saw a rapid growth in multilateral concessional development assistance. The Pearson Report, published in 1969, indicated that in the mid-1960s bilateral aid accounted for almost 90% of ODA to developing countries, and the report argued that it was necessary to strengthen multilateral channels (which at the time were perceived to be more efficient and less politicized) (Pearson Report 1969). Multilateral assistance expanded faster than bilateral aid, and its share in total development assistance grew to nearly 25% in the mid-1970s, even without counting the funds the EEC provided. Multilateral concessional aid also began to diversify, with the creation of several new mechanisms to provide low-interest loans and grants to developing-country borrowers, including the African Development Fund, attached to the African Development Bank (AfDB); the Asian Development Fund (AsDF), attached to the Asian Development Bank (AsDB); and the development funds of the Arab–Organization of Petroleum Exporting Countries (OPEC). All these institutions were established in the early and mid-1970s. Complementing the range of multilateral development-assistance programs and institutions were the regional initiatives, such as the Regional Program for Scientific and Technological Development of the Organization of American States and the Colombo Plan, through which several bilateral donors provided support for education in South and East Asian countries.

NGOs played a limited role in channeling the assistance provided by religious groups and private foundations in the early years of the development experiment but became more visible and active during the 1960s and 1970s in both donor and recipient countries. As a growing number of donor-country NGOs began to play the role of aid intermediaries, a symbiosis evolved between the NGOs and the bilateral development-assistance agencies providing the funding. NGOs were often very helpful in this period in reaching small groups of beneficiaries difficult for government agencies and multilateral institutions to reach, but in many cases they increased the cost of delivering assistance; they became excessively dependent on resources provided by official agencies; and they generated frictions with government agencies, local organizations, and grass-roots groups in the recipient countries. Multilateral institutions remained largely aloof from NGOs and would only begin to work with them in the late 1980s.

A major reorientation of aid philosophy toward the perceived common global problems — poverty alleviation, urban development, and basic human needs — also contributed significantly to strengthening donor support for multilateral initiatives. During the 1970s, total multilateral concessional assistance expanded by a factor of 6.5 in nominal terms; concessional flows through IDA increased nearly sevenfold; flows through EEC and the United Nations system increased about five times each; and concessional resources channeled through the regional development banks (comprising the funds for special operations of the AfDB, AsDB, and IDB) almost tripled. This expansion occurred for three reasons.

First, the United States became more interested in multilateral initiatives, particularly as the capacity of its aid-delivery organizations began to reach its limits. The growing demands of an increasing number of developing countries, following the process of decolonization, together with the shift from reconstruction of war-torn economies to more complex development programs, made it more difficult for the United States to respond adequately on its own to these demands. In addition, under provisions of the 1973 "New Directions" amendment to the *Foreign Assistance Act*, resources for development assistance were reoriented toward issues such as poverty alleviation, basic human needs, and agricultural and rural development, which were common to many developing countries and could be better addressed through multilateral initiatives.

As a result, between the mid-1960s and the mid-1970s, the US share in multilateral development assistance more than doubled to 30%. A concern with "burden-sharing" between donors emerged. Moreover, with the expansion of the postwar world economy, other industrialized countries became interested in development assistance as a way to maintain international political and economic stability. This led to the widespread use of matching-funds arrangements for multilateral concessional assistance, in which each donor pledged to cover a predetermined proportion of the total cost of a program.

Second, Canada, the Netherlands, and the Nordic countries (Denmark, Finland, Norway, and Sweden) responded quite vigorously to the United States' appeal for burden-sharing and gave high priority to multilateral channels. The aggregate share of these six countries in total ODA increased from 2.7% in 1960/61 to 10.4% in 1975/76, whereas the US share decreased from 46.3 to 21.2%. This was due in part to the strong domestic constituencies these non-US countries had to support poverty alleviation in the developing regions and the disproportionately large size of their assistance in relation to the technical and administrative capacities of their aid agencies. (The ratios of ODA to gross national product [GNP] of the Nordic countries have been exceptionally higher [at around

1.0%] than the average of 0.35% for all donors.) As well, these countries actively promoted the idea that aid should be provided through mechanisms that involve the participation of both donors and recipients. As a consequence, these countries tended to allocate significant resources for development assistance through multilateral institutions, particularly through the agencies of the United Nations system, such as UNDP.

The third reason was that multilateral development-cooperation institutions significantly improved their administrative and technical capacities and were thus able to attract strong support from bilateral donors. Particularly notable were the major changes brought about in the World Bank under the McNamara presidency (1968–81), including a significant reorientation toward antipoverty projects, the creation of entirely new units to address poverty-related problems, and the strengthening of the World Bank's research capacity. The UNDP also expanded its in-house technical and administrative capabilities, particularly during Bradford Morse's term as UNDP Administrator, and built a strong network of resident representatives in most developing countries.

However, even as official aid began to shift from bilateral to multilateral channels, which were presumably less politicized, several critics did not see multilateral organizations as any less likely to pursue the political and commercial interests of rich donor countries than the well-being of the poor in the developing regions (see Chapter 5). Hidden motivations were suspected behind the policies of major institutions like the World Bank, IMF, USAID, and other development-assistance agencies, which critics saw as engaging in a conspiracy to preserve an unjust international economic system (Hayter 1971; Hensman 1971). Other authors saw increasing multilateral-aid flows as disguised bilateral transfers, with harmful effects less obvious but no less real than those of bilateral aid (Goulet and Hudson 1971).

Following this rapid rise through the mid-1970s, the share of multilateral channels in total development assistance stabilized at about 28–30% during the 1980s (including contributions to the EEC). However, this stability concealed a trend toward "bilateralism in multilateral aid," which became evident as the international context for development assistance began to change. The dominant position of the United States weakened significantly in the second half of the 1980s as its share of total ODA declined to about 18% and its share of multilateral concessional aid declined to about 16%. This reduction coincided with a shift toward greater emphasis on bilateral security and political interests in the provision of aid, in contrast to the priority awarded to multilateral initiatives a decade earlier. For example, the security-oriented Economic Support Fund, which provides assistance to countries of strategic interest to the United States, grew faster than other types of development assistance and accounted for about 50% of total United States bilateral aid in the late 1980s, with 90% of its funds earmarked for five countries (Egypt, El Salvador, Israel, Pakistan, and the Philippines).

All through the 1960s and 1970s, Japan was among the top five donor countries, but during the 1980s its development-assistance program expanded rapidly and shifted from rather narrow bilateral economic interests, such as promoting exports and investments in the Asian region, to broader multilateral considerations related to international economic and political stability. Japan's increasingly important role in the world economy, added to the relative weakness of its development-assistance organizations, led to a growing reliance on multilateral institutions to channel Japanese aid. This took the form of greater participation in multilateral concessional assistance funds, such as IDA at the World Bank and AsDF at the AsDB, cofinancing arrangements, and trust funds of international financial institutions. These initiatives allowed Japan to exert greater influence on the policies and practices of these organizations, maintain a separate identity for its aid funds, and pursue a policy of "moderate bilateralism" in multilateral assistance.

European donors also expanded their participation in multilateral channels for concessional development assistance during the 1980s, particularly through the European Community. Nevertheless, with the exception of the Nordic countries and the Netherlands, European donors continued to rely on their long-standing bilateral-aid arrangements — or on regional funds administered by the European Community (such as the European Development Fund linked to the Lomé Convention) — rather than on United Nations agencies or on international financial institutions, for channeling their aid.

Following the international debt crisis triggered in 1982 by the Mexican default of its commercial loans, the role of multilateral development finance changed significantly. The IMF established the Structural Adjustment Facility and the Enhanced Structural Adjustment Facility (ESAF), and the World Bank launched Structural Adjustment Lending. This helped many developing countries to weather their liquidity and insolvency crises during the 1980s, but at the price of adopting painful economic-adjustment policies. The "disciplinary functions" of these institutions increased with the growing importance of highly conditioned lending, and having an agreement with the IMF became a condition not only on loans and concessional assistance from multilateral institutions but also on cofinancing from bilateral donors and loans from commercial banks. The Special Program of Assistance to Low-Income Debt Distressed Countries in Sub-Saharan

Africa, launched in 1988, provided a clear example of the increasing reliance of bilateral donors on multilateral institutions. A Policy Framework Paper, drawn primarily by the IMF and the World Bank (in consultation with government authorities), became a prerequisite for mobilizing large amounts of bilateral funds from donor countries.

The structural adjustment programs designed by the World Bank for a number of Sub-Saharan countries have been particularly controversial examples of the disciplinary functions exercised by multilateral institutions in the 1980s and 1990s. Although these mostly very poor nations made dramatic liberal reforms, their economies have nevertheless shown "exceptionally poor performance" (Mkandawire and Soludo 1999, p. 81). This conclusion applies not only to indicators of economic growth but also to the fight against poverty. The World Bank itself has tended to blame this poor economic and social performance on the African governments' poor implementation or the bank's ineffective imposition of its conditionality, rather than looking at flaws in the model behind the design of the adjustment programs. It has been argued that although it is easy for the multilateral organizations to impose this type of external conditionality on the poorest countries, as they have few alternatives for development financing, it is unlikely to work. Rather, what is needed is more indigenous "ownership" of policies, along with local approaches to development work, rather than having governments — and societies — carrying out programs they do not believe in and have never participated in designing (Helleiner 1997).

In short, from the late 1940s to the late 1980s — a period that spanned Hobsbawm's Golden Age and most of the Crisis Decades — development-assistance organizations grew in number, size, and complexity, and their mandates shifted and evolved to accommodate changing circumstances. New institutions, programs, funding mechanisms, and procedures were created in most developed countries to assist developing nations. The World Bank significantly expanded its regular lending program, using resources obtained from international capital markets; established the IDA as a soft-loan window, with contributions from donor countries; and created an affiliate to provide financing to the private sector. New multilateral development banks were created at the regional level; specialized institutions served the needs of Africa, Asia, and Latin America; and other institutions, such as the European Investment Bank and the Islamic Development Bank, focused on narrower constituencies.

The European Community and Japan significantly expanded their development-assistance programs. Several technical- and financial-assistance programs were merged in the United Nations to create the UNDP. New agencies were established to cater to some specific needs of developing countries. In parallel with these government and intergovernmental initiatives, private giving by foundations, charitable institutions, and religious groups supported a growing number of programs and projects throughout the developing world. Following a trend toward reliance on multilateral institutions during the 1960s and 1970s, there was a shift toward bilateralism in multilateral and regional development assistance in the following decade.

Concluding remarks

While the events described in the preceding sections unfolded there emerged a vast, dense, and at times almost impenetrable forest of development-assistance organizations. As these agencies demanded counterparts, a corresponding assortment of government organizations and NGOs was often established in developing countries to work with donor agencies, international financing institutions, and private aid entities. By the time the development experiment reached its fourth decade, in the late 1980s, the growing and increasingly complex set of organizational arrangements (a result of incremental institutional innovations) became too heavy and unwieldy. Turf battles became the norm; accountability all but disappeared; many development-assistance organizations lost their sense of purpose and direction; and all these problems were exacerbated by a diminishing amount of resources available for development cooperation.

During the 1980s the limitations and shortcomings of the decades-old institutional arrangements for development cooperation became evident. This coincided with a new ideological orientation of the governments of many industrialized nations. Seeking to reduce government spending, conservative politicians in several developed countries found an easy target in foreign-aid programs, which were depicted as being wasteful and ineffective. Individual initiative and the private sector were heralded as the new harbingers of economic growth and development, and government programs to assist the poor were questioned and abandoned. In its more extreme manifestations, the "greed-is-good" syndrome portrayed development assistance as nothing but a series of dependency-generating handouts. This happened at a time when a large number of developing countries had experienced several years of economic downturn and a severe debt crisis, which made the 1980s a "lost decade" in terms of any improvement in living standards for most of Africa and Latin America and many Asia countries.

Before examining how the development-cooperation experiment began a radical, and as yet unfinished, transformation during the 1990s, it is useful to examine the main features of the international order that began to emerge clearly during the 1980s. A multiplicity of trends and changes, crystallizing in the emerging fractured global order, provide a backdrop against which to explore the future of development cooperation as we move into the 21st century.

CHAPTER 3

A NEW CONTEXT

In plastic historical periods like the one we are living through at present, when almost anything seems possible, it is important to identify the underlying forces shaping the future of international relations. This chapter reviews the major political, economic, social, environmental, cultural, governance, and knowledge transformations, whose implications have been the subject of heated debate during the 1990s, and that are creating a new global and increasingly interconnected context for development cooperation.[4]

International security in a postbipolar world

The end of the Cold War undermined the ideological, military, and political foundations of the international order that had prevailed after the late 1940s, a period in which the concept of development emerged as the new incarnation of the Western idea of progress.

We are well along the way in the transition to a postbipolar world order (Stremlau 1989), whose nature is being defined, but which requires a profound reexamination of the means to provide national, regional, and international peace and security, as preconditions for the pursuit of development objectives. Some elements of this new order include the unquestioned military predominance of the United States, a greatly diminished threat of an all-out nuclear war between the Russian Federation and the United States, an increase in the number and intensity of violent local and regional conflicts, the transformation of the means of waging war (including the persistent threat of chemical warfare and the emergence of electronic warfare), the likelihood of a more cooperative approach to conflict

---

[4]   Among the various authors who discuss the features of the emerging international order are Cetron and Davis (1991), Liepietz (1992), Amin (1992), Brown (1992), Hogan (1992), Takahashi (1992), Taylor and Taylor (1992), Carnoy et al. (1993), South Centre (1993), Slater et al. (1993), Singer and Wildavsky (1993), Groupe de Lisbonne (1995), Kennedy (1993), Barney et al. (1993), Davidian (1994), Sakamoto (1994), Kincaid and Portes (1994), O'Brien (1994), Kapstein (1994), Commission on Global Governance (CGG 1995), Holm and Sorensen (1995), Korten (1995), Bressand and Distler (1995), Santos (1995), Saul (1995), Athanasiou (1996), Kaplan (1996), Huntington (1996), Mander and Goldsmith (1996), Castells (1996), and Greider (1997).

resolution among key political and economic players, and an emerging larger role for international institutions in fostering and maintaining international security (Carnegie Quarterly 1993, 1996; Nolan 1994; Sahnoun 1994; Rubin 1997; The Economist 1997a).

The demise of East–West rivalry has complex implications for national security and governance. The Cold War imposed a certain logic in the organization of conflicts between and within nations. Most of these conflicts were not left to run their own course (if they ever had one) but were enlisted in the service of the East or the West (Hogan 1992). Although this suppressed many legitimate grievances and often led to repressive regimes supported by either East or West, it also provided an order of sorts that contained conflicts and limited their escalation, lest the two superpowers became involved in local wars with unpredictable but possibly catastrophic consequences. Moreover, within developing countries, conflicts and insurgencies based on Cold War ideology and once generously financed by the two superpowers have vanished, as has the possibility of developing countries playing one camp against the other.[5]

Some of the international security threats of the Cold War have disappeared, but they have been replaced by others just as ominous. Although the prospects of nuclear Armageddon have receded, the current potential for arms proliferation has led to a situation in which the likelihood of the use of nuclear weapons — either in a regional conflict or by terrorist groups — is probably greater now than in the bipolar era. The mid-1998 test of nuclear weapons conducted by India and Pakistan has led to a major escalation in South Asia and may run the risk of provoking China into conducting further tests. Moreover, an economically driven global arms trade — which has the implicit support of the United States and the major European powers — may lead to the proliferation of both conventional weapons and weapons of mass destruction. In an environment in which the arms trade is controlled increasingly by profit-oriented corporations engaged in strategic alliances across borders, which are responsive primarily to the concerns of their shareholders and largely unaccountable to the citizenry, access to all types of weapons has become easier and difficult to control. Biological weapons are particularly insidious because the destructive potential of their constituent pathogens is quite unpredictable; they are relatively inexpensive; and their

---

[5]   In a rather prescient statement, Stavrianos (1981, p. 796) pointed out that "the self-evident fact is that if a geologic cataclysm were to remove the Soviet Union from the face of the globe, the deplored 'hot spots' and 'international terrorism' would persist undiminished."

components are much easier to obtain than, for instance, those of nuclear weapons (Keller and Nolan 1997–98).

Catastrophic terrorism, with weapons that range from nuclear devices to computer viruses, has been identified as an eminent threat that even the United States is not quite ready to deal with. It has been suggested that meeting this new challenge will require joint efforts of the international community to design innovative systems to prevent, deter, and respond to such threats (Carter et al. 1998).

Ethnic and religious tensions within countries and regional conflicts over natural resources — such as water, oil, or tropical forests — and over environmental spillovers are creating new sources of political instability (Brown 1993; Myers 1993). In particular, religious-fundamentalist terrorism in Algeria and Egypt; the persistence of ethnic and religious violence in Israel, Lebanon, Northern Ireland, Palestine, and Spain; and the persecution of ethnic minorities in Iraq clearly indicate that religious and ethnic allegiances have become a dangerous source of strife and violent conflict. These tensions and conflicts may be kept in check by concerted actions of the major military powers, regional and international organizations, or a combination of both. But so far, despite diminished global superpower rivalry, there is no evidence of a decline in regional disputes, civil wars, or organized violence of ethnic groups, secessionist movements, terrorists, criminals, or drug traffickers.

However, local ethnic and religious conflicts have the potential to ensnare the major military powers — or at least those in the West — as the 1998–99 Balkan conflict clearly shows. The recently enlarged North Atlantic Treaty Organization began a bombing campaign in early 1999 that threatens to escalate and might become a protracted exercise with unforeseen consequences for European and international security.

New threats to national and international security have now emerged, often resulting from the actions of nonstate actors and so-called rogue states. We are witnessing an increase in, and the convergence of, criminal and terrorist activities: "Previously distinct issues — proliferation, terrorism, arms control, and organized crime — are now merging; the roles of organized crime and foreign corruption are especially neglected by most policy analysts who work on the proliferation issue" (Sopko 1996–97, p. 16). Terrorism, once associated chiefly with political motivations, has become linked in this turbulent context with widespread ethnic and religious conflicts. Terrorist activities, including those supported by rogue states, seem likely to intensify in a world of easily available weapons of mass destruction and advanced information and communications technology (Cetron and Davis 1991).

At the same time, states are becoming less important as political units, in the sense of being able to control whatever phenomena, whether economic, social, environmental, or technological, taking place in the world at present. The preeminence and sovereignty of states are being eroded in many aspects of foreign and economic policy, as highlighted by the renewed importance of the United Nations in conflict prevention and resolution, the proliferation of regional trade and economic agreements, the growing economic power of international corporations and private investors, the rise in power of international NGOs, and the conditions established by international financial institutions on obtaining access to resources under their control. However, the state is far from disappearing or becoming obsolete, and we are still struggling to understand the changed role of the nation-state, one of the most remarkable institutional innovations of the last three centuries (Mathews 1997).

The need for international cooperation in assuring political stability, preventing and resolving deadly conflicts, and fighting against cross-border criminal activities has grown significantly during the last three decades. Not even the richer and more powerful nations can ignore the fact that a more dense and complex web of engagements, which should involve countries at all levels of development, is required to create an international environment conducive to steady improvements in living standards and human well-being. Although the movement toward supranational forms of action and regulation is likely to proceed by fits and starts, with temporary reversals and renewed bouts of nationalism, it will probably gain momentum in the early years of the 21st century.

Political pluralism, popular participation, democratic movements, and pressures to ensure respect for human rights are everywhere becoming a fact of life, in the East, West, North, and South. International protest and, in a few cases, economic and political sanctions are sending a clear signal that repressive political regimes are no longer considered — at least in principle — acceptable members of the community of nations. Nevertheless, there is also plenty of evidence that indifference and disaster fatigue are dampening the expressions of sympathy for the plight of countries torn by internal conflicts and suffering human-rights abuses. Similarly, political expediency and narrowly defined economic interests often displace considerations of human rights and democratic governance in the exercise of foreign policy. Perhaps the most striking example of this is the fact that China and Indonesia, two countries considered to have repressive regimes, were respectively the third and fourth largest recipients of aid from established democracies in 1996 (The Christian Science Monitor 1997).

During the early 1990s, Eastern European countries had their first open elections in half a century; almost all the countries of Latin America had democratic regimes; Mexico advanced toward multiparty democracy; peace agreements were reached in Central America; the Middle East peace process moved forward; and a military coup failed in the Russian Federation. In addition, the Central Asian states of the former Soviet Union were struggling to become modern nations; multiparty elections were held in Romania and Taiwan; Hong Kong returned peacefully to China, without major disruptions or social conflicts; white rule disappeared in South Africa; and attempts were made to abolish one-party rule in several African countries.

However, steady advances toward democracy, respect for human rights, and peaceful coexistence are by no means guaranteed. The 1990s witnessed civil wars in Afghanistan, Albania, Angola, Cambodia, Congo, Rwanda–Burundi, Somalia, the former Yugoslavia, and Zaire; the overthrow of democratic regimes in Haiti and Nigeria; and a self-inflicted coup in Peru. In addition, the firm and deadly grip of the North Korean dictatorship, which appears ready to starve millions to maintain political control, and the tribulations of democratic regimes in Ecuador, South Korea, and Venezuela, among many others, give ample testimony to the precarious character of advances toward democratic forms of governance. Moreover, even though electoral processes are becoming an established feature of political life all over the world, democratic practices — including, checks and balances, an independent judiciary, respect for the rights of minorities, transparency, and accountability, among others — appear to lag far behind in many countries (Carothers 1997; Kaplan 1997; Zakaria 1997).

Growing economic and financial interdependence

Major transformations are taking place in the patterns of world economic interdependence, which include the rapid growth and globalization of financial markets, a major expansion in the volume of world trade, major shifts in trade patterns, significant increases in the volume of direct foreign investment and in short-term portfolio investments, and new situations in key countries that affect the world economy.

International financial markets now comprise a tight web of transactions involving global securities trading, arbitrage in multiple markets and currencies, portfolio investments through a bewildering array of international funds, and massive trans-border capital movements. Financial transactions have acquired a life of their own and are becoming uncoupled from the production and distribution of goods and services. The combined daily average of trade in the foreign-exchange markets reached $1.260 trillion in 1995, 15 times the 1980 level and 70 times the average daily volume of international trade in goods and services (Eatwell 1996). Another indication of the uncoupling of finance and production is the fact that, in 1993, stock-market transactions grew 45% in Germany and 22% in France, a year in which both countries experienced severe recessions (Plihon 1995).

Deregulation, advances in communications and information technology, the search for higher returns and risk diversification, and the internationalization of production are the main forces behind the globalization of finance. Oddly enough, the increasingly global character of financial markets has been the result of an explosive growth in transactions between the financial centres of just a few cities located primarily in the rich countries (Amsterdam, Chicago, Frankfurt, Hong Kong, London, New York, Paris, Tokyo, Zurich, and so on) and even in a few blocks within these cities.

By the end of 1997, twenty-five cities controlled 83% of the world's equity under institutional management, and three cities — London, New York, and Tokyo — accounted for nearly 60% of the global foreign-exchange market (Sassen 1999). In fact, the number of main international financial centres may be reduced further, as deregulation at the international level may make it unnecessary to sustain financial centres for each nation. Currently, one can speak of only three great financial centres that stand above the rest: London, New York, and Hong Kong. It is predicted that global finance will eventually need little more than one principal financial centre for each of the world's regions (The Economist 1998).

Even though the recent growth of the emerging capital markets of Asia and Latin America is beginning to register on the screen of international financial transactions (primarily because of the relatively high returns they yield to investors), these markets are a long way from challenging or even joining the established centres of global finance. For example, although stock market capitalization increased dramatically from $95 billion in 1985 to $1 371 billion in 1996 in the 18 principal emerging markets, this figure is still small in comparison with that of industrialized nations: the United States alone had a stock-market capitalization of $8.478 trillion, more than six times that of all principal emerging markets (World Bank 1997b). The emergence of an integrated global financial marketplace raises a series of issues of general concern, particularly for developing countries. The huge surge in private-capital flows in the 1990s, both in direct foreign investment and portfolios (invested through pension and mutual funds in the stock and bond markets), to developing countries has brought with it the realization of the potential risks and increased volatility of interconnected financial markets. At $240 billion, net private-capital flows to developing countries in 1996 were six times larger than they were in 1990; total private-capital flows were five times larger than official flows in that same year. From an emerging-economy perspective, these substantial inflows can be seen as an engine for sustainable growth, but it has been noted that financial integration must be carefully managed.

A recent World Bank (1997b) report points to several areas that must be strengthened to enable developing countries to achieve "productive financial integration" and avoid the serious pitfalls of injudicious financial opening and hasty deregulation. Particularly important are maintaining macroeconomic stability, strengthening banking systems, ensuring well-functioning stock markets, having a base of domestic investors to shield against flow reversals, and containing lending booms, which are characteristic of the initial stages of financial integration. Yet, as the recent stock-market, currency, and banking crises in several East Asian countries — including once unassailable South Korea — show, even the most advanced among developing countries are far from achieving the elusive goal of productive financial integration.

Major changes have also taken place in the volume, direction, and content of international trade, such as the rapid progress toward trade liberalization during the post-World War II period, as a result of several rounds of negotiations within the framework of the General Agreement on Tariffs and Trade (GATT), the emergence of the North Pacific as the world's largest trading area (with the North Atlantic taking second place), the rise of regional trading blocks (most notably the European Union and the North American Free Trade Area), and the rapid growth of intraregional trade in Southeast Asia and the Southern Cone of Latin America (Association of Southeast Asian Nations and Southern Cone Common Market). In addition, at the end of 1994, international trade received a major boost with the successful conclusion of the Uruguay Round negotiations, the most comprehensive of the GATT agreements, which paved the way for the creation of the World Trade Organization (WTO). Yet, unless regional markets are seen primarily as an intermediate step to establishing truly global markets for products and services, the rise of regional trading blocks may slow the pace toward worldwide trade liberalization. Moreover, an insistence in maintaining nationalist or even regionalist trade policies in this new context may be counterproductive (Schwab and Smadja 1995).

World trade has grown markedly in the last two decades. The total value of all imports and exports in 1994 was more than twice that of 1980. The rate of growth in world trade has exceeded that in the growth of world production: for example, in 1994, world merchandise trade grew 9.2%, more than three times faster than world GDP, whereas in the 1970s and 1980s trade grew only 1.5 times faster than production. During the 1990s, this has led to a process described as "globalization through trade integration" and to a decoupling of world trade and output (Otsubo 1996). In addition, the content of international trade has shifted away from primary commodities (exported primarily by developing countries) and toward high-technology services and manufactured products, which are typically industrialized-nation exports, as the rate of growth in trade in these services and products has exceeded that of primary commodities. Another feature of current trade patterns is the growing share of international trade taking place within corporations. It has been estimated that between 40 and 50% of imports and exports of major economies like Japan and the United States correspond to intrafirm transactions (Greider 1997).

The rapid growth and globalization of the world economy are also illustrated by the recent surge in flows of direct foreign investment, which are considered increasingly interrelated to trade as a factor behind growth and development. In fact, the recent growth in direct foreign investment has been even faster than that in trade, reaching a record high of $315 billion in 1995. Although a large part of these investment flows go between the largest developed economies, flows of direct foreign investment to developing countries were also at a record high of $100 billion in 1995. Another important indicator of economic globalization is the value of cross-border mergers and acquisitions, which totaled $229 billion in 1995, doubling the figure for 1988 (UNCTAD 1996).

The production of goods and services has also expanded and spread at an uneven pace throughout the world, and this has led to significant regional shifts and to a more balanced worldwide distribution of productive activities. Three centres of power — East Asia, North America, and Western Europe — are now in a position of strategic economic parity (Schwab and Smajda 1995). Services have become an increasingly important part of the world economy, and their average annual growth rate during 1990–95 has been 5.3% (8.8% in East Asia and the Pacific), more than twice the 2% growth rate of the world's total output of goods and services.

A new web of commercial linkages between transnational corporations has now emerged, covering manufacturing, finance, trade, and services. Strategic alliances between corporations in precompetitive research and development, coupled with fierce competition in final-product markets, are a prime example of these new trends, which demand new corporate and national strategies. A significant shift is taking place in the organization of productive and service activities in the globalized segments of the world economy. The economic unit is no longer the enterprise, either local, international, or transnational, but a specific network created for a particular purpose at a particular time, which operates in large part independently of the various enterprises that established it. As Castells pointed out,

> Under different organizational arrangements, and through diverse cultural expressions, [the new organizational forms of the informational economy] are all based on networks. *Networks are the fundamental stuff of which new organizations are and will be made.* And they are able to form and expand all over the main streets and back alleys of the global economy because of their reliance on the information power provided by the new technological paradigm.
>
> (Castells 1996, p. 168, his emphasis)

A core of strategic economic activities — capital markets, business services, travel and tourism, technology, and a few production lines such as automobiles, computers, and electronic goods — now sets the pace for the evolution of the globalized economy, operating in real time and simultaneously in many parts of the planet. Many parts of the world that do not share in these activities — both in the developing and in the industrialized nations — are at the same time being marginalized and run the risk of becoming, at best, appendices to the globalized centres of production and, at worst, irrelevant to the functioning of an increasingly globalized economy. The explosion of private-capital flows in the early 1990s, for example, largely bypassed most of the nations of sub-Saharan Africa. As the Indian social scientist Rajni Khotari once said, "for the first time in history, the rich do not need the poor" (R. Khotari, personal communication, Cairo, 1981). Little wonder, then, that most developing countries have shed their erstwhile antagonistic stance toward transnational corporations. After the often hostile way in which they viewed foreign investment in the 1960s and 1970s, developing countries now welcome, seek, and court direct foreign investment.

On another plane, the last two decades have seen completely new situations in several key countries and regions that affect significantly the world economy. During the 1980s, for the first time in recent history, the United States became a net debtor nation, although by the mid-1990s it appeared poised to cut its fiscal deficit and achieve a balanced federal budget in the early years of the next century. Despite setbacks during the early and mid-1990s, Japan remains a dominant economic and financial actor on the international scene and now — after the bankruptcy of several important financial enterprises — appears ready to restructure its aging and inefficient financial system.

Hesitations of some countries notwithstanding, following the 1986 accord on a Single Act, Europe is steadily moving toward economic, monetary, and maybe some form of political unity, a path that appeared unthinkable during the years of "Eurosclerosis" in the late 1970s and early 1980s. The Soviet Union was dissolved, and its former constituents are undergoing a painful transition to becoming market economies, a path followed earlier by Central and Eastern European countries that has yielded handsome economic dividends for some of them. However, as the mid-1998 downturn of the Russian stock market indicated, economic reforms are proving to be quite painful and uncertain. China has undergone an astonishing economic transformation while eschewing political liberalization. As a result of embracing market economics and introducing major of policy reforms, China has experienced very high rates of growth during the 1990s; it has become a major player in the world economy and received huge amounts of direct foreign investment; and Hong Kong has again become part of China, bringing with it all of its economic resources and entrepreneurial spirit.

Latin America has weathered the debt crisis of the 1980s, and, after a decade of stagnation, its policy reforms led to renewed growth in the early 1990s and to sustained economic expansion by the late 1990s. Most African countries saw the precarious gains of several decades reversed during the 1980s, although policy reforms and external assistance restored growth in a few of them during the 1990s. Political instability and strife in the Middle Eastern countries has not fostered an environment conducive to economic growth. After two decades of rapid economic growth, the newly industrialized economies of Southeast Asia have experienced the collapse of their currencies, major stock-market upheavals, and severe financial setbacks in mid- and late 1997. Since the early 1990s, India has been experimenting with economic-policy reforms and liberalization, which are likely to spur economic growth, while other countries in the Asian region are trying to begin a difficult process of economic reconstruction and political reconciliation after decades of war.

After the collapse of the Soviet Union and the general failure of centrally planned economies, capitalism has emerged unchallenged as the only feasible path to prosperity. However, as the competition between centrally planned and market economies disappeared, it became possible to focus attention on the variations within capitalism and on the differences in the ways various market economies function. Albert (1991) contrasted the "neo-American" and "Rhenanian" varieties of capitalism as alternative models for the organization of market economies. The first emphasizes individual competition and short-term financial performance in enterprises and limits the range of social services provided by the state. The second emphasizes consensus and collective action and long-term productive performance in enterprises and considers a wider range of state interventions in the provision of public goods. Along similar lines and based on an extensive worldwide survey of managers, Hampden-Turner and Trompenaars (1993) identified seven distinct "cultures of capitalism," based on the values that drive the activities of firms; even a distinct Chinese strain of capitalism has been recently identified (Redding 1997). As economic competition intensifies between the key regions in the global economy — East Asia, Europe, and North America — each is putting forward its own version of capitalism as the model to be followed by the rest of the world.

Persistent inequalities and economic uncertainty

The increasing economic and financial interdependence characteristic of globalization coexists with persistent and growing inequalities in living standards between and within nations. Despite dramatic improvements in life expectancy in many parts of the world during the last 40 years, there are still enormous and enduring economic differences between rich and poor countries and between regions within countries.

According to the World Bank, in 1995, the average per capita GNP for the 49 low-income economies was $430, whereas the average for the 26 high-income economies was $24 930, almost 58 times higher. Moreover, if large and rapidly growing China and India are excluded from the group of low-income economies, their average per capita GNP would reach only $290, about 84 times less than the corresponding average for the high-income economies. The total population of the low-income countries was approximately 3.2 billion in 1996–97, nearly 3.5 times as many as the 902 million of the high-income countries, even though both groups of countries cover roughly the same area (World Bank 1996c, 1997d).

Moreover, during the last three decades, the share of world income for the richest 20% of the global population rose from 70% to nearly 85%, whereas the share of the poorest 20% declined from 2.3% to 1.4%. In the early 1990s, the ratio of income shares of the richest to the poorest 20% was about 61 to 1, and the ratio of the average income of the poorest 20% in the United States to the poorest 20% in Tanzania was 130 to 1 (UNDP 1996). Among developing countries, a few outstanding successes, notably those of Southeast Asia, coexist with a large number of stagnant or even regressing situations, particularly in sub-Saharan Africa, but also in Asia, Latin America, and the Middle East. Within many developing countries, too, the distribution of income continues to be highly skewed. The richest 20% of Chile's population received 61% of national income in 1994, whereas the poorest 10% only received 1.4% of national income. Similar distributions are found in countries such as Brazil, South Africa, Venezuela, and Zimbabwe (World Bank 1997d).

Although the divide between poverty and affluence has proven to be one of the most enduring and alarming features of the international economic order, the gap between rich and poor has also been increasing significantly in the industrialized nations in recent years. The case of the United States illustrates this clearly. Between 1950 and 1978, the poorest 20% of the United States population increased its income by 140%, whereas that of the richest 20% increased by 99%. However, between 1977 and 1994, the poorest 20% lost ground and its income was reduced by 16%, whereas that of the richest 20% increased by 25%. In the United Kingdom, the share of income earned by the richest 20% of the population increased from 43% to 50% between 1979 and 1996, whereas that of the poorest 20% increased only from 2.4% to 2.6%. The skewed pattern of wealth distribution is clearly visible in France, where the richest 20% of the population concentrates about 69% of assets and 44% of income and the poorest 20% accounts for only 0.45% of assets and 6% of income (Lind 1995; Julien 1995; The Economist 1997b).

In parallel with these persistent inequalities, the uncertainty and volatility of the international economy have been steadily increasing during the last two decades. The abandonment of fixed exchange rates in 1971, the oil-price shocks of the 1970s and 1980s, and the globalization of finance during the 1980s and 1990s have created a rather unpredictable international economic environment. In the early 1990s, the range and diversity of possible outcomes in practically all aspects of the international economy appeared much larger than at any time during the preceding three decades, and this uncertainty increased toward the mid- and late 1990s. Growing interdependence, spurred by advances in telecommunications and information technologies, has created an international economic environment that transmits disturbances and magnifies disruptions. A prime example is the impact of the virtually instantaneous transmission of information on the volatility of currency, stock, and derivatives markets. This volatility is often amplified by the pervasiveness of computer trading; only extreme measures, such as halting trading in stock markets, have been able to limit its negative impact to a certain extent.

Although world-trade expansion and economic growth have provided a steady backdrop against which to project the sudden shifts and swings of economic indicators, the accelerated and uneven process of economic globalization and the high degree of uncertainty associated with it have raised questions about the need for better international economic governance. Issues such as the reform the international monetary system, coordination of macroeconomic policies among the major world economies, regulation of international transactions and financial flows, establishment of standby mechanisms to assist countries in financial distress, and financing of development and reconstruction efforts (including the reform of the Bretton Woods institutions) all point to the need for closer cooperation among governments, as well as for greater cooperation between governments and private financial institutions (Solomon 1991; Griesgraber 1994; Kennen 1994; Stewart 1995).

The need for a new architecture of international finance has acquired particular urgency after the East Asian crisis of 1997–98, which, when added to the collapse of Russian finances in 1998, has had serious negative repercussions in Latin America and other emerging markets. Although a design acceptable to all major actors on the international financial scene is still far from articulated, much less agreed on, the urgent need for a new system to guarantee greater stability has been expressed by many academics, businesspeople, and policymakers. Even the President of the United Stated weighed in with the view that "the global economy simply cannot live with the ... systemic disruptions that have occurred over the past year" (Bill Clinton, cited in Business Week 1998b, p. 38).

Sudden withdrawals of private capital from emerging markets, a significant contributing factor behind the financial problems that have affected several developing countries in the last 2 years, could be viewed as the international equivalent of a "bank run" on entire economies. As financier George Soros (Soros 1998–99, p. 58) has forcefully argued, there are no mechanisms at present to prevent such major disruptions and reduce the negative impact of the high volatility of financial flows: "Market discipline is desirable, but needs to be complemented by another kind of discipline: Public-policy measures are needed to stabilize the flows of international finance required by the global capitalist system and to keep the inherent instability of financial markets under control." Moreover, the impact of the Asian crisis on developing countries has been so severe that the much-celebrated triumph of capitalism is beginning to be questioned. Global capitalism has been said to be "under siege" (Business Week 1998a) as the 1990s come to an end and some countries (Malaysia and Russia, for example) begin to have second thoughts about financial liberalization, economic deregulation, privatization, and the adoption of the Washington Consensus on economic-policy reforms.

An important concern in the evolution of global economic governance is the degree to which the interests of poor countries, along with those generally of countries without economic power, will be taken into account in the design of international economic-governance structures. This concern is made more acute by the fact that even in the Bretton Woods institutions and regional development banks — whose main objectives are to finance development projects, support economic policy reforms, and assist in reconstruction efforts — developing countries have a very limited say in setting policies and running the organizations.

Social conditions

The last several decades have witnessed a rather contradictory situation in the evolution of social conditions throughout the world. The *Human Development Report 1996* (UNDP 1996, pp. 17–18) indicated that

> Human development over the past 30 years is a mixed picture of unprecedented human progress and unspeakable human misery — of human advances on several fronts and retreats on several others. ... The developing countries have in many respects covered as much distance in their human development during past 30 years as the industrial world managed over a century.

Since 1960 average life expectancy in developing countries has increased by more than one-third; the population with access to safe water has doubled to nearly 70%; primary-school enrollment has increased by nearly two-thirds to 77%; real per capita income has increased at an average of 3.5% a year; the infant mortality rate has been cut to less than one-half to 70 per thousand live births. Between 1980 and 1995, the total fertility rate in developing countries dropped from 4.1 children per woman to 3.1 children per woman.

But enormous challenges remain: 99% of the 20 million people who died in 1993 from communicable diseases lived in the developing countries; around 17 million people die each year from curable infections and parasitic diseases; 90% of the 18 million HIV-infected people live in developing countries; more than 130 million primary-level and 275 million secondary-level school children are out of school; nearly 800 million people do not get enough food; 500 million people are chronically malnourished; and about one-third of the people in developing countries — 1.3 billion people — live in poverty. Moreover, as pointed out in the preceding section, the gap between the rich and poor continues to widen. In 1997, about 20% of the world's population, well more than a billion people, lived on the equivalent of less than $1 a day, whereas an unprecedented 3 million people had liquid assets of more than $1 million dollars.

The negative side of this mixed picture of advances and misery is partly the result of an explosive growth in social demands in the developing regions, which was largely triggered by population increases during the last 50 years. Coupled with a significant slowdown in population growth in the industrialized nations, this has led to a highly skewed worldwide distribution of social needs, demands, and expectations, on the one hand, and the capabilities to satisfy them, on the other (United Nations 1993).

A significant drop in the population growth rate of industrialized countries is to be expected in the transition to the 21st century, from an annual average of 0.54% in 1985–90 to only 0.38% in 2000–05. This implies a rapid rise in the number of aged people, particularly in Japan, Europe, and the United States, where the proportion of people aged 65 or more will exceed 30% of the population by 2025, and the ratio of dependents (children and old people) to active workers will increase significantly. Aging in industrialized nations will have a major impact on the demand for social services, as well as important consequences for the patterns of consumption, employment, savings, and the direction of technical progress.

Peter Peterson has warned about the dire consequences of the "graying new world older" during the first decades of the 21st century for international security, economic interdependence, and the emergence of an "old/young fault line," which may replace the North–South divide (Peterson 1999, p. 43–44).

In developing countries, rapid population growth is expected to continue into the new century, although at a moderately slower pace, dropping from an average rate of 2.11% a year in 1985–90 to 1.74% during 2000–05. As a consequence, youth will remain by far the largest segment of the population in most of these countries, whose economies must expand at rates significantly above those of their populations to satisfy the growing demand for work. Yet, the countries with apparently the least promising prospects have populations that continue to grow most rapidly. During 1990–95, sub-Saharan Africa's annual population growth rate was around 3%, almost twice the world average of 1.5%. China, with its 1.2 billion inhabitants in 1995, presents a rather special problem, particularly in view of its "one-child" policy, which poses a dilemma between higher population growth rates in the short term and an aging population in the long term (United Nations 1991; The Economist 1996).

World population imbalances have raised the possibility of uncontrolled mass migrations from poor to rich nations, a prospect that elicits xenophobic reactions among significant segments of the population in the advanced economies. However, as Amartya Sen has pointed out, "the explanation for the increased migratory pressure over the decades owes more to the dynamism of international capitalism than to just the growing size of the population of the third world countries" (Sen 1994, p. 70). Sen argued that in addition to world population growth imbalances, it is necessary to consider "the growing demand for immigration to the North from the South," which is related to revolutions in transport and communications, reductions in obstacles to labour movements, and "the growing reach and absorptive power of international capitalism (even as domestic politics in the North have turned more inward-looking and nationalistic)" (Sen 1994, p. 70).

Although the massive inflows of workers from Northern Africa and Western Asia has failed as yet to materialize, in several Western European countries there is already a backlash against foreigners and growing support for right-wing nationalistic political movements. The United States has adopted stern measures to stem the flow of illegal immigrants from Central and South America, and some of its states have even reduced social benefits available to legal immigrants. In Asia, migration pressures are likely to build as a result of the growing demographic imbalances between Japan and the poorer overpopulated countries of the region. Despite increased participation of women in the labour market, the Japanese will experience a decline in the labour force after 2000, and labour shortages will be compounded by moves to reduce the number of working hours.[6]

The increased flows of refugees from civil wars, particularly in Africa, Asia, and Europe, add to the perception of a growing threat from population growth. In Africa alone, there were nearly 12 million refugees in 1995, almost four times the estimate for just 10 years earlier (World Bank 1997d). The spread of ethnic and religious conflicts in several regions, particularly in the Middle East, South Asia, and the former Soviet Block, might aggravate this situation and give rise to greater concerns, even alarmism, about population growth and migration.

The dynamics of population growth strongly condition the demand for food, education, employment, housing, and other social goods. Food and nutrition requirements have multiplied many times over, particularly in the poorest countries, and although world aggregate food production has been increasing and is sufficient to provide each and every human being with adequate nourishment, existing political, social, and institutional arrangements — at both the national and international levels — have proven incapable of doing so. Armed conflicts,

---

[6]   Matthew Connelly and Paul Kennedy highlighted the fear of uncontrolled migration, indeed of invasion, by impoverished migrants from the poor regions of the world. Inspired by French novelist Jean Raspail, they described the arrival of the first wave of "a million desperate Indians who, forsaking the ghastly conditions of downtown Calcutta and surrounding villages, commandeer an armada of decrepit ships and set off for the French Riviera" (Connelly and Kennedy 1994, p. 61).

droughts, and natural disasters have conspired to make it even more difficult to ensure access to food in many violence-ridden regions of the developing world.

Demands for basic health care and elementary education expanded at a rapid pace during the last three decades, and developing countries made significant efforts to improve the provision of these services to their growing populations. Nevertheless, abysmal disparities remain between rich and poor countries in access to social services. For example, although there is 1 doctor for every 390 people in the industrialized countries, the corresponding figure is 1 doctor for every 6 700 people in the developing countries (CPBN 1992; FAO 1996).

The increased mobility accompanying improvements in transportation technology has made it easier for diseases to spread widely and rapidly, as shown by the worldwide AIDS epidemic. This problem is not restricted to the developing regions but also affects the transition economies. For example, throughout the former Soviet Union, particularly in Russia, risky sexual behaviour and increased drug use led to an epidemic rise in cases of AIDS. About 800 000 people may be HIV positive by the year 2000 in these countries (Reid 1995). By 2000, about three-quarters of the world population living in urban agglomerations will be in developing countries. Migration and accelerated urbanization have created huge demands for housing, sanitation, transportation, and energy supply, a situation that adds unmet urban needs and widespread urban poverty to the deprivation of rural populations throughout the developing world.

Unemployment has emerged as perhaps the most difficult and urgent problem in the developing regions of the world. It has also begun to affect the rich countries during the last two decades. In most developing countries, the inability of the modern sectors of the economy to absorb new entrants into the labour force has led to a variety of "informal" arrangements for workers to earn their means of subsistence, largely in self-generated, low-productivity jobs that barely allow people to make ends meet. Developing countries face the difficult challenge of raising labour productivity while absorbing the growing number of entrants into the labour force. As yet, this fundamental problem seems to have no adequate solution. This challenge was clearly summarized in the *World Development Report 1995: Workers in an Integrating World*, prepared by the World Bank:

> About 99% of the 1 billion or so workers projected to join the world's labour force over the next thirty years will live in what are today's low- and middle income countries. Some groups of relatively poor workers have experienced large gains in the past thirty years — especially in Asia. But there is no worldwide trend toward convergence between rich and poor workers. Indeed, there are risks that workers in poorer countries will fall further behind, as lower investment and educational attainment widen

disparities. Some workers, especially in Sub-Saharan Africa, could become increasingly marginalized. And those left out of the general prosperity in countries that are enjoying growth could suffer permanent losses, setting in motion intergenerational cycles of neglect.

(World Bank 1995, pp. 7–8)

Differences in social and economic indicators between men and women throughout the world are a prominent and most disturbing feature of the global social situation. Despite two decades of efforts dedicated to women in development, women and children remain the poorest of the poor, and in terms of development indicators the gender gap is widening. In industrialized countries, gender discrimination appears in employment and wages, with women often getting less than two-thirds of the employment opportunities and about one-half of the earnings of men. In developing countries, the greatest disparities between males and females are in education, the job market, health care, and nutritional support. For example, women make up two-thirds of the world's illiterate population and get only 55% of years of schooling. The 1989 United Nations survey on the role of women stated that women do two-thirds of the world's work, own one-tenth of the land, and have only one-hundredth of the world's income (United Nations 1993; Rowbotham and Mitter 1994).

Growing social demands, population imbalances, gender differences, and constraints on the access to basic services will tax to the limit the capacities of most developing-country governments, development-cooperation institutions, and international organizations. New conceptions of social policy and new institutional arrangements will have to be developed to cope with the growth in social demands.

Environmental sustainability

During the last several decades, we have began to reexamine our views on the linkages between human beings and nature, primarily because we have gradually realized that it is no longer possible to ignore the growing impact of human activities on the biophysical environment. As a result, environmental concerns have risen to the top of the international public-policy agenda. There is now greater awareness of how the regenerative capacities of natural ecosystems impose limitations on human activities, as well as of the dangers of the uncontrolled exploitation of natural resources (fisheries, forests, land, rivers) and the overloading of the capacity of the Earth to absorb waste (air and water pollution, acid rain, toxic and nuclear wastes).

The contemporary concern with environmental sustainability can be traced to the warnings issued during the 1960s and 1970s about the negative impact of the patterns of economic growth pursued by the high-income countries. Rachel Carson's description of the destruction caused by chemical pesticides in the early 1960s created considerable controversy and forced a reexamination of agricultural practices in the United States (Carson 1962). The spectre of a shortage of natural resources was raised by *Limits to Growth*, a report of the Club of Rome, whose publication preceded by a few months the quadrupling of oil prices by OPEC in 1973 (Meadows et al. 1972). In subsequent years, other authors and organizations — such as Lester Brown at the Worldwatch Institute and Gerald Barney in *The Global 2000 Report* — raised similar concerns and sought to inform citizens in the industrialized nations about excessive energy consumption, unsustainable agricultural practices, toxic wastes, and similar issues (Brown 1984; Barney 1980).

These concerns were extrapolated to developing countries, with a focus on the effects of rapid population growth. In many instances, particularly during the 1970s and early 1980s, these preoccupations were seen as a form of "environmental colonialism" (De Almeida 1972). It was argued that the preservation of the environment is primarily a responsibility of developed countries, that the high-income countries developed the practices that pollute the environment, that they use a disproportionate share of natural resources, and that they are trying to prevent developing countries from achieving economic growth and high standards of living. To a large extent, these views were responsible for the rather limited advances of the 1972 Stockholm United Nations Conference on Environment and Development.

During the 1970s, Ignacy Sachs and Maurice Strong introduced the idea of "ecodevelopment" and suggested strategies and policies to harmonize environmental and economic-growth objectives (Sachs 1977, 1980). *Our Common Future*, the Brundlandt Report, of the World Commission on Environment and Development (WCED 1987, p. 1), put forward "the possibility for a new era of economic growth, one that must be based on policies that sustain and expand the environmental resource base" and offered specific recommendations at the national and international levels to achieve this. But it is also clear that the opportunities to achieve development while sustaining and expanding the environmental resource base are not unlimited and that the scope for taking advantage of what have been called "win–win" situations in environment and development may be rather constrained (Cairncross 1991; World Bank 1992b).

It is now widely accepted that the problems of environmental sustainability and resource use are closely related to population growth and poverty in the developing countries, as well as the often wasteful consumption habits of rich nations — one-fifth of the world's population living in the rich countries consume more than 80% of the world's resources (Durning 1992). Moreover, as they grow and industrialize rapidly, the large developing countries may considerably increase the pressures on the environment; for example, carbon dioxide emissions in China and India nearly doubled between 1980 and 1992 and reached 3 450 t in the latter year, out of a world total of 21 350 t (World Bank 1997d). Major changes in values and institutions in both groups of countries will be essential to seriously addressing the problem of environmental sustainability.

From a broader perspective, ideas about the relationship between environment and development have evolved gradually over the past five decades. From a primordial dichotomy between "frontier economics" and "deep ecology," other paradigms — environmental protection, resource management, and ecodevelopment — have evolved in a progression that involves a greater integration of economic, ecological, cultural, and social systems in the definition of development and the organization of human societies (Colby 1990). In particular — as testified by several reports, public statements, and projects financed by international organizations — the transition from concepts and ideas to strategies, policies, and practices to harmonize objectives for the environment and economic growth has accelerated since the early 1980s.

An important milestone in the incorporation of environmental sustainability into development thinking and practice was the adoption of Agenda 21 at the 1992 Earth Summit in Rio de Janeiro, a wide-ranging world program of action to promote sustainable development. However, the negotiations during that conference exposed the divergence of perspectives between industrialized and developing nations on approaches, strategies, and policies to achieve sustainable development. Questions of lifestyles, national sovereignty, barriers to trade, and financial assistance, in addition to access to less polluting technologies, are now at the centre of the international debate on sustainable development (UNCED 1992; IDRC 1993a, b). Five years after the Rio Summit, more than 65 heads of state gathered in New York at the United Nations' Rio+5 Conference to assess the progress made on the 1992 agreements. Although some advances were made, such as the Basel Convention on hazardous materials, the overall progress on significant sustainable-development issues (such as assistance from industrialized countries) has been deemed rather unsatisfactory and disappointing.

In addition to concerns about the environment at the national level, truly global environmental problems emerged in the 1980s. The depletion of the ozone layer and the threat of climate change, often referred to as "global warming" or "the greenhouse effect," have underscored the possibility that human activities can cause irreversible environmental damage. However, despite expanded research efforts, considerable uncertainty and controversy remain regarding global environmental problems and, in particular, climate change. Average temperatures have been rising throughout the globe, and it is now beyond reasonable scientific doubt that human activities are having an effect on the climate. But it is very difficult to unequivocally determine the extent to which humans are responsible for this global-warming trend, primarily because of climatic variability, the various possible sources of atmospheric temperature change, the shortness of the monitoring record, and the nonuniform character of changes over the planet (IPCC 1996).

Regional changes in climate may be more important than global changes, particularly in economic and social terms. Some areas may even get cooler while others get warmer, with the aggregate average showing little or no change. The rise in sea level accompanying polar or overall warming will have a more severe impact on low-lying and island countries; tropical and temperate zones will see major changes in precipitation patterns; mountainous and polar regions may see glacier coverage receding; and ocean currents may experience major shifts. In the last analysis, the fact that deviations from familiar climatic patterns may become larger is of greater importance (Sagasti and Colby 1993). This means that severe, unusual events (hurricanes, floods, precipitation patterns, monsoon seasons, and droughts) will probably become both more extreme and more common. All of these changes will have major economic, social, and political implications, as demonstrated by the unusually severe appearance of the El Niño global weather phenomenon in 1997–98, which altered weather patterns all over the world and caused major destruction.

The supply of fresh water for a growing population is another global environmental question particularly central to the prospects for human development and welfare, one that may spark international conflict in the coming decades. United Nations estimates indicate that by 2025 "two thirds of humanity will face shortages of clean freshwater" (Work in Progress 1998, p. 1). The impact of a growing human population on the world's oceans, rivers, and lakes has been considerable in terms of pollution and imbalances between urban and rural water supplies. Population growth alone has determined that "per capita water supplies as we enter the 21st century are one third lower than they were in 1970" (Work in Progress 1998, p. 24). There is a clear potential for international conflict in this area, as waterways often cross several countries and water supply is intimately linked to a number of environmental factors. In fact, disputes over water rights have already become a very real issue in regions such areas the Middle East and in the European nations on the Danube River.

The international and global dimensions of environmental change have led to proposals to redefine national security in environmental terms (Mathews 1989; Myers 1989). Another consequence of the greater importance of environmental concerns is that international economic relations, particularly commerce and trade, will become increasingly linked to environmental issues. Similarly, access to development cooperation and to finance from international institutions will be more and more conditioned on adopting meaasures to protect the environment. Moreover, some industrialized countries — notably Japan and Germany — are positioning themselves to compete in what will be one of the most dynamic markets of the future, environmentally sound technologies. Being able to provide environmentally friendly technologies is rapidly becoming a source of competitive advantage in the global search for new markets (Rath and Herbert-Copley 1993).

Culture, religion, and ethical concerns

One of the striking features of the contemporary scene is the degree to which questions of a cultural nature, which were usually neglected or given scant attention at the international level, have acquired renewed importance. After a brief interlude in the late 1950s and early 1960s when sociological and cultural explanations of development held sway (Hagen 1962; Lerner 1962; McClelland 1962), most of the post-World War II period has been dominated by economic perspectives and accounts of the way to improve the human condition.

Samuel Huntington put forward the prospect of a "clash of civilizations" as the dominant force in international affairs in the transition to the 21st century, suggesting that the great divisions and dominating sources of conflict will be cultural (Hutington 1996) and that "culture and cultural identities, which at the broadest level are civilizational entities, are shaping the patterns of cohesion, disintegration, and conflict in the post-Cold War world" (Huntington 1996, p. 20; see also Huntington 1993). Other authors have advanced cultural explanations of economic and political success, arguing that contemporary analysts tend to underestimate culture as an essential factor shaping society (Inglehart 1990). Some economic historians now even argue that "the most important influence on a nation's responsiveness to change probably is its social attitudes, religious beliefs, and culture" (Kennedy 1993, p. 16).

Even international institutions like the World Bank, previously known to focus exclusively on economic and social questions, are beginning to pay attention to cultural questions (Serageldin and Taboroff 1994). In addition, the rise of religious fundamentalism and fierce ethnic rivalries, which have reemerged in violent form throughout the world, are a powerful reminder of the renewed and growing importance of the largely neglected nonmaterial and cultural dimensions of development.

Three powerful cultural forces are shaping the international scene in the transition to the 21st century: the growing importance of religious values and the rise of religious fundamentalism as a main driving force in economic and political actions in many parts of the world; the tensions between pressures to homogenize culture, attributable to the pervasive influence of mass media, and the desire to preserve cultural identity; and the emergence of moral and ethical issues at the forefront of choices about inter- and intragenerational equity, particularly in relation to human rights, the environment, income distribution, and poverty reduction.

The revival of religious and spiritual concerns has been a characteristic of the last two decades of the 20th century, which have witnessed the renaissance of Islamic values in northern Africa, Central Asia, and the Middle East; a revival of the Orthodox Christian Church in Eastern Europe and the former Soviet Union; the spread of evangelical churches in Latin America and other developing regions; a surge in the popularity of the Roman Catholic Pope; the growing influence of Christian fundamentalism in North American political life; and the renewed interest in mysticism and Oriental religions, often associated with "New Age" movements that eschew rationality. All of this points to the fact that, probably because of the overriding concern with improving material well-being and standards of living, the spiritual dimensions of human development have been neglected during the mostly secular post-World War II period (Beckford 1986; Macy 1986; Wright 1986; Barney et al. 1993; Johnston and Sampson 1994; Ryan 1995).

As a consequence of the globalization and pervasive influence of mass media — a direct result of technological advances in telecommunications during the past two decades — two contradictory cultural forces can now be seen at play. On the one hand, there are pressures to standardize (Westernize?) aspirations and cultural values throughout the world, but there is, on the other hand, the desire to reassert individuality and preserve cultural identity (O'Neill 1993). These two contradictory forces create cultural tensions and emotional stresses, particularly in developing countries, where the images of affluence brought by television programs from high-income nations contrast sharply with the harsh reality of mass poverty and the fact that those worlds of plenty are simply unattainable for the vast majority of the population.

Fernando Fajnzylber coined the term "frustration space" to describe the area between the rising curve depicting the number of television sets per 1 000 inhabitants and the declining curve depicting the minimum urban wage in Latin America during the 1980s (Fajnzylber 1992). This frustration space has continued to expand as the gap between rich and poor widens and access to mass media, particularly television, increases throughout the developing world. For example, in Peru there were 52 television sets and 159 radio receivers per 1 000 inhabitants in 1980; by 1993, when real urban wages had dropped to about one-half of their 1980 level, the corresponding numbers had nearly doubled to 99 and 253, respectively.

Moral and ethical questions, once the province of academics and religious activists, are finding their way into public debates on the rights of future generations in relation to sustainable development and on a variety of other issues, such as racism, abortion, corruption, arms proliferation, crime prevention, and drug traffic. A renewed concern with human rights throughout the world has led many to question the principle of nonintervention in the internal affairs of states where governments do not respect basic human rights (ODC 1992; Damrosch 1993; Brauman 1995; Ramón Chornet 1995). Finally, reversing the trend that prevailed during the 1980s, equity considerations are finding their way into the political agenda of many industrialized and developing countries at the same time as the moral and ethical aspects of economic behaviour have begun to receive greater attention (Dasgupta 1993; Nussbaum and Sen 1993). However, this does not mean that solidarity, compassion, and concern for the well-being of others have become the guiding principles of national and international policy-making.

Changes in the cultural sphere indicate that a new set of issues has been added to the international agenda. These include the need to consider the views of religious leaders in national and international institutions, the importance of taking into account the impact of the transfer of information and of mass media images, and the need to incorporate ethical, moral, and human-rights issues into the conduct of international affairs.

Moreover, the 1998 arrest of former Chilean dictator Augusto Pinochet in the United Kingdom and the possibility of his being tried for human-rights abuses have set the stage for a new era in which such crimes are not committed with impunity (Lagos and Muñoz 1999; Slaughter 1999).

Governance and democracy

A host of issues related to governance — that is, to the ways power and authority are exercised in pursuit of economic and social objectives — have acquired great prominence throughout the world since the end of the Cold War. The broken spell of East–West confrontation, which kept most of us mesmerized by the relentless struggle between communism and capitalism, and the victory of the West, market economics, and democratic politics have forced us to wake up to the reality that there are many kinds of capitalism and many types of democratic regimes.

But the end of the Cold War is not the only reason why questions of governance have become important in rich and poor countries, regional and international organizations, and even corporations and civil-society organizations. During the last two decades, a gradual change has been occurring in the roles played by the public sector, the private sector, and the organizations of civil society. In Europe and the United States — as well as in Eastern Europe, the former Soviet Union, and in many developing countries — thousands of public enterprises have been privatized, and the provision of many public services has been contracted out to private firms. This has been, in large measure, a response to the growing share of total government expenditures in the GDP of most countries — particularly of the industrialized nations, which has more than doubled since 1960 and now stands at about 45% of GDP (World Bank 1997d). During the 1990s, the role of the state has been reexamined from the perspective of improving accountability, responsiveness, transparency, openness, and institutional capabilities. As a result, after expanding relentlessly for decades, the public sector has come under pressure to become smaller, stronger, and more efficient.

In addition, NGOs and other civil-society organizations focusing on human rights, the preservation of the environment, poverty and hunger reduction, the delivery of basic social services, humanitarian relief, and consumer rights, among other issues, have become important players on the national and international scenes. All of this has altered the division of labour between the public, the private, and the social sectors in the provision of what were until very recently considered public goods and services (Nerfin 1987; Picciotto 1995). As a result, the governance debate incorporates a host of new issues going well beyond public-sector reform.

Therefore, governance has become a subject of concern for society at large. Good government is no longer an exclusive concern of the public sector; it has also become a preoccupation of private enterprises and civil-society organizations (trade unions, professional associations, environmental groups, advocacy groups for human rights and for all sorts of other causes, grass-roots movements, religious organizations, neighbourhood associations), as well as of international institutions and development-cooperation agencies.

The salience of governance issues has also been reinforced by the impact of technological advances in telecommunications, mass media, and information processing, which are changing the nature and functioning of representative democracies (Council of Europe 1981; Rosell 1993, 1994). These advances were instrumental in hastening the demise of one-party rule in Eastern Europe and the Soviet Union, opening up the possibility of direct forms of democracy in which citizens may change the roles of their state representatives, and in creating a more open and transparent setting for politics everywhere.

In the industrialized nations, several political events have led to what has been perceived as a widespread crisis of governance in the early and mid-1990s. Corruption scandals have undermined public trust in the political system in France, Germany, Italy, Japan, Spain, and the United States; for the first time in recent memory, right-wing armed militias brought terrorism to the heartland of the United States; xenophobic political groups emerged in France, Germany, and the United Kingdom; and constitutional crises and conflicts surfaced in Australia, Canada, and Japan. The spread of organized crime and drug traffic throughout Europe, Japan, and North America — not to speak of Central Asia, Eastern Europe, and the former Soviet Union — has also generated insecurity and fear and has made the task of governing more difficult.

Through the ballot box, citizens in rich countries have expressed their dissatisfaction with the ways their economic and political systems function, as is evident from the setbacks experienced by traditional and ruling parties in Asia, several countries of Europe, and even in North America. The crisis that the decades-old welfare state is experiencing in practically all advanced economies, primarily because it is becoming financially unfeasible, has added to the sense of insecurity and instability that is breaking the social compact between the state and civil society and between governments and the citizenry in these countries. The need to balance economic flexibility and social cohesion in the transition to the 21st century has prompted calls to reorient the welfare state, renew the decision-making and participatory processes, and improve systems of governance (DAC 1996, 1997b).

Governance problems have intensified in developing countries because of the sharp contrast between the growth in social demands and the capacity of the institutional frameworks — including the institutions of the state, the private sector, and civil society — to process and satisfy them. As indicated before, during the 1980s and 1990s, this has coincided with attempts to redefine the roles of the public and private sectors and markets and states in fostering economic growth, social justice, and environmental sustainability. Government failures in economic-policy management, productive activities, and provision of social services — added to renewed confidence in the positive role that market forces can play — prompted the international development community to pay greater attention to the ways power and authority are exercised through state institutions in pursuit of development objectives. This was brought sharply into focus by the extreme cases of poor governance in collapsed states such as Afghanistan, Cambodia, Liberia, Rwanda, and Somalia. In addition, civil-society organizations and particularly grass-roots movements have shown in many parts of the world that they can provide basic social services to the poor, especially in situations in which government agencies and the private sector are either incapable of providing such services or uninterested in doing so.

Governance and good government have also emerged as areas of concern for international development organizations during the last two decades. Throughout most of the post-World War II period, development assistance focused primarily on investment projects in infrastructure, agriculture, industry, and the social sectors. However, by the early 1980s, it became clear that many of the projects supported with external technical and financial resources failed to yield the anticipated rates of return. One reason was that investments were made in highly distorted policy environments, which prevented benefits from materializing. By the end of the 1980s, most developing countries had accepted the need for policy reforms and sought a better balance between market forces and state intervention. These developments underscored the importance of the government's capacity to formulate and manage policy reforms, as well as the capabilities of the private sector to assess the impact of the policy environment on enterprise performance (CCSTG 1992; World Bank 1992a).

The growing importance of democratic governance has highlighted the importance of "social capital," which, according to Robert Putnam, consists of such features of social organization as the patterns of stable connection between individuals and the moral resources available to the group, including trust, shared norms, and networks of civic engagements. Over time, social capital can improve the efficiency of society by helping people to overcome the dilemmas of collective action that can hinder cooperation. The availability of social capital explains the institutional success and the high degree of cooperation found in some societies, as well as the prevalence of democratic forms of governance: "building social capital will not be easy, but it is the key to making democracy work" (Putnam 1993, p. 185). Although Putnam focused on the patterns of social organization along the North–South division in Italy, recent work has shown that in developing nations, too, social capital can lead to higher incomes, better quality of social services, and increases in well-being (World Bank 1997d).

The policy reforms of the last decade and a half in developing countries have had important negative social consequences, such as an increase in the number of poor people, cuts in the provision of basic social services, and increased unemployment, the severity of which was not anticipated in the early 1980s. According to Ernest Stern, a former senior official of the World Bank,

> we at the World Bank — and everyone else, I believe, underestimated the political difficulty of protected adjustment. Economists here and elsewhere often tend to believe that we need only do our analysis, reach our conclusions, and write a report; the rest will follow. We do not have much experience with the political processes of change. We fail to give weight in our own thinking to the fact that structural adjustment means a major redistribution of economic power and hence of political power in many of the countries undergoing this process.
>
> (Stern 1991, p. 4)

Without interventions to ameliorate the impact of policy reforms, including macroeconomic stabilization, trade liberalization, deregulation, and privatization, social conditions worsened in many developing countries. This prompted a renewed concern with the political sustainability and feasibility of economic reforms, focusing attention on the ways governments exercise power and authority. Therefore, the need to marshall political support for economic reforms, the precarious nature of new democracies, and the need to have legitimate and effective mechanisms for citizen participation have all highlighted the importance of governance in the poor regions of the world (Sagasti et al. 1995).

Even though serious concerns about the nature of the democratic regimes have emerged in the developing regions, it is clear that the new international political context has altered the balance in favour of democratic forms of governance (Schmitz and Gillies 1992; Slater and Bennis 1990; Diamond and Plattner 1993; Held 1993; Diamond 1995). Without the justification of East–West conflict, it has become more difficult for Western countries to accept authoritarian rule in the developing world. Statements like "they may be bastards, but they are our bastards," when referring to pro-Western dictators, and distinctions between "friendly authoritarian" and "hostile dictatorial" regimes have become much harder to make (Kirkpatrick 1979). With the collapse of one-party regimes and the spread of democratic practices, former East-block countries are in no mood to support authoritarian regimes that violate human rights in the developing countries, even if they could afford it. Finally, advances in information and communications technologies have also helped in furthering democratization processes, giving citizens greater access to information, bypassing traditional methods of censorship, and putting new channels of communication at the disposal of rulers and citizens.

In short, the new international context places extraordinary demands on the capacity to legitimately, fairly, and effectively exercise power and authority. At the national level, governance has become an exceedingly difficult process of mediation between interests and aspirations that have their roots both within and outside a country. New global and international phenomena have appeared in full view, and for many of these phenomena there is no precedent for international cooperation, let alone willingness to surrender sovereignty — particularly for the more powerful countries (CCG 1995; Falk 1995; Righter 1995; South Centre 1996).

The knowledge explosion and the knowledge divide

Scientific advances and technological innovations are at the root of the complex transformations that have taken place during the last half century. Since World War II the products of scientific research and technological innovation have become more and more deeply enmeshed in all aspects of human activity, to the extent that many see a "knowledge society" as having emerged during the last several decades. This has profound implications for the organization of human activities and will radically modify relations between workers involved in the production and distribution of knowledge and those engaged in various forms of manual labour (Machlup 1962, 1980; Drucker 1968, 1994; OECD 1996).

Four features of science and technology merit particular attention as we enter a new century: the changes taking place in the conduct of scientific research, the increasingly systemic character of technological innovation, the emergence of a new "technoeconomic paradigm," and the persistence of the knowledge divide. All of these have a profound impact on the prospects for developing countries and for the future of development cooperation.

In the five decades since World War II, knowledge has grown at an astonishing pace. The explosive growth in knowledge has been described by David Linowes in the following terms:

> It took from the time of Christ to the mid-eighteenth century for knowledge to double. It doubled again 150 years later, and then again in only 50 years. Today it doubles every 4 or 5 years. More new information has been produced in the last 30 years than in the previous 5,000.

(Linowes 1990)

The growth of scientific research, supported by advances in information and computer sciences, has been primarily responsible for this explosion of knowledge. There have also been increased interpenetration and cross-fertilization between scientific research, technological innovation, and the commercial exploitation of research results.

The institutional settings for the conduct of basic research, applied research, and the development of new products and processes are undergoing significant change, particularly because of shifts in sources of funding and the more prominent role the private sector is playing in financing and conduct of research. Links between universities and industries are being strengthened, collaborative industrial research and technological alliances have become an imperative in certain fields, and venture-capital firms and some specialized government agencies are playing increasingly important roles in providing capital for new technology businesses. These changes have been taking place primarily in the rich countries, although several newly industrializing nations — particularly those in Southeast Asia — are also moving in this direction.

Organizational arrangements for the conduct of scientific and technological activities have changed largely in response to major increases in the cost of basic and applied research, which are also bringing about greater concentration in fields of research in which large facilities are needed and results may take a long time. Certain fields of research have become increasingly dependent on advanced and expensive instruments that, as in the case of chemical synthesis and advanced microelectronics research, combine advances in electronics, materials sciences, optics, analytical techniques, and information processing. The high cost of advanced instruments and financial constraints have been creating a difficult situation for university laboratories in industrialized nations and have effectively put many fields of research out of the reach of the vast majority of scientific institutions in developing countries.

However, advances in microelectronics, computers, and telecommunications have at the same time opened up new possibilities for the active participation of researchers from all parts of the world, including the poorer regions. Not only is there greater access to libraries and other sources of written information, but also it is possible to interact in almost real time with peers from all over the world in electronic conferences and to send data for analysis to centres with more advanced facilities. Although these opportunities are still being explored, it is clear that there is ample scope for developing countries to become actively involved in many aspects of scientific research, even in areas that would appear at first sight closed to them (Salam 1991; World Bank 1998).

The innovation process, which turns the results of research into productive activities, has also changed significantly, particularly in science- intensive industries and services. Innovation is becoming more complex and systemic, as well as more expensive, involves greater sophistication in management techniques, and is giving rise to new forms of appropriation of technological knowledge. As a result, both international collaboration and competition have intensified, and the role of governments in the support of innovation has been transformed.

The systemic nature of the innovation process has at least two manifestations: the complementarity of specific technical advances required to materialize a particular innovation and the larger network of institutions and support services needed for innovation to take place. New technologies are differentiated from old ones by their greater combinative and contagious character, largely because individual advances in information technology, automation, new materials, chemical synthesis, and biotechnology, among many others, cannot be applied on their own without complementary inputs from other technologies. This has become clearly noticeable in automation and computer-aided manufacturing, where microelectronics, computers, telecommunications, optoelectronics, and artificial intelligence are fusing together into an integrated technology system, as well as in fields like aircraft production and the development of new drugs.

The increasingly systemic character of innovation is also reflected in the larger number of actors involved in bringing major innovations to the market. In addition to the firms directly involved in this process, there may also be subcontractors, suppliers of inputs and equipment, laboratories, other organizations providing technological services, management consultants, educational and research institutions, market-research units, distributors, trading companies, financial institutions, and venture-capital firms. All of these are complemented by various government agencies and departments engaged in the formulation and implementation of policies that directly or indirectly affect the innovation process. The concept of "national systems of innovation" has been put forward to account for the growing complexity of the institutional arrangements required to facilitate the innovation process (Nelson 1993).

As a result of the more complex and systemic character of innovation, the costs of incorporating research results into productive and service activities and of bringing new products to the market have been steadily increasing during the past few decades. The higher costs of innovation and the larger risks faced by firms in a more competitive environment have in effect increased barriers to entry in many fields of industry. Paradoxically, the increase in competitive pressures has generated a host of cooperative arrangements between industrial firms, primarily in precompetitive research and marketing. However, only firms with substantive financial or technological assets (including small firms with a focus on specific technology niches) can expect to become players in the game of international technological alliances (Freeman and Hagedoorn 1992; Groupe de Lisbonne 1995).

The more systemic the character of innovation, the more it requires an emphasis on management skills and capabilities. To realize the full potential of new technologies, it has become necessary to introduce innovations in organization and management, a task for which advances in information technology have provided the tools. A well-developed physical infrastructure is also required to support innovation, including a good network of roads and transport facilities, telecommunications and data-transmission networks, reliable electricity supply, access to waste-disposal facilities, and clear-water supply. In addition, it may be necessary to count on advanced repair and maintenance services for a variety of laboratory and industrial equipment.

The changes in the innovation process have mixed effects on the prospects for developing countries. On the one hand, there is the possibility of incorporating advanced-technology components into traditional and conventional technologies in developing countries, that is, "technology blending," which can lead to more appropriate and higher productivity technologies (Bhalla 1993). On the other hand, the comparative advantage of developing countries is shifting away from low labour costs and natural resources, which is forcing major changes in education and industrialization policies. In addition, the physical and institutional infrastructure required to support increasingly complex innovation processes may well be beyond the existing capabilities of most developing countries, although it must also be kept in mind that a significant proportion of products and services in these countries is produced, distributed, and consumed locally. This may to a certain extent ease the pressures arising from the taxing demands of the innovation processes in more competitive fields.

The interactions of science, technology, and economic growth after World War II can be interpreted as the latest manifestation of a series of cyclical phenomena in the history of economic activity of the last 200 years. Carlota Pérez and Christopher Freeman have proposed the most widely known and accepted interpretation of such long waves of economic activity in recent times. They suggest that the transition from one long wave to another involves changes in the dominant technoeconomic paradigm. A technoeconomic paradigm is a combination of interrelated product, process, technical, organizational, and managerial innovations, embodying a significant jump in potential productivity for all or most of the economy and opening up an unusual range of investment and profit opportunities.

A major characteristic of the diffusion pattern of a new technoeconomic paradigm is its spread from initial industries and services to the economy as a whole (Freeman and Pérez 1988).

The organizing principle of each paradigm is to be found most of all in the dynamics of the relative cost structure of all possible inputs to production. In each paradigm, a particular input or set of inputs (the "key factor") fulfills the following conditions: (1) low and rapidly falling relative cost; (2) apparently almost unlimited ability of supply over long periods, which is an essential condition for the confidence to take major investment decisions; and (3) clear potential for use or incorporation of the new key factor or factors in many products and processes throughout the economic system, either directly or through a set of related innovations that both reduce the cost and change the quality of capital equipment, labour, and other inputs into the system.

The key factor in the technoeconomic paradigm that has now matured is energy (especially oil), whose falling cost, apparent unlimited supply, and widespread use reorganized the production of goods and services at the world level from the 1930s to the 1980s. Transport-related industries (automobiles, trucks, tractors, aircraft, motorized armaments), consumer durables, and oil-based products (petrochemicals, synthetic materials), accompanied by the expansion of the physical and institutional infrastructure to make full use of these products (highways, airports, gasoline distribution systems, consumer credit), set the pace for economic growth during what has also been called the "Fordist mass production Kondratieff wave." This wave extended through the 1980s and early 1990s and included the 1950–73 Golden Age of economic growth, a period of unprecedented economic and trade expansion following World War II (Maddison 1995).

A new technoeconomic paradigm began to emerge in the 1980s. The microelectronic chip is replacing energy as the key factor, and information and telecommunications industries and services (computers, electronic capital and consumer goods, robotics, telecommunications equipment, optical fibres, ceramics, software, and information services) are taking the lead in the process of economic growth. Satellites, digital-telecommunications networks, and special-purpose computers are providing the infrastructure for the expansion of information and communications services, which will continue well into the 21st century.

This transition has profound implications for the way production is organized in enterprises, for competitive strategies, and even for the institutional arrangements to support productive and service activities at the national and international levels. The well-proven set of common-sense guidelines derived from decades of successful experience in increasing efficiency within the framework of the technoeconomic paradigm based on energy is now giving way to a new set of efficiency principles and practices associated with the new possibilities opened up by the microelectronic chip (Pérez 1989).

As a result, the role that knowledge now plays in all human activities has become so critical that the concepts of development and progress need to be redefined in terms of the capacity to generate, acquire, disseminate, and use knowledge. The presence or absence of this capacity constitutes a crucial divide between rich and poor nations and societies, between those parts of the world in which individuals have the potential to decide and act with autonomy and those in which people are not yet empowered to realize their full potential as human beings (Sagasti 1980, 1988, 1995, 1997a).

Differences in scientific and technological capabilities that have persisted over a long time and are rather difficult to surmount constitute a distinguishing feature of the emerging international order. Scientific and technological capacities are distributed in an even more lopsided way than economic power. The high-income countries of the OECD account for about 85% of total world expenditure in science and technology; China, the newly industrializing countries of East Asia, and India account for a further 10%; and the rest of the world accounts for only about 4% (UNESCO 1996). Moreover, although the average income per capita of the 24 rich countries of the OECD is about 60 times greater than that of the roughly 50 countries classified by the World Bank as "low-income economies," average expenditures on science and technology per capita in the former are 250 times greater than those in the latter.

The distribution of human resources devoted to science and technology is more balanced: about 50% of the world's supply of scientists and engineers is concentrated in the OECD countries; 17%, in Central and Eastern Europe and the Commonwealth of Independent States; 15%, in China, India, and the newly industrializing countries of East Asia; and the rest, mostly in the developing regions. However, the fragility and vulnerability of most research-and-development organizations in poor countries, which face the constant threat of losing their best people to institutions and firms in more advanced economies, make it difficult to consolidate and sustain the growth of scientific and technological activities.

The distribution of the world's scientific and technological output, measured with the rather imperfect indicators of scientific publications and registered patents, also shows a rather extreme degree of concentration of capabilities to generate modern knowledge. Nearly 80% of world scientific output is produced in nine highly industrialized countries, and Eastern Europe, India; the OECD countries contribute 94% of the indexed scientific literature; and measures of inequality between countries are more pronounced in scientific publications than in income, population, or land. Similar degrees of concentration are found in patent indicators: more than 96% of world patents are registered by Japan, the countries of Western Europe, and the United States (Annerstedt 1993; Shrum and Shenhav 1995).

These imbalances have prompted calls to use the scientific and technological potential of rich countries to address the problems of the poor regions of the world. The 1970 World Plan of Action on Science and Technology for Development, prepared by the United Nations Advisory Committee on Science and Technology, suggested that 5% of research-and-development expenditures in rich countries should be focused on the problems of poor nations, a request that was repeated in many international gatherings in subsequent years. However, with the notable exception of a few fields, such as health care, the mobilization of developed-country scientists to deal with problems found mainly in the developing world has not been very successful.

All this suggests that the scientific and technological capabilities of most developing countries are far too limited to deal adequately with the challenges of economic advance, social progress, and environmental sustainability. With the exception of a few large countries (China, Brazil, India, Mexico) and some newly industrializing countries (Malaysia, Singapore, South Korea, Taiwan) that have built a significant base of scientific and technological activities, low- and middle-income countries do not have the capabilities to generate knowledge or to effectively select, absorb, adapt, and use imported knowledge. Severe resource constraints and growing social demands tend to undermine their long-term efforts to build scientific and technological capabilities. Difficult choices must be made between alleviating poverty in the short term and building capacities to generate and use knowledge in the long term.

The limitations of developing countries are made even more acute by the changes taking place in scientific research and technological innovation. Notwithstanding the opportunities that the change in technoeconomic paradigm and the expanded access to information networks may offer to some developing countries, the increasing costs of research and innovation, the accelerating obsolescence of scientific and technological capabilities, and the growing complexity of the institutional settings for research and innovation are making it more difficult to take advantage of advances at the frontiers of knowledge. As time passes and knowledge continues to increase at an explosive rate, the cumulative impact of imbalances in scientific and technological capacities is likely to create almost impenetrable barriers for those who wish to cross the knowledge divide and mobilize knowledge to improve the condition of the majority of human beings who live in the poor regions of the world.

Concluding remarks

The various trends reviewed in this chapter indicate rather clearly that the context for development efforts has changed radically during the last two decades, particularly since the end of the 1980s. In this new international context, it is not surprising that the habits of thought, practices, and institutional arrangements associated with the decades-old development-cooperation experiment have begun to experience serious difficulties. However, before focusing in some detail on the main features of the transformation that development cooperation is now experiencing, we shall examine some of the interpretations offered to account for these trends and their interactions and will also propose a characterization of the fractured global order to provide a backdrop for development-cooperation efforts in the future.

CHAPTER 4

THE EMERGING FRACTURED GLOBAL ORDER

The multiplicity of changes and trends reviewed in the preceding chapter indicate that an accelerated, segmented, and uneven process of globalization is under way. The worldwide expansion of productive and service activities, the growth of international trade, the diminishing importance of national frontiers, and the intensive exchange of information and knowledge throughout the world coexist with a concentration of "global" activities in certain countries, regions, even neighbourhoods, and certain firms and corporations. The simultaneous integration and exclusion of countries — as well as of peoples within countries — are two intertwining aspects of the multidimensional processes of globalization and fragmentation under way in our turbulent period in history, a time that is witnessing the emergence of a fractured global order.

This chapter examines some of the interpretations offered to account for the process of globalization, proposes a characterization of the emerging fractured global order, and focuses on the knowledge fracture that is now creating a great divide between societies with the capacity to generate and use knowledge and those without it. The processes leading to a fractured global order have major implications for development finance and international cooperation, which will be dealt with in the next two chapters.

Interpretations of globalization: an overview

Many interpretations have been offered to account for the complex trends leading to the emergence of a new world order (see Table 1 for a summary). A few examples will give an idea of the wide variety of concepts and metaphors proposed to apprehend and explain the new realities of the fractured global order.

Table 1. Main features of the emerging fractured global order.

International security in a postbipolar world	• End of the Cold War and demise of East–West rivalry • Virtual elimination of the threat of an all-out nuclear war and of conflicts based on Cold War ideology • Emergence of new security concerns: environmental conflicts, terrorism, drug traffic, international crime syndicates, proliferation of chemical and biological weapons, proliferation of small-scale nuclear devices • Erosion of the power of nation-states as political units (both from below and from above) • Increase in number and intensity of regional conflicts (ethnic conflicts, religious conflicts, conflicts over resources) • Larger role for regional and international institutions, particularly the United Nations, in maintaining security
Economic and financial interdependence	• Rapid growth and globalization of financial markets • Changes in trade patterns: shift of the content of trade in favour of high-technology services and manufactured products, emergence of the North Pacific as the largest trading area, multiplication of regional trade agreements, growth of intrafirm trade, creation of the World Trade Organization • New situations in key countries (China, East Asian newly industrializing countries, European Community, Japan, Russian Federation, United States)
Persistent inequalities and economic uncertainty	• Persistent and growing disparities between industrialized and developing countries • Growing inequalities of income and opportunities within both rich and poor countries • Greater instability of the international economic system • Increasing concern and demands for better international economic governance
Social conditions	• Demographic imbalances (low population growth and aging populations in rich countries versus relatively high population growth in developing countries) • Growing social demands (food, education, health, housing, sanitation) in poor countries • Unemployment: developing countries face the challenge of having to raise labour productivity while absorbing a growing number of entrants into the labour force; developed countries face structural changes in employment patterns • Widespread and growing social exclusion (gender, ethnic, age, poverty, education) in both developed and developing countries
Environmental sustainability	• Greater awareness of the problems of resource depletion • Threats to environmental sustainability and appropriate resource use: poverty in developing countries; wasteful consumption in rich nations • Security also defined in environmental terms • Need for and development of environmentally sound technologies • Acknowledgement of the danger posed by global environmental problems
Culture, religion, and ethical concerns	• Growing importance of religious and spiritual values • Rise of religious fundamentalism (Islamic, Christian) as a driving force of economic, social, and political actions • Conflict between cultural homogeneity and cultural identity, as a result of globalization of mass media, communications, and transportation • Growing importance of moral and ethical issues in equity and human-rights issues

(continued)

Table 1 concluded.

Governance and spread of democratic practices	• Crisis of governance in high-income and poor nations (representation versus efficiency; social demands exceeding institutional capabilities) • Political pluralism, democracy, and popular participation spreading throughout most world regions • Redefinition everywhere of the roles of the public sector, of the private sector, and of civil-society organizations • Governance problems exacerbated by the social impact of economic-policy reforms • Information technology having major impacts on political systems and governance • Growing importance of social capital and of institutional development
Knowledge explosion and knowledge divide	• Exponential growth of knowledge • Greater importance of knowledge as a factor of production; emergence of the "knowledge society" • Changes in the conduct of scientific research: increasing costs, greater specialization, importance of information technology • Increasingly systemic character of technological innovation: more and greater diversity of inputs required; more actors involved • Change of technoeconomic paradigm: from energy intensive (key factor = oil) to information intensive (key factor = microchip) • Transformation of production and service activities by major advances in information and communications technology, in biotechnology, and in materials technology • Extreme and cumulative inequalities between S&T capabilities of industrialized countries and those of developing countries • Limited S&T capacity of developing countries to face economic, social, political, cultural, environmental, and knowledge challenges

Note: S&T, science and technology.

Images and concepts of world order

Holm and Sorensen (1995) offer a framework to classify the forces that shape the emerging fractured global order in terms of two dimensions: type of process and scope of change. Along the first dimension, they differentiate two meanings of globalization. One considers globalization "as a somewhat trivial trend toward increasing interconnectedness between peoples and individuals. It is, moreover, identified by some observers as a cyclical trend, and it is not immediately clear that interconnectedness (including economic interdependence) has increased unremittingly over time." The other meaning views globalization "as leading toward a fundamental, qualitative shift in the conditions of people's lives. Globalization increases risks and opportunities for individuals who become both objects of and participants in global processes." Furthermore, drawing on the contributions of the authors of their edited volume, particularly Sunkel (1995), they indicated that "the process of globalization is uneven both in intensity and in geographical scope and depth" (Holm and Sorensen 1995, pp. 4–7). Along the second dimension, which refers to the scope of globalization, they distinguish between considering globalization primarily in economic terms and viewing it as a broader process of social change. Table 2 summarizes their framework for the analysis of globalization.

Table 2. Dimensions of globalization.

	Range or scope of change	
Type or scope of process	Quantitative (more of the same)	Qualitative (epochal shift)
Narrow: focused primarily on economics	Intensified interdependence: increased economic interactions between national economies	Consolidated global marketplace for production, distribution, and consumption
Comprehensive: considers broad social changes	Increased interconnectedness between peoples and individuals (in addition to economies)	Globalized societies: fundamental shift in the conditions of people's lives

Source: Adapted from Holm and Sorensen (1995).

Joseph Nye has viewed the new international situation as "a three-dimensional chess game," with the United States the only player on the top, military board; three players — Europe, Japan, and the United States — on the middle, economic board; and many players on the bottom, transnational-relations board. According to Nye, the games played on these boards have become quite complex: "one must play games of power that are not only horizontal across any given board but at the same time vertical" (Nye 1994, p. 380).

Huntington has suggested that — rather than having a unipolar, bipolar, or multipolar international system — we now have "a uni-multipolar system with one superpower and the several major powers," which creates new tensions between the United States as the only superpower and several regional powers, such as Germany and France in Europe, China and potentially Japan in East Asia, India in South Asia, Iran in Southwest Asia, Brazil in Latin America, and South Africa and Nigeria in Africa. These major powers "are preeminent in certain areas of the world without being able to extend their interests and capabilities as globally as the United States" (Huntington 1999, pp. 36–37). This state of affairs is presumably temporary, as Huntington predicts it will transform itself into a truly multipolar system during the 21st century

Meghnad Desai stressed the complex and unstable character of the relations between the major players in the international arena:

> we have the paradox of unequally powerful nations, among which there is *too little inequality* to make one nation state dominant and *too much inequality* to establish a symmetrical framework of the Rule of Law. The world of nation states is neither ready for a Lockean contract for a democracy, nor for a Hobbesian Absolutist monarch. There are querulous barons of unequal size — too many for comfort — but with no one powerful enough to lay down the law.
>
> (Desai 1995, p. 11, his emphasis)

Brazilian political scientist, Helio Jaguaribe, has seen two options for the evolution of the world order in the post-Cold War period. One of these options is the emergence of an "American World Empire," in which the "hegemonic conditions of the United States" would be expanded and consolidated, a process that may happen regardless of the will of the American people. The other option is for the European Union to evolve well beyond economic and monetary integration and articulate a "common political project," possibly complemented with a recovery of the Russian economy and the consolidation of China as a great international power, which would lead to a multipolar system with three levels. At the first level would be a few powers capable of having influence at the global level. They would form some kind of "World Directorate" operating directly or through the United Nations. At the second level would be countries with an important role in regulating the political and economic interests of a specific region, and at the third level would be the majority of countries, which would have no significant international role (Jaguaribe 1998).

For Richard Cooper, "confusion is a more apt term [at present] than order. We are at a climax of collapsing and changing orders" (Cooper 1993, p. 13). In his view, the colonial order, Cold War, balance-of-power system in Europe, and imperialist order have all collapsed. What is now emerging is "a divided world, but one that is divided quite differently from the days of the East–West confrontation" (Cooper 1993, p. 14). It comprises a premodern world in which there is no order and in which "the state no longer fulfils Weber's criterion of having the legitimate monopoly on the use of force" (Cooper 1993, p. 14); the modern world in which there is order, but also risks, and in which the nation-state is still the great engine of modernization; and a postmodern world in which "the state system is also collapsing, but unlike the pre-modern it is collapsing into greater order rather than into disorder" (Cooper 1993, p. 16). This accords with Peter Drucker's remark that "we are not facing the 'new world order' today's politicians so constantly invoke. Rather, we are facing a new world disorder — no one can know for how long" (Drucker 1993, p. 113).

Louis Emmerij introduced the metaphor of a "two-track" evolution of the world economy, according to which the developing world is falling far behind the rich nations, with little prospect for catching up. He argued that the world is entering into a new era that

> is likely to be characterized by rapidly changing international competitive strengths and weaknesses as between different countries and regions; increasing globalization combined with growing multipolarity and thus fragmented economic hegemony; growing dualism among (and within)

countries in terms of economic participation; and a growing impotence of
purely national decision-making.

(Emmerij 1989, p. 25)

Jorge Nef argued that our conceptual frameworks must reflect the
"complex, nuanced and dynamic nature of our age of extremes" and suggested that
the changes we are experiencing fall under the following three categories: the
"broader and long-ranging changes of our age of pervasive technology," the "alterations in the ideologico-political matrix which define the cultural polarities of the
system," and the "alterations in the economic fabric of the world order," which
he defined as "perhaps the most important set of circumstances" at present (Nef
1995, p. 5).

In an attempt to make sense of what William Greider described as the
"bewildering facts" of the emerging international order, he identified "four broad,
competing power blocks — each losing or gaining influence over events." These
four blocks are labour, which is identified as the most obvious loser; national governments, which have lost ground on the whole; the multinational corporations,
which are collectively "the muscle and brains" of the new system, and their success has "weakened labour and degraded the control of governments"; and finance
capital, which is viewed as the "Robespierre of this revolution." Global finance
is seen as acting collectively as the "disinterested enforcer" of the imperative of
"maximizing the return on capital without regard to national identity or political
and social consequences." Greider concluded that some form of regulation or control over global capital will be necessary to avoid the problems of uncertainty and
instability that are now emerging into full sight, and which may create serious
social and political upheavals (Greider 1997, pp. 24–25).

Max Singer and Aaron Wildavsky argued that it is necessary to examine
the "real world," rather than focusing on the "world as it should be." They have
viewed the contemporary world as divided into two zones: "The key to understanding the real world order is to separate the world into two parts. One part is
zones of peace, wealth and democracy. The other part is zones of turmoil, war and
development." They added that "unfortunately, only 15 percent of the world's
population lives in the zones of peace and democracy. Most people now live in
zones of turmoil and development, where poverty, war, tyranny, and anarchy will
continue to devastate lives." Despite their pessimistic — they would argue,
"realistic" — approach, Singer and Wildavsky managed to state confidently that
"we have good reason to look forward to the current world order with hope and
confidence. It will be better than any that preceded it" (Singer and Wildavsky
1993, pp. 3, 6, 12).

Dani Rodrik, a mainstream economist, has been concerned that globalization may lead to social disintegration and engender a backlash against trade expansion. For Rodrik, the processes associated with the worldwide integration of markets for goods, services, and capital are creating three sources of tensions:

> First, reduced barriers to trade and investment accentuate the asymmetries between groups that can cross international borders ... and those that cannot. In the first category are owners of capital, highly skilled workers, and many professionals ... . Unskilled and semiskilled workers and most middle managers belong in the second category. ...
>
> (Rodrik 1997, p. 4)
>
> Second, globalization engenders conflicts within and between nations over domestic norms and the social institutions that embody them. As the technology for manufactured goods becomes standardized and diffused internationally, nations with very different sets of values, norms, institutions, and collective preferences begin to compete head on in markets for similar goods ... . Trade becomes contentious when it unleashes forces that undermine the norms implicit in domestic practices [workplace practices, legal rules, social safety nets].
>
> (Rodrik 1997, p. 5)
>
> Third, globalization has made it exceedingly difficult for governments to provide social insurance — one of their central functions and one that has helped maintain social cohesion and domestic political support for ongoing liberalization throughout the postwar period. ... The increasing mobility of capital has rendered an important segment of the tax base footloose, leaving governments with the unappetizing option of increasing taxes disproportionately on labour income.
>
> (Rodrik 1997, p. 6)

Rodrik concluded that "the most serious challenge for the world economy in the years ahead lies in making globalization compatible with domestic social and political stability" (Rodrik 1997, p. 2), which implies ensuring that international economic integration does not lead to domestic social disintegration.

Structures and forces in the world order

Yoshikazu Sakamoto has postulated that the Cold War and the international order emerging after its demise are particular manifestations "of a deeper contradiction that underlies modern historical developments" (Sakamoto 1994, pp. 18–19). This contradiction is expressed along three dimensions, which account for all major conflicts and changes in recent history: capitalism versus socialism, state nationalism versus internationalism, and democracy versus authoritarianism. Each of these dimensions is considered "a driving force that generates historical changes with a particular orientation toward 'structuration' " (Sakamoto 1994, p. 19). This framework has been used by Sakamoto to place various historical processes in different regions; for example, a capitalism–nationalism–democracy model is seen to have obtained in what he has called the "advanced countries" of the West during the 19th century (Sakamoto 1994, p. 21), whereas a socialism–nationalism–authoritarianism model prevailed in the countries of the East block during the Cold War and characterizes China at present. Sakamoto also pointed out that one of the fundamental features of modern history is "uneven development" (Sakamoto 1994, p. 20), which is expressed in a variety of ways related to the three dimensions of the contradiction mentioned above, and he has stressed that the role of the state — as well as the roles of the market and civil society — varies in the different models of historical development.

Barbara Stallings put forward the idea that the emerging global order is the result of "two sets of interrelated changes that have taken place since the early 1980s." The first is a "dramatic transformation of the international political economy," which arose out of a significant shift in the political divisions of the world and a sharp increase in economic interdependence; the second is a "rapidly growing differentiation among third world countries" (Stallings 1995, p. 349). Stallings has attempted to reconcile what appear to be two different interpretations of these changes, one that "projects a continuation and deepening of the multilateral, interdependent global system," and the other, which "argues that regionalism is the trend of the future" (Stallings 1995, p. 352). In her view, what we have at present is "a semiregionalized world economy — regionalized from the viewpoint of the third world countries, but much less so from the triad [Europe, Japan, the United States] perspective" (Stallings 1995, p. 353).

In the second edition of a rather influential book, Barry Jones put forward the view that the emergence of a new global economic order is marked by a sharp break with the past, leading to what he considered a paradigm shift of major proportions. He identified 16 elements that clearly mark this discontinuity — ranging from the rise of postindustrialism to the decline of ideology, to the availability of smart machines, to major transformations in demand and employment, among others — which are all rooted in the diffusion of major technological advances during the last few decades. He argued that the nature of work and employment has changed in a fundamental way and that this will necessarily lead to a reaccommodation in international economic relations (Jones 1995).

Rather than listing 16 major sources of discontinuity, as Jones did, the United Nations Research Institute for Social Development (UNRISD) examined

6 broad trends affecting large parts of the world: the spread of liberal democracy, the dominance of market forces, the integration of the global economy, the transformation of production systems and labour markets, the speed of technological changes, and the media revolution and consumerism. The UNRISD report concludes that "these processes may seem to operate independently and be part of the inevitable march of human progress. But, in reality, they are interdependent and shaped by strong political forces, determining who gains and who loses." The report also argues that "technological advance would have inevitably speeded up and intensified international contacts. But the form of globalization has been shaped by, and continues to follow the contours of, existing international power relations." UNRISD (1995) also highlighted the problems associated with the emergence of a global order, such as the growth in refugees, the international breakdown of law and order, the endless war on drugs, ethnic and religious conflicts, and civil wars, which require concerted international action to confront.

Other conceptual frameworks offered to apprehend the main features of the emerging global order stress the need to maintain the stability of the international system. For example, Kazuo Takahashi, editor of the report to the Global Commission for a Post-Cold War Global System (Takahashi 1992), has seen the contemporary world as fraught with conflict. He argued that "the emergence of a new global order is not yet in sight. Despite its precarious condition, the world society will have to deal with an increasing number of crisis situations in the period immediately ahead." Therefore, according to the members of the Global Commission, as reported by Takahashi, "it is vitally important for the world community to formulate a long-term vision at a time when crisis management is the essential task of its political leaders" (Takahashi 1992, p. 14). The Global Commission's vision emerged out of an appreciation of the changing parameters, actors, and structures of the emerging global society, which lead to two sets of scenarios. The first set comprises "evolutionary scenarios" based on strengthened global partnerships and a transition from regionalism to globalism, and the second set of "disruptive scenarios" results from the collapse of major powers, a global depression, worldwide economic disturbances, an intensification of national and ethnic conflicts, and the globalization of terrorism (Takahashi 1992, p. 69).

In contrast, focusing on international finance, Ethan Kapstein argued that there is already a system in place to help deal with some of the major instabilities and problems created by globalization. In his view, what he has called "international cooperation based on home country control" has evolved as a "two level structure, with international cooperation at the upper level and home country control below" (Kapstein 1994, p. 2). In the case of international finance, this structure has helped to maintain a balance between national regulation and international competition. It requires intensive consultations and negotiations between financing institutions and regulatory agencies at the national level, as well as between regulatory agencies in different countries. Kapstein also examined the cases of pollution from oil tankers and telecommunications and argued that "something of a generic policy solution to economic globalization has emerged in those issue-areas which threaten to unleash cross-border externalities (that is, unwanted events like pollution or a financial crisis) in the event of a systems breakdown." In his view, even though "perhaps supranational agencies would provide the global economy with more effective supervision of multinational firms and transactions ... international cooperation based on home country control provides a way for national states to enjoy the benefits of interdependence while maintaining national responsibility for the sector in question" (Kapstein 1994, p. 180).

In Michael Bruno's preface to the 1995 edition of the World Bank's *Global Economic Prospects and the Developing Countries*, the former chief economist of the World Bank emphasized the ambiguous character of the globalization process and its opportunities and risks:

> the ... central message is that the increasing integration of the developing countries into the global economy constitutes perhaps the most important opportunity for raising the welfare of both developing and industrial countries over the long term. But the process of integration will not without frictions that give rise to protectionist pressures. ... Globalization comes with liberalization, deregulation and more mobile and potentially volatile cross-border capital flows, which means that sound macroeconomic management command and increasingly high premium. Penalties for policy errors rise. Globalization thus requires closer monitoring and quicker policy responses at the country, regional, and global levels.
>
> The process of integration will affect countries unevenly and could increase international disparities. ... The global outlook is in general bright, but masks wide differences across regions and countries —for many, global optimism coexists with local pessimism.
>
> (Bruno 1995, p. 5)

Pessimism and resistance to globalization

However, in contrast to studies like Bruno's, which have focused on both the benefits and costs of globalization, most accounts and interpretations of the emerging global order have expressed a rather pessimistic view of the prospects for developing countries. For example, in their examination of the implications of the emerging world order for developing countries, Slater et al. (1993, pp. 361–362) reached a gloomy conclusion:

> for those countries that comprise much of the Third and Fourth Worlds, the picture remains bleak ... . There are tremendous obstacles to overcome as countries attempt to deal with an uneasy mix among political, social, and economic variables in a global system and isolates and marginalizes the most burdensome cases.

In *The Economist*'s 1994 annual survey of the global economy (The Economist 1994), it anticipated a "war of the worlds" between the "so-called industrial economies that dominate the globe" and the "newly emerging economic giants" during the next quarter century. It pointed out that shifts in economic power are rarely smooth and that "a number of people in the rich industrial nations are already urging their governments to prepare for battle against the upstarts," which include the East Asian, Eastern European, and Latin American nations. Other authors have focused on the economic and political downside of the process of globalization, and some — such as Anderson (1994) and Sterling (1994) — have focused particularly on the spread of illegal activities, organized crime, and money laundering.

One of the most clear expressions of the pessimism with which analysts from the industrialized nations view the prospects of poor countries in the emerging global order was provided by Paul Kennedy:

> as we move into the next century the developed economies appear to have all the trump cards in their hands — capital, technology, control of communications, surplus foodstuffs, powerful multinational companies — and, if anything, their advantages are *growing* because technology is eroding the value of labour and materials, the chief assets of developing countries.
>
> (Kennedy 1993, p. 225, his emphasis)

Elaborating on this point of view, Matthew Connelly and Paul Kennedy characterized the emerging international order in the following terms:

> Perhaps the global problem of the early twenty-first century is basically this: that across our planet a number of what may be termed demographic–technological fault lines are emerging, between fast-growing, adolescent, resource-poor, undercapitalized, and uneducated populations on one side, and technologically inventive, demographically moribund, and increasingly nervous rich societies on the other.
>
> (Connelly and Kennedy 1994, pp. 78–79)

Kennedy's perspective on the problems of the emerging international order appears to be marked by a sense of futility, perhaps even despair, although tempered by what may be called hopeless optimism:

> in the unlikely event that governments and societies do decide to transform themselves, we ought to recognize that our endeavors might have only a marginal effect on the profound driving forces of today's world. ... Nothing is certain except that we face innumerable uncertainties; but simply recognizing that fact provides a vital starting point ... . Thus, despite the size and complexity of the global challenges facing us, it is too simple and too soon to conclude gloomily that nothing can be done.
>
> (Kennedy 1993, pp. 348–349)

Little wonder that the process of globalization has elicited many negative reactions. Jerry Mander and Edward Goldsmith edited a volume with 43 contributions, *The Case Against the Global Economy and a Turn Toward the Local*, gathering a plethora of arguments for resisting the forces of economic globalization. The gist of their case rests primarily on environmental considerations. As Goldsmith pointed out in the concluding chapter,

> If the world's environment is being degraded so rapidly, with a corresponding reduction in its capacity to sustain complex forms of life such as the human species, it is because it cannot sustain the present impact of our economic activities. To increase this impact still further, as we are doing by creating a global economy based on free trade, is both irresponsible and cynical. The only responsible policy must, on the contrary, be *to drastically reduce this impact*, and it is only in the sort of economy in which economic activities are carried out on a far smaller scale and cater primarily to a local or regional market that we can hope to do so
>
> (Goldsmith 1996, p. 510, his emphasis).

A similar point was made by Tom Athanasiou, who argued that globalization has become "an euphemism for a commercial imperative unbuffered by ethical scepticism, care for the weak and vulnerable, environmental protection and even democracy." In his view, the forces of globalization must be resisted, and "it is *not* too late to act, or to recall the old imperative to 'educate, agitate, and organize,' or to remember that the deepest springs of hope lie in engagement, in making the choice to make a difference" (Athanasiou 1996, pp. 44, 306, his emphasis).

This call to arms against globalization reaches a high point with the arguments of Samir Amin, for whom "the world system is in crisis. There is a general breakdown of accumulation, in the sense that most of the social formations of the

East (formerly called socialist) and the South (third and fourth worlds) are unable to reproduce on an extended scale, or even in some cases to hold their own" (Amin 1992, p. 12). In Amin's view, this crisis "constitutes a historical limit for capitalism," and a solution to this problem would require "a reallocation of capital on a global scale that is unattainable under the short-term profitability criteria that now rule the market. A market solution of the problem is bound to generate growing social, national, and international imbalances that will turn out to be unbearable." He argued for a "reconstruction of the world system on a polycentric basis" (Amin 1992, p. 13), which would require Third World countries to subordinate their relations with others to the imperatives of internal development, rather than adjusting their international agendas to the world expansion of capital. Without going as far as advocating autarky or self-exclusion from the world economy, Amin proposed a "delinking" strategy, as expressed in workers' refusal to submit to "the demands of economistic alienation," in political responses to natural-resource waste and environmental degradation, and in geopolitical and cultural conflicts between states and civilizations (Amin 1992, p. 14).

Despite all the warnings about the nefarious effects of globalization, the idea that the processes of globalization are moving swiftly and inexorably has remained unchallenged by any but a few analysts. For example, an article in *Fortune* magazine posed the question "Global — or Just Globaloney?" (Farnham 1994). Farnham argued that globalization is taking place in some narrow sectors of the world economy while the rest remains relatively untouched by the pressures of globalization. Following this line of reasoning, even though it is necessary to acknowledge the growing importance of the global reach of international finance, mass media, and certain industries, such as automobiles and computers, it is also important to remember that many segments of the world economy remain firmly anchored in, and even limited to, regional and local scales. This is particularly the case of many agricultural activities, small industries and crafts, a wide range of services of restricted geographical scope, and practically all activities linked to subsistence economies. Although it is difficult to estimate the proportion of the world's population remaining outside the circuits of globalized production, trade, finance, and consumption, it is likely that a significant majority of those who live in the poor or developing regions do not take part in such activities and remain little affected by them.

Knowledge and culture as driving forces of global change

Most of the interpretations and accounts of the trends shaping the new international order, such as those reviewed in the preceding sections, put emphasis on economic and power relations between states and, to a lesser extent, on those between states and corporations. From this perspective, the main features of the emerging global order are explained in terms of economic, military, security, social, and political interactions between international actors. However, other authors privilege a different set of driving forces to explain the world order that is crystallizing as we move toward the 21st century: (1) knowledge acquisition, generation, and use; and (2) cultural values and attitudes.

Authors such as Machlup (1962, 1980), Drucker (1968, 1993), and Castells (1996) have consistently focused on the role that knowledge and information play in shaping the emerging international order. For example, according to Castells, we now live in a new economy — what he has called an "informational economy" — characterized by five main features related to each other in a systemic way: (1) the increasing dependence of the sources of productivity on the application of science and technology and the quality of information and management; (2) the shift taking place in advanced capitalist societies from material production to information processing in the proportion of GNP and in that of the population employed in these new activities; (3) the deep transformation in the organization of production and the economy in general; (4) the cross-border organization of capital, production, management, markets, labour, information, and technology in the new global economy; and (5) the fact that these economic and organizational changes are occurring in the context of one of the most important technological revolutions in history, which is based on information technology and has, with its major scientific discoveries and applications, transformed the material basis of the world in less than 20 years (Castells 1996).

The main consequence of all these changes is the emergence of a completely new world situation:

> Toward the end of the second millennium of the Christian Era several events of historical significance have transformed the social landscape of human life. A technological revolution, centered around information technologies, is reshaping the material basis of society. Economies throughout he world have become globally interdependent, introducing a new form of relationship between economy, state, and society, in a system of variable geometry.
>
> There has also been an accentuation of uneven development, this time not only between North and South, but between the dynamic segments and territories of societies everywhere, and those others that risk becoming irrelevant from the perspective of the system's logic. Indeed, we observe the parallel unleashing of formidable productive forces of the

informational revolution, and the consolidation of black holes of human
misery in the global economy.

(Castells 1996, pp. 1–2).

Castells' three-volume inquiry takes technology as a point of departure, even
though he has placed this technological revolution "in the social context in which
it takes place and by which it is being shaped." Similar viewpoints have been
expressed by Sagasti in a series of articles (1980, 1988, 1990, 1997a, b). Castells
also argued against the false dilemma of technological determinism and
emphasized the reciprocal influences between technology and its social context.

As indicated in the preceding chapter, one of the salient features of the
emerging international order is the greater attention paid to cultural, religious, and
ethical concerns. Indeed, Huntington argued that the world of the future will be
characterized by "clash of civilizations," in which cultural conflicts "along the
fault lines between civilizations" will become more dangerous than economic or
ideological conflicts (Huntington 1996, p. 28; see also Huntington 1993). Reviewing and discarding accounts of world order given in terms of "One world: Euphoria and Harmony," "Two Worlds: Us and Them," "184 States, More or Less,"
and "Sheer Chaos," Huntington concluded that

> the post-Cold War world is a world of seven or eight major civilizations.
> Cultural commonalities and differences shape the interests, antagonisms,
> and associations of states. The most important countries in the world
> come overwhelmingly from different civilizations. The local conflicts
> most likely to escalate into broader wars are those between groups and
> states from different civilizations. The predominant patterns of political
> and economic development differ from civilization to civilization. The
> key issues on the international agenda involve differences among civiliza-
> tions. Power is shifting from the long predominant West to non-Western
> civilizations. Global politics has become multipolar and
> multicivilizational.

(Huntington 1996, p. 29).

Analysts who focus on culture and values as the main forces shaping the
emerging international order tend to place Western civilization in a broader perspective and to emphasize the increasingly important role that non-Western cultures will play in the future. For example, Walker criticized the ethnocentrism
implicit in the long-entrenched claims to universality of the various aspects of
Western culture and anticipated that "we are entering an epoch that will be characterized increasingly by a clash of civilizations and a decline of the current hege-
mony of Western cultural forms" (Walker 1984, p. 3). Friberg and Hettne focused

on the possible contributions of non-Western social movements to the emergence of "post-materialist" cultural forms that may respond better to concerns for the environment (Friberg and Hettne 1988, p. 356). Arguing that a "Green strategy has been independently developed in many locations," they postulated that it will lead to "a truly global dialogue, ideology and movement with natural anchorage in all corners of the world" (Friberg and Hettne 1988, p. 358).

Jack Weatherford has forcefully argued that cultural variety plays a most important role in an increasingly global society. He noted that "the emergence of a world culture failed to obliterate local cultures. Instead, ethnic and cultural identities grew stronger, everywhere ... rather than blending into a homogenized world culture shared by all, the various tribes, nations, religions, and ethnic groups accentuated their differences to become more varied than ever." He concluded that

> Today all of us are unquestionably part of our global society, but that common membership does not produce cultural uniformity around the globe. The challenge now facing us is to live in harmony without living in uniformity, to be united by some forces such as worldwide commerce, pop culture and communications, but to remain peacefully different in other areas such as religion and ethnicity. We need to share some values such as commitment to fundamental human rights and basic rules of interaction, but we can be wildly different in other areas such as life-styles, spirituality, musical tastes, and community life.
>
> (Weatherford 1994, p. 290)

This highly selective and rather succinct review of interpretations of the emerging world order illustrates the variety of perspectives taken on the simultaneous processes of globalization and fragmentation.[7] There is no dearth of images and conceptual frameworks to account for the trends observed in the last two decades. It is also interesting to note that most of these interpretations have been provided by analysts from industrialized and rich nations. Therefore, without too

---

[7]   In addition, several analysts have begun to offer integrative perspectives on the emerging world order: Ramón Tamames (Tamames 1991), the Spanish economist and politician, presented a rather comprehensive review of the forces shaping the new international order; Richard Falk (Falk 1992) offered what he called a "post-modern" view on the prospects for a new world order; the Central Bureau of Planning of the Netherlands (CPBN 1992) prepared a report exploring three different scenarios in which economic, environmental, social, and institutional issues are put together to offer alternative views on how the world economy may evolve over the next 25 years; Bushrui et al. (1993) edited a volume in which they gathered scientific, technological, and cultural perspectives on the emergence of a fractured global order; and a volume edited by Diamond and Plattner (1993) examines the democratization dimension of the global order.

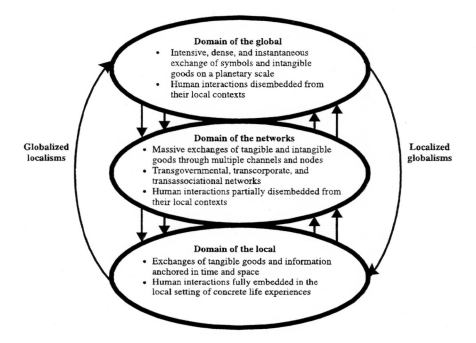

Figure 1. The three domains of the fractured global order.

much exaggeration, it may be possible to say that people in the South risk becoming passive consumers of the global futures dreamt for them in the North. This is particularly troublesome because of the pessimism prevailing among Northern analysts regarding the future prospects of poor countries and regions.

A fractured global order

From the perspective of the developing regions of the world, that is, from a noncentral (or excentric) point of view, the transition to the 21st century is marked by the emergence of a fractured global order (Sagasti 1989a, b, 1990). This is an order that is global but not integrated, that puts us all in contact with one another while simultaneously maintaining deep fissures between diverse groups of countries and between peoples within countries, and that is benefiting a small percentage of humanity while segregating a large portion of the world's population.

The structure of the fractured global order can be conceptualized in terms of three closely interconnected and partially overlapping domains, each of which has its own specific features and ways of interacting with the other two: the domain of the global, that of the networks, and that of the local (Figure 1).

The domain of the global comprises primarily the intensive, dense, and nearly instantaneous exchanges of symbols and intangible goods on a planetary scale, characteristic of the information age. Advances in information and communications technologies have allowed us to free our activities and interactions from the constraints imposed by our immediate and concrete experiences of time and space and to restructure those activities and interactions almost at will in the abstract domain of the global. The separation and delinking of time and space from each other and from their concrete experiential settings are what make the domain of the global possible. Social relations are thus "disembedded" or "lifted out" from their local contexts (Giddens 1990), transformed into vast and complex symbolic arrays that represent myriad social interactions, and projected into the realm of the global, where they become free to roam and intermingle in a rather fluid fashion.

The stuff of which the domain of the global is made comprises images, sounds, and words that blanket the planet and quickly reach almost everywhere through mass media; cultural products and icons — music, movies, television programs, sports and fashion, ideas and concepts, and even aspirations and values — that link societies far apart and virtually unknown to each other; and the enormous exchange of messages, data, and information through telecommunication networks and the Internet. In this domain, it is rather difficult to trace the paths followed by a specific transaction, for interactions take place at high speeds, are rather ephemeral, and can involve many agents simultaneously. The communications networks that sustain the domain of the global now allow human beings to converse with each other in a variety of many-to-one, one-to-many, and many-to-many patterns that were impossible until just a few years ago.

The domain of the networks consists of a bewildering multiplicity of combinations of exchanges of tangible and intangible goods — trade in products and services, power and influence relations, transfers of data and information — which flow through a myriad of identifiable channels and nodes interconnecting social groups all over the world.[8] Interactions in the domain of the networks involve all kinds of organizations — public institutions, private corporations, and civil-society associations — whose interrelations create a tangled web of overlapping and intertwined networks of networks. The domain of the networks is constantly transforming itself, as connections between its constituent units are established and severed,

---

[8]   Castells (1996, p. 168) suggested that "under different organizational arrangements, and through diverse cultural expressions, [the organizational forms of the informational economy] are all based in networks. *Networks are the fundamental stuff of which new organizations are and will be made*" (Castells' emphasis).

new channels and nodes are created, old ones are destroyed, and the network units mutate and evolve.

Transgovernmental, transcorporate, and transassociational networks, along with the thick sets of relations between them, are the main types of structural arrangements found in the domain of the networks. As the hold of nation-states on international affairs has weakened during the last three decades, a host of new cross-border linkages between public agencies has emerged in full view. These transgovernmental networks involve regulatory agencies, executives, courts, armed forces, and legislatures that now routinely exchange information and coordinate their activities (Slaughter 1997). Transcorporate networks, comprising multi-national enterprises and private firms operating at the international level through wholly owned subsidiaries, foreign partners, representatives, and agencies, together with strategic alliances of all types, have long been an established feature of the international economic scene. Also, a variety of civil-society organizations — ranging from citizens' groups and professional associations to environmental and human-rights activists — have now formed regional and worldwide alliances, thus configuring a new set of transassociational networks whose international weight has increased considerably. Although states will continue to be the main unit for political decision-making in the fractured global order, the erosion of sovereignty is making them more porous and allowing transgovernmental, transcorporate, and transassociational relations to proceed in an increasingly decentralized manner.

The social relations reflected in the combinations of tangible and intangible goods exchanged in the domain of the networks are both partially embedded in, and partially disembedded from, the time- and space-bound local contexts of inter-action. Long in the making, the domain of the networks owes its present richness to the technological innovations in transport and communications of the last five decades, which have facilitated new and more intensive few-to-many, few-to-few, and few-to-one — as well as one-to-few and many-to-few — patterns of interrela-tion and communication between human beings.

The domain of the local comprises those relations and transactions that are anchored in time and space and primarily constitute the production, exchange, and consumption of tangible goods and services, together with the corresponding information resources and personal interrelations needed for human beings and social groups to exist and evolve. This domain has been in existence since the dawn of humanity, and the social relations reflected in the transactions and inter-actions that comprise it are firmly embedded in the settings of our concrete lived experiences.

In the domain of the local, where most of the daily lives of people unfold, transactions are relatively easy to trace, and in this domain the prevailing patterns of interrelation and communication between human beings one to few, few to one, and few to few. This domain contains the extraordinarily rich range of face-to-face interactions between individuals that allows us to convey to each other, not only information about things, but also feelings, emotions, aspirations and values, which stand at the root of what it means to be human and confer on human beings their unique character.

As these three domains overlap, it is possible to identify social interactions located in the interfaces between them. For example, financial transactions that take place on a global scale — as well as money that never rests and moves constantly throughout the world's financial channels and hubs — straddle the domain of the global and that of the networks. Point-to-point trade in goods and services through clearly identifiable routes initially requires localized production and ultimately involves localized consumption and therefore spans both the domain of the local and that of the networks.

In addition, some activities circumscribed in time and space can rise from the domain of the local, be processed and leveraged through the domain of the networks, and reach the domain of the global (for example, American English as the language of the Internet, tastes for Chinese food and Brazilian music, Western market-economy concepts and policies typified in the so-called Washington Consensus, designs derived from local cultures in developing regions). The reverse also frequently happens, as interactions in the domain of the global filter down through the domain of the networks and reach that of the local (for example, the tourist and travel industries focusing on countries and regions with rich historical heritages, the technique of music videos used to present local compositions and talent, highly mobile financial assets invested in medium- and long-term projects in a specific location). Santos (1995, p. 263) called the former "globalized localisms"; and the later, "localized globalisms." Santos pointed out that in the context of a highly asymmetric fractured global order, the rich, or "core," countries specialize in globalized localisms, whereas the poor, or "peripheral," countries are left primarily with localized globalisms.

In economic terms, the domain of the local comprises what are known as "nontradeable goods," such as personal services, retailing, local transportation, and heavy goods with high transport costs; the domain of the network comprises all types of tradeable goods, services, and information that are transportable and exchangeable over a fairly long distance; and the domain of the global includes what may be called "hypertradeable goods" and impersonal services, which can be sold, bought, and transferred in a nearly instantaneous fashion all over the world. Many of these goods and services are exchanged at a frenetic pace (currency trading, for example).

The emerging fractured global order, along with its three domains, shows a multiplicity of fault lines of political, economic, social, environmental, cultural, scientific, and technological nature; these faults overlap partially and often shift direction; they sometimes reinforce each other and at other times work at cross purposes. The overall picture they present is one of turbulence and uncertainty, in which a variety of contradictory processes open up a wide range of both opportunities and threats defying established habits of thought. Integration and exclusion coexist uneasily side by side in all domains and aspects of the fractured global order. All this is certainly in line with what characterizes periods of profound and fundamental transformation, such as the Renaissance (Heller 1981), and this is also the nature of the transition on which we are now embarked toward a post-Baconian age (Sagasti 1997a, b).

It has been argued that the fractured global order has long been in the making. Proponents of the "world-systems" view (Wallerstein 1974, 1983, 1995; Hopkins and Wallerstein 1980) and others (Ferrer 1996, for example) have maintained that the fractures that accompany the globalization process emerged as far back as the 16th century, with the first wave of Western European capitalist expansion. There is ample merit in tracing the historical roots of the fractured global order over several centuries — most notably to balance the lack of historical awareness of some analysts who view it as a fairly recent phenomenon.

Although we fully acknowledge the importance of a centuries-old perspective on globalization, we argue that the processes of accelerated political, economic, social, environmental, cultural, scientific, and technological change that have unfolded since World War II — and have rapidly acquired a planetary character — are creating a new setting for the evolution of interactions among the world's peoples. In contrast to previous bursts of globalized exchanges, all of which took place within the framework of the Baconian program, the emerging fractured global order is deeply embedded in the transition to a post-Baconian age and is also having in a major effect on the character of this transition. Among other things, this transition demands a reinterpretation of progress and development, particularly in view of the fundamental changes taking place in our conceptions of the human condition.

The multiplicity of processes giving birth to a fractured global order contain ambiguities and inconsistencies that generate widespread confusion and uncertainty. It is necessary to dispel the notion that the variety of forces at play in the three domains of the fractured global order are all pointing in one general direction, whether positive or negative. Each and every one of these forces, along with any combination of them, can produce "good" or "bad" results. This depends on, among other things, the perspective from which they are viewed, the structure of power relations in the domains and aspects of the fractured global order under consideration, and the capacities of developing countries and regions to design and carry out strategies for overcoming their disadvantages.

The ambiguous nature of the fractured global order means that a premium must be placed on an accurate reading of rapidly shifting and closely interrelated trends. Even those that may be considered as having a positive effect can, at times, end up creating more harm than good, particularly in developing countries. For example, the increased availability of private capital in the financial markets of developing countries, resulting from the globalization of finance, may appreciate local currencies and make exports less competitive. Increased food aid, resulting from humanitarian concerns and the growing awareness of the impact of natural and human-made disasters, may discourage efforts to increase food production in the recipient countries. The desire to spread Western democratic practices, closely associated with the worldwide dissemination of the ideas about human rights and democratic governance, may lead to the imposition of inappropriate — even counterproductive — political conditions on access to markets in developed countries and international finance, considering local circumstances. Even the end of the Cold War, which was a clear international "good" by most accounts, is seen by some analysts as opening the door to a variety of long-suppressed regional conflicts (Mearsheimer 1990).

At the same time, some trends that may be considered as having negative effects may create new opportunities for developing countries and regions. Global warming, a clear negative for all humanity, may generate new initiatives for international cooperation and for transfer of resources from rich to poor countries. In the agreements reached at the 1997 Kyoto Conference of Parties of the International Panel on Climate Change, which set the target of a 5.2% reduction in global emissions from 1990 levels by 2008–12, a provision is included regarding "Clean Development Mechanisms," or payments from industrialized to developing countries to preserve forests that function as carbon dioxide sinks. Costa Rica is among the first countries poised to take advantage of this agreement. Similarly, the accelerated development of new technologies, which has increased the knowledge gap between rich and poor countries, can be seen as a development that expands the pool of available technologies for developing countries to tap into. The newly industrialized countries of Southeast Asia have done this over the last three decades. Also, enormous growth is occurring in social demands, which already tax the capacities of most developing countries to provide basic social services but can also be seen as a force that spurs institutional innovations to increase popular participation and reinforce democratic practices, thus transforming the roles of the state, the private sector, and civil society. This is illustrated by the growing role of grass-roots organizations providing social services in Latin America and South Asia.

In every transformation of "bads" into "goods" within the framework of the fractured global order, the capacity to adopt a perspective that highlights opportunities and the ability to design and put into practice strategies to take advantage of such opportunities becomes a critical asset for anyone who wishes to avert the apparently unfavourable consequences of globalization. A major adjustment of mind-sets will be required to fully exploit the room to manoeuvre offered in the turbulent context of the emerging fractured global order. For example, many dichotomies once deeply embedded in our habits of thought — competition versus collaboration, market forces versus state intervention, democracy versus authoritarian rule, global actions versus local solutions — are losing their sharp edges as contradictory forces appear to converge and reinforce each other at specific times and places. Corporations that compete fiercely in some markets form strategic alliances in others; government guidance and regulation are required to make markets work effectively; authoritarian rule coexists with free elections and a free press; and "think globally, act locally" solutions are now part of mainstream thinking and policy-making, especially on the environment.

Holm and Sorensen (1995, p. 6) suggested that "uneven globalization is best conceived as a dialectical process, stimulating integration as well as fragmentation, universalism as well as particularism, and cultural differentiation as well as globalization." Yet, rather than a dialectical process in which thesis and antithesis lead to a synthesis, which is then transformed into a new thesis, the multiplicity of trends constituting the fractured global order would be better characterized as a set of paradoxical processes, in which mutually inconsistent and contradictory trends coexist without the prospect of resolution, at least in the near future. Changing circumstances may even turn these contradictions into convergences and coincidences.[9] Moreover, unexpected turns of events in a turbulent

---

[9]   Morrison (1983, cited in Smith and Berg 1987, p. 3) stated the importance of paradoxical mind-sets in the following terms: "We stand in a turmoil of contradictions without having the faintest idea how to handle them: Law/Freedom; Rich/Poor; Right/Left; Love/Hate — the list seems endless. Paradox lives and moves in this realm; it is the art of balancing opposites in such a way that they do not cancel each other but shoot sparks of light across their points of polarity. It looks at our desperate either/ors and tells us they are really both/ands — that life is

environment suggest that social actors who would be unable to exert any influence in a more stable context may have the opportunity to shape the outcomes of the multiplicity of processes now unfolding on the world scene. This prompted Harland Cleveland to suggest that we are facing "an open moment for international leadership" (Cleveland 1993).

The knowledge fracture and the two civilizations

Because of its particular importance and the pivotal role it plays in shaping all the other dimensions of the fractured global order and its domains, the knowledge fracture merits special attention. Long ago, science superseded other ways of generating knowledge, and scientific research is now the main source for technological innovation. As a consequence, scientific and technological capabilities have become perhaps the most important asset in the quest to improve living standards.

However, modern science and technology have always had an ambiguous character, even though the cultural context in which they developed from the 17th to the mid-20th century ignored the dark side of their promises and the threats they posed. Over centuries, and especially during the last five decades, we have learned that science and technology do not always bring about improvements in the areas of human activity they affect. Despite the promises of Enlightenment rationalism and, even more, 19th-century positivism, progress in science and technology does not necessarily coincide with that in morality, society, or even the economy. The complex and rapidly shifting context of the emerging fractured global order, in which scientific and technological fractures are highly visible, is making this point in a painfully obvious way as we embark on the transition to the post-Baconian age. For example, in contrast to the Enlightenment vision of knowledge as a free and widely shared good, to be used for the benefit of all human beings, the growing economic value of research has generated a host of initiatives to secure property rights over scientific and technological knowledge. These mechanisms to appropriate that intangible good, knowledge, are primarily designed by government agencies, corporations, and institutions from countries with high levels of scientific and technological capability and imposed on poor countries without these capacities through international regimes over intellectual property rights.

---

larger than any of our concepts and can, if we let it, embrace our contradictions." For arguments in favour of an "incoherent" approach to foreign policy, which is quite close to the idea of a paradoxical stance in facing the fractured global order, see Luttwak (1998).

The great divide between people with and those without the capacity to generate and use knowledge may rapidly become an impassable abyss. Given the great variety of national and local situations, to focus sharply on this divide it may be appropriate to speak metaphorically of "two civilizations" (Sagasti 1980). In each domain, the interaction of the two civilizations is asymmetrical: the first civilization has more of an affect on the second than vice versa.

The first civilization is based on the growth of science as the main activity generating knowledge, the rapid evolution of science-related technologies, the incorporation of these technologies into productive and social processes, and the emergence of new forms of working and living, deeply influenced by the world-view of modern science and scientific technology. Most of the high-income countries — where science, technology, and production are closely intertwined and form an endogenous scientific and technological base — belong to the first civilization (Sagasti 1979). The second civilization has a low capacity to generate scientific knowledge; a broad traditional technological base, on which a thin layer of modern imported technologies is superimposed; and a productive system with a rather small modern segment, closely linked to the economies of high-income nations, together with a larger traditional segment that is relatively isolated from the international economy. Most of the low-income countries of the developing world — where scientific research, technological development, and productive activities remain separate — have an exogenous scientific and technological base and would belong to the second civilization.

However, even though the distance between the first and second civilizations may be widening as a consequence of the knowledge explosion, during the past three decades a handful of developing countries have begun to establish the foundations to develop an endogenous scientific and technological base. In parallel, some high-income nations have been losing ground in scientific research, technological development, and the linkage of these two to productive activities. As a result, it is possible to find nations that have features of both the first and second civilizations.

Disjointed and even contradictory cultural forms coexist in the nations of the second civilization. These nations face difficult choices regarding the importance of tradition, with its hierarchies, codes, and rites, and the weight to be placed on reason — the foundation of modern science — with its capacity to create order or disorder and to transform or destroy. Taken to extremes, scientific and technological thinking threatens to reduce human beings to purely rational automatons. Conversely, attacks on scientific rationality — leveled from particular faiths, cultures, or traditions — threaten to retard or prevent change and may lead to stagnation.

In a fractured global order, the main challenge to the nations of the second civilization — with their legitimate diversity of cultures, perspectives and world-views — is to harmoniously integrate science and technology, along with its material and intellectual manifestations, into the social and cultural heritage with which they achieve their sense of identity.[10]

Concluding remarks

The conceptual framework of the fractured global order does not postulate the existence of an overall coordinator to decide on the course of the contradictory processes of globalization and fragmentation, let alone of a conspiracy to run the world to exploit and debase the majority of its population. As has been the case throughout history, nobody is "in charge" of the turbulent processes creating a few winners and many losers. The various interconnected systems that make up the three domains of the fractured global order run according to their own logic and the logics of the interactions between them. Although this is no consolation to those who experience the anxieties and the pain of the transition to a new world situation, it suggests that the first task in confronting the threats of the fractured global order and taking advantage of the opportunities it affords is to understand the multiple driving forces of its domains and components, their changing nature, and the logic that animates them. Only then will it be possible to design strategies and policies to improve the condition of the excluded and marginalized.

Nevertheless, the absence of a deus ex machina to control the processes leading to the fractured global order does not mean they lack an overall direction. Their direction emerges from the prevailing promarket and antistate way of thinking in our times. It is leading, albeit in jagged and paradoxical manner, toward both greater integration and greater fragmentation in all realms of human activity. Moreover, those who benefit from such a state of affairs (primarily private firms and individuals associated with highly mobile capital and knowledge resources) exert a dominant influence in the world's centres of political power. They also appear determined to thwart any effort to slow the pace of globalization

---

[10]   The late Argentinean physicist, Jorge Sabato, a pioneer of Latin American scientific and technological studies and policies, clearly stated the need to harmonize the Western drive for material progress with cultural traditions that confer a sense of identity: "We want development, but with *siesta*" (J. Sabato, at the Andean Pact conference, Lima Peru, Oct 1970).

or even to reflect on where are we now and explore whether the emerging frac-tured global order is where we want to be.[11]

The processes leading to the emergence of the fractured global order can be appropriately characterized using the metaphor of the "juggernaut" that Anthony Giddens used to describe the process of modernization:

> a runaway engine of enormous power which, collectively as human beings, we can drive to some extent, but which also threatens to rush out of control and which could render itself asunder. The juggernaut crushes those who resist it, and while it sometimes seems to have a steady path, there are times when it veers away erratically in directions we cannot foresee. The ride is by no means wholly unpleasant or unrewarding; it can often be exhilarating and charged with hopeful anticipation. But so long as the institutions of modernity endure [we would substitute "frac-tured global order" for "institutions of modernity"], we shall never be able to control completely either the path or the pace of the journey. In turn, we shall never be able to feel entirely secure, because the terrain across which it runs is fraught with risks of high consequence.
>
> (Giddens 1990, p. 139)

The main responsibility for finding ways to improve the living conditions in developing countries and regions that have so far not benefited from (or even been harmed by) the trends giving shape to the globalization juggernaut lies squarely on the shoulders of the leaders in these countries and regions. But they cannot help by railing against the forces shaping the fractured global order; the real choice is not about how to best fight globalization but about how to govern and manage it. Perhaps the juggernaut metaphor should give way to that of the surfer who rides huge waves and safely reaches the shore. He or she cannot control the complex and powerful movements of the waves but is nevertheless able to guide the surfboard to take advantage of the slightest changes in the direc-tion of sea currents and winds. The surfer may even be allowed to hold the illu-sion that he or she is "steering" the waves to make them reach the shore.

---

[11] A notable example of the refusal even to allow thinking about alternatives to the manic pace of globalization was the bill introduced by US Senator Robert Dole at the Second Session of the 104th Congress, in 1996, which sought to deny "any voluntary or assessed contribution to the United Nations or any of its specialized and affiliated agencies ... unless the President certifies that the United Nations or such agency, as the case may be, is not engaged in any effort to develop, advocate, promote, or publicize any proposal concerning taxation or fees on United States persons in order to raise revenue for the United Nations or any such agency." The target of Senator Dole was the proposed "Tobin Tax" on international financial transactions, which is aimed both at reducing volatility in global financial markets and raising revenues for countries and international agencies, which UNDP staff and consultants were exploring at that time (Raffer 1998).

However, even the most determined and well-designed efforts of leaders in developing countries and regions will yield no results if the international context remains heavily biased against their efforts. Thus, the international communities of nations, corporations, and civil-society associations have a most important role to play in removing constraints and creating favourable conditions for those who embark in the uncertain road to "development," whatever meaning we may eventually give this word as we move into a new century and the post-Baconian age. As Streeten pointed out, "strategies should aim to select the positive impulses of globalization and encourage them, while minimizing the impact of negative impulses, or cushioning the losers against them. This cannot be done by combining globalization with laissez faire" (Streeten 1998, p. 45).

Perhaps the most important challenge the international community faces in the transition to the 21st century is to prevent the multiplicity of fractures that span all the domains of the emerging global order from creating self-contained, partially isolated pockets of mutually distrustful peoples, ignorant and suspicious of each other's viewpoints, aspirations, potentials, and capabilities. It is essential to prevent these fractures from creating inward-looking societies — both between and within rich and poor nations — that relate to one another only through symbolic links forged by mass media or narrowly circumscribed economic transactions and that interact in ways fraught with conflicts that threaten human and environmental security. Efforts to meet this challenge imply a commitment to building bridges across the multiple fractures of the emerging global order and particularly the will to prevent the knowledge fracture leading to a world with two distinct and diverging civilizations and to give human beings — both individually and collectively — the opportunity to realize their full potential.

CHAPTER 5

TRANSFORMATION IN THE 1990S

By the mid-1990s, the context for the development-cooperation experiment had been radically transformed. A multiplicity of changes and trends that had begun to assert themselves since the early 1980s, each with its own speed and intensity, crystallized with the emergence of a fractured global order. These changes and trends have altered beyond recognition the landscape that prevailed at the time when the development-cooperation experiment began, and they have important implications for the resource flows, motivations, and institutional arrangements of development assistance.

As a consequence, the effectiveness and appropriateness of established approaches to development cooperation, largely centred on the flow of official aid through bilateral and multilateral channels, came under serious question during the 1990s. A new mix of enduring and emerging motivations for engaging in development cooperation, not only for rich nations, but also for private corporations and civil-society associations, will require fundamental changes in the way the enterprise of development cooperation is organized and managed. As befits the context of the paradoxical fractured global order, it is by no means certain that the multiplicity of objectives that ODA is supposed to achieve can all be accomplished simultaneously, as they may often work at cross purposes.

This chapter looks at the transformations development cooperation is now undergoing and the responses that these changes are eliciting from bilateral agencies, multilateral institutions, and other actors involved in development assistance. After examining the recent evolution of resource flows to the developing world and the decreasing availability of ODA resources — what has been called the "ODA squeeze" — we will shift attention to the prevailing sense of dissatisfaction and uneasiness with development cooperation and with multilateral institutions in particular, which is leading to a profound questioning of the organizational arrangements for development assistance. We then mention briefly the new demands on international development cooperation, focusing on the challenges of conflict prevention, peacemaking, and postwar reconstruction. This chapter ends with a review of some initiatives developed in response to the demands to transform development cooperation in the context of the emerging fractured global order.

Resource flows in the 1980s and 1990s: the ODA squeeze

After experiencing a rapid growth during the 1970s, roughly in parallel with the growth of development-cooperation organizations, total resources for development assistance began to level off during the 1980s and decline in the 1990s. ODA disbursements have actually decreased in real terms since 1988 (Figure 2). Along the way, the participation of various groups of donors remained stable, with the exception of the relative shares of Japan and the United States (Figure 3). In effect, in the 20-year period from 1975–76 to 1996–97, the share of the United States in the total flows from the countries of the Development Assistance Committee (DAC) was more than halved, from more than 30% to less than 15%, whereas that of Japan more than doubled, from about 8% to nearly 20%. This has made Japan the largest donor and appears to be one of the indications of the end of a long period of American leadership in the field of development assistance.

But the changes in the structure of total financial flows to developing countries during the past 15 years have been even more dramatic than those in relative shares of ODA donors (Figure 4). In 1980, private flows represented 57% of total net financial flows to developing countries and multilateral institutions; official flows, 24%. After the debt crisis of the early 1980s, the volume of private flows dropped significantly, to the point that by 1990 ODA flows were larger (43%) than private flows (39%). Moreover, considering only the resources provided by the countries of the DAC, private flows in market terms (excluding grants provided by NGOs) accounted for just 13% of official and private flows to developing countries and multilateral organizations in that same year (Table 3).

However, the rebound of private flows was quite spectacular: from 1990 to 1996, they increased nearly fivefold in current terms and rose from 39% to 77% of total financial flows to developing countries. The World Bank estimated that net private capital flows to developing countries exceeded $240 billion in 1996, which was about five times the size of official flows in that year. Yet, it is important to add that private flows are highly concentrated: just 12 developing countries received 80% of these flows in the period from 1990 to 1995. Meanwhile, the total volume of ODA remained practically stagnant in current terms during this period (Figure 5), and fiscal constraints in most donor countries appeared to be transforming "aid fatigue" into outright "aid exhaustion." There was also a significant change in the nature of private flows from the early 1980s to the mid-1990s, with portfolio investments and direct foreign investment replacing lending by commercial banks to developing-country governments as the main vehicle for private flows. Although direct foreign investment has emerged as the

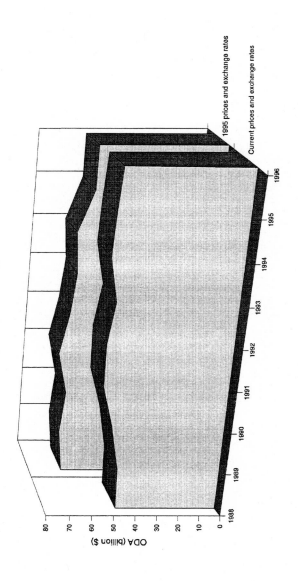

Figure 2. Total official development assistance (ODA) at current prices and exchange rates and 1995 prices and exchange rates. Source: DAC (1997b).

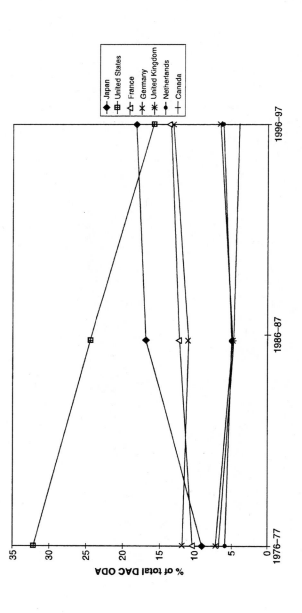

Figure 3. Share of total OECD Development Assistance Committee (DAC) official development assistance (ODA) at current prices and exchange rates. Source: DAC (1998).

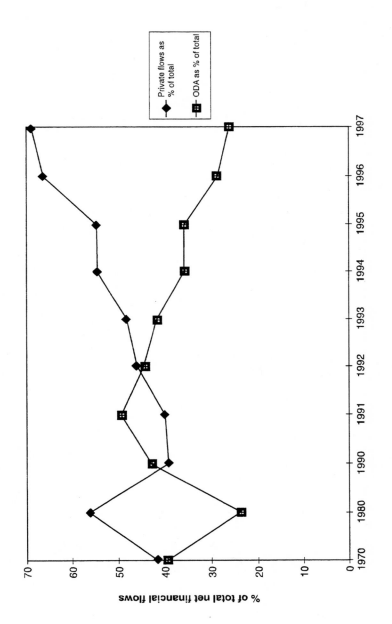

Figure 4. Official development assistance (ODA) and private flows as percentage of total net financial flow to developing countries and multilateral organizations. Source: DAC (1993, 1998).

Table 3. Official and private flows from OECD DAC countries to developing countries and multilateral organizations, 1980, 1985, 1990–96.

Type of flow	1980	1985	1990[a]	1991[a]	1992[a]	1993	1994	1995	1996	1997
ODA (million $)[b]	26 195	28 755	52 955	56 678	60 850	56 486	59 152	58 926	55 485	48 324
% of total	35	65	69	60	53	42	36	36	28	26
Bilateral grants and grant-like flows (million $)[b]	12 968	17 026	30 754	34 629	32 913	33 416	35 185	36 184	36 506	31 197
% of total	18	38	40	37	28	25	21	22	19	17
Bilateral loans (million $)[b]	4 015	4 164	6 377	6 624	8 336	5 943	6 115	4 444	2 585	1 147
% of total	5	9	8	7	7	4	4	3	1	1
Contributions to multilateral institutions (million $)[b]	9 212	7 566	15 824	15 425	19 601	17 127	17 852	18 299	16 347	15 981
% of total	12	17	21	16	17	13	11	11	8	9
Other official flows (million $)[b]	5 037	3 144	8 631	7 062	8 900	7 918	10 456	9 872	5 562	6 113
% of total	7	7	11	7	8	6	6	6	3	3
Private flows at market terms (million $)[b]	40 316	9 505	9 790	25 519	40 052	65 316	90 238	89 824	128 939	128 525
% of total	55	21	13	27	34	48	54	55	66	69
Net grants by NGOs (million $)[b]	2 386	2 884	5 077	5 403	6 005	5 692	6 046	5 973	5 568	4 628
% of total	3	7	7	6	5	4	4	4	3	2

Source: DAC (1993, 1994, 1995a, 1996, 1997b, 1998).
Note: DAC, Development Assistance Committee; NGO, nongovernmental organization; ODA, official development assistance; OECD, Organisation for Economic Co-operation and Development.
a Excluding debt forgiveness of non-ODA claims.
b Current prices.

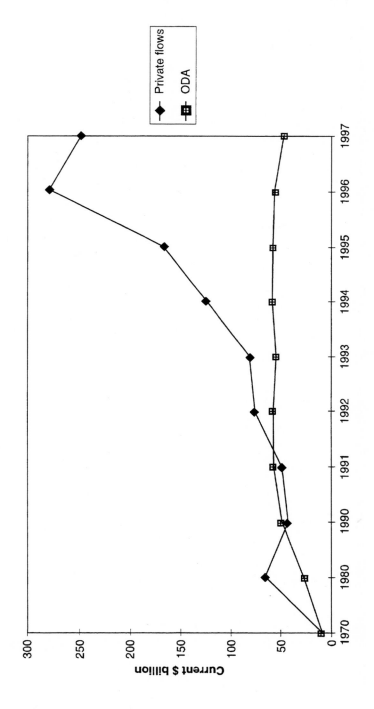

Figure 5. Evolution of total net financial flows to developing countries and multilateral organizations. Source: DAC (1993, 1998). Note: Data for 1997 are provisional; ODA, official development assistance.

most important component of private-capital flows in the 1990s, portfolio flows have also increased sharply and by 1996 represented a third of total private-capital flows (World Bank 1997b).

Together with the worldwide trends toward economic liberalization, privatization, deregulation, and the spread of market economies, these changes in the structure of flows are leading to a redefinition of development finance. During the 1950s and 1960s, before the trends reviewed in the preceding chapters led to the emergence of a fractured global order, official sources of finance — both bilateral and multilateral — played the dominant role in structuring the flow of external resources to developing countries. The surge in commercial bank lending to developing countries from the mid-1970s to the early 1980s changed this pattern, but the 1980s debt crisis reduced significantly the role of private sources in development finance and reasserted the preeminence of official flows. This situation has changed once again during the 1990s, with the spectacular increase of foreign investment and portfolio flows.

The dozen or so developing countries that have been the major recipients of private-capital flows have not found it easy to manage them: in many cases these flows have led to overvalued exchange rates and have increased the vulnerability of domestic capital markets. This has increased the requirements for sound and sophisticated macroeconomic management and for designing appropriate policy responses (Fernández-Arias and Montiel 1996). At the other extreme, "the overwhelming majority of developing countries, in particular the smaller low-income economies, still need to create the conditions to attract private capital and must depend on declining official flows" (World Bank 1997b, p. xi).

It is also clear that private financing — which follows primarily the logic of the market — is not an adequate substitute for ODA, particularly for the poorest countries. Flows of direct foreign investment are highly concentrated in just a few relatively better-off developing countries, difficult to steer toward regions or activities where they would have greatest social impact, and generally not oriented toward the long-term task of building local capabilities. This prompted the OECD's DAC to state that "the international community needs to sustain and increase the volume of official development assistance in order to reverse the growing marginalisation of the poor and achieve progress toward realistic goals of human development" (DAC 1996, p. 4).

Donors have shown a clear preference for multilateral channels, over which they are able to exert more influence. It is also becoming apparent that a greater concern with accountability, targeting, and efficiency is pushing donors in the direction of multilateral channels and programs that reduce delivery costs and allow them to trace the impacts of their contributions. This is reflected in the growing proportion of multilateral ODA channeled through IDA, the World Bank affiliate, where weighted voting prevails, in relation to contributions to the core budget of UNDP, where one-country, one-vote is the rule. Contributions to the latter diminished steadily from 2.2% of total ODA resources in 1985 to 1.6% in 1993, whereas those to the former have risen from 6.8% in 1985 to 8.9% in 1993 (they reached a peak of 10.4% of total ODA resources in 1992). In addition, although core contributions to UNDP tripled in nominal terms during the period of 1973–93, in real value they remained practically constant and even declined slightly. Whereas IDA has faced serious difficulties during the 1990s, UNDP has experienced even worse problems in terms of securing contributions to its core budget, but this has been compensated for, in part, through voluntary contributions tied to specific programs or activities (Sagasti 1994).

The troubles ODA faced during the 1990s have also been exacerbated by difficulties in securing the resources agreed on for the 10th (1994–96) and 11th (1997–99) replenishments of IDA, the concessional-assistance window of the World Bank group, which provides long-term, low interest, extended-grace-period loans to the poorest countries. For example, the IDA-10 negotiations failed to raise additional resources for the "Earth increment," which was agreed to at the 1992 United Nations Conference on Environment and Development in Rio de Janeiro to help in the transition toward environmentally sustainable development. Moreover, the United States, which had pledged $3.75 billion to IDA-10, reduced its third-year (1996) contribution from $1.3 billion to $700 million, bringing its total overdue payments to IDA-9 and IDA-10 to $934 million by early 1996. As the President of the World Bank indicated, "if every government cut [its pledges] by the same rate, IDA — which deals with 67 countries and more than 2 billion people of whom 1.2 billion live on under a dollar a day — would have been cut from $6 billion a year to a bit over $3 billion" (Wolfensohn 1996). This forced other donors to establish an interim fund of 2.2 billion Special Drawing Rights (about $3.2 billion), without the participation of the United States, to secure resources for projects to be financed as part of IDA-11.

Even though the provisional trust fund allowed IDA to maintain an annual level of disbursements close to $6 billion between 1995 and 1997, the troubled IDA-11 negotiations may have signaled the end of nearly three decades of steady increases in multilateral concessional assistance. Moreover, in January 1997, the Board of Directors of the World Bank increased the number of poor countries eligible to receive IDA soft loans to 79, bringing the combined population of these countries to about 3.3 billion, or 57% of the world's total. The difficulties in IDA financing have led some to suggest alternative approaches to raising the resources needed to keep IDA in operation at a steady level indefinitely — for example, the establishment of a fund to subsidize the interest rates of regular loans provided by the World Bank (delivered through the European Bank for Reconstruction and Development [IBRD]) (Sanford 1997).

During the early 1990s, several poor countries experienced serious problems in their financial relations with multilateral development institutions, and for some of them repayments of old loans exceeded the inflow of new capital. For example, considering all developing countries, World Bank net transfers (disbursements minus amortization and interest payments) to developing countries were negative during the first half of the 1990s, and the regional development banks were in a somewhat more favourable position (Ohlin 1994; World Bank 1996b). The problem was most acute for some of the poorest developing countries that rely on soft loans from IDA and other concessional resources from multilateral and bilateral agencies.

By the end of 1996, the IMF had established the ESAF–Heavily Indebted Poor Countries fund, and the World Bank had established the Heavily Indebted Poor Countries (HIPC) trust fund, both designed to help heavily indebted poor countries reduce their financial obligations to multilateral institutions. The AfDB and the IDB, as well as several bilateral agencies, had agreed to take part in these initiatives to ease the multilateral-debt burden of countries such as Bolivia, Burkina Faso, Côte d'Ivoire, and Uganda. Considering that the World Bank made an initial contribution of $500 million from its net income to the HIPC trust fund and that most of the net income of this institution comes from its borrowers' loan repayments, such contributions effectively constitute a transfer of resources from the middle- and low-income World Bank borrowers to the heavily indebted poor countries. Unless the rich countries that dominate the World Bank's board make additional contributions to the HIPC trust fund, a significant share of the burden of financing the HIPC trust fund will fall on the middle-income developing countries that borrow from the IBRD window of the World Bank group at near market rates.

In general terms, considering the new composition of resource flows to developing countries, there appears to be an implicit emerging trend toward allocating official aid resources to the tasks of social and sustainable development, whereas private financing takes care of economic growth. Multilateral institutions have announced they will give greater priority in lending to the social sectors (education, health, population) for environmentally sustainable development, the

Table 4. Official aid disbursements from OECD DAC countries to Part II CEECs and NISs, 1990–95.

	1990	1991	1992	1993	1994	1995	1996	1997
Total DAC ODA (million $) [a]	52 961	56 678	60 850	56 486	59 152	58 926	55 438	48 324
ODA to Part II CEECs and NISs	2 248	7 128	6 948	7 092	7 468	9 202	5 694	5 056
% of total ODA	4.24	12.58	11.42	12.56	12.63	15.62	10.27	10.46

Source: DAC (1995a, 1996, 1998, 1998).
Note: CEECs, Central and Eastern European countries; DAC, Development Assistance Committee; NIS, newly independent state; ODA, official development assistance; OECD, Organisation for Economic Co-operation and Development.
[a] Current prices.

reform of public administration, and improvement in governance. Even the financing of physical infrastructure, particularly transport and energy, which was a traditional preserve of multilateral development banks, is now increasingly left to the private sector, which is often expected to work in partnership with international financial institutions and bilateral export-development agencies. In addition to social, sustainable, and governance development — to which many donors add the task of promoting their exports to developing countries — in the post-Cold War period official flows also began to finance tasks like conflict prevention, peacemaking, and peacekeeping in developing regions. It is beginning to be understood that assistance for such purposes is part of the development effort, in the sense that many violent conflicts are only an intensification of the struggle for power inherent in the process of economic, social, and political development (Miller 1992).

As ODA stagnates in nominal terms and reaches historical lows as a proportion of GDP in rich countries (Figure 6) a significant proportion of official assistance is being channeled to nontraditional recipients like the former socialist regimes of Eastern Europe and the former Soviet Union, which in 1995 received $9 billion, or about 15% of the resources provided by the countries of the DAC (Table 4). An increasing share of what is left of ODA is being allocated to emergency relief, both for natural and human-made disasters — which means that it is not really focused on the long-term tasks of environmentally sustainable economic and social development. For example, the number of grants for refugee relief grew from 177 in 1988 to 1 975 in 1993, a more than 10-fold increase in just 5 years, whereas total ODA funds for emergency and distress relief grew from about $350 million in 1980 to about $600 million in 1985 and then soared to nearly $3.5 billion in 1994 and almost $3.1 billion in 1995 (Figure 7).

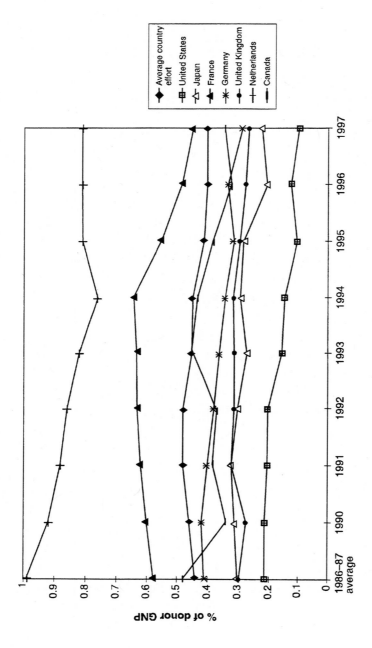

Figure 6. Official development assistance (ODA) as a percentage of donor gross national product (GNP). Source: DAC (1997b, 1998).

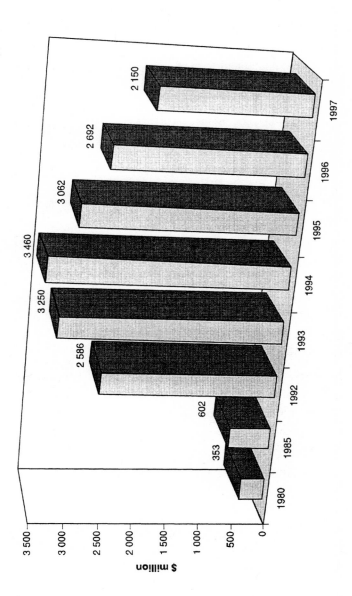

Figure 7. Official development assistance (ODA) for emergency and distress relief (excluding emergency food aid) from OECD Development Assistance Committee countries. Source: DAC (1996, 1998).

Taken together, all of these trends in the structure of development finance point toward a "squeeze" on traditional forms of development assistance, particularly from the perspective of the poorer developing countries that are unattractive to private investors and have relied on official sources of finance to prevent a further deterioration of their already low standards of living (for example, in 1994–95, ODA to Mozambique and Rwanda represented, respectively, 95.7 and 123% of their GNP).

Finally, the role that multilateral and some bilateral agencies played in the East Asian financial crisis of 1997–98 has also intensified the ODA squeeze. For example, in late 1997 the World Bank agreed to provide about $10 billion — roughly half of its total annual lending volume — to South Korea, of which nearly $3 billion was disbursed during the first quarter of 1998 (this compares with the nearly $7.3 billion that the World Bank group provided to South Korea between 1963 and 1990). In addition, South Korea received a $4 billion loan from the AsDB, 43% of its total 1997 lending volume, as part of the IMF-led rescue package. A similar situation is likely to develop in the case of the Russian Federation — an "emergent" transitional market economy with more than 10 000 nuclear warheads — as a result of the stock-market crash of mid-1998, which will require a major injection of funds that the international financial institutions do not have the capacity to provide, at least not without substantial increases in the resources available to them.

Indonesia, Malaysia, and Thailand, among other countries, have also requested significant resources from multilateral financial institutions and from bilateral sources (most notably from the Japanese government and its aid agencies). Moreover, to strengthen its balance sheet, the Board of Directors of the AsDB recommended that in 1998 no profits should be transferred to the AsDF, the soft-loan window providing resources for the poorest countries of the region, and that, instead, profits should be used to increase provisions and reserves to deal with the additional risk brought about by the crisis. Therefore, unless there is a major, but rather unlikely, increase in ODA and in the resources available to multilateral institutions, funds will be reallocated away from low- and middle-income countries and toward the relatively better-off East Asian countries that experienced financial crises in late 1997 and 1998, further aggravating the ODA squeeze.

Questioning development cooperation and the role of multilateral institutions

In parallel with the ODA squeeze, in the last decade, there has been an intense reexamination of the purposes, means, and impacts of development assistance. As early as the 1960s, when the development-cooperation experiment was less than two decades old, there were many criticisms, some rather harsh, of the motivations, choice of channels, conditions, and impacts of development assistance. Although notable advances have been made in social conditions in the developing world in the past 50 years, there is no consensus that financial and technical assistance from the rich nations have been decisive in achieving these gains.

During the 1990s, as the ODA squeeze focused attention on the effectiveness of international cooperation for development, these criticisms have reemerged with force. Keith Griffin and Terry McKinley articulated this sentiment clearly:

> Looking back over four and a half decades of international economic assistance to the developing countries, it is clear that expectations of rapid and dramatic progress were too high, the economic analysis was faulty and the political assumptions were simplistic. In short, the supporters of foreign aid were embarrassingly naive. ... First, it is evident that foreign aid, contrary to original expectations, has not contributed to a noticeable acceleration of the rate of growth of developing countries. ... Second, where aid inflows are large in relation to the recipient's national product, relative prices are distorted in an anti-development direction. ... Third, the availability of foreign aid has made it easier for the governments of recipient countries to increase unproductive current expenditure, to expand the military and to reduce taxation. ... Fourth, there is no evidence apart from the occasional anecdote that either bilateral or multilateral aid programs have succeeded in reaching the poor.
>
> (Griffin and McKinley 1994, pp. 3–4)

Other critics, such as Paul Blustein, see the whole development-cooperation experiment as a colossal waste of money: "the billions of dollars in foreign aid showered on poor countries since 1970 has produced no net impact on the overall economic performance of the Third World, nor on the economic policies of the recipient countries" (Blustein 1997).

Graham Hancock has gone even further, arguing that "aid is not bad, however, because it is sometimes misused, corrupt or crass; rather, it is *inherently* bad, bad to the bone, and utterly beyond reform" and that aid is "the most formidable obstacle to the productive endeavors of the poor." However, not even the most acerbic critics of development assistance have surpassed the vituperative level of Hancock's characterization, on the donor side, of "the notorious club of parasites and hangers-on made up of the United Nations, the World Bank and the bilateral agencies," who have reached "record breaking standards [of] self-serving behavior, arrogance, paternalism, moral cowardice and mendacity" and, on the recipient side, of the "incompetent and venal" leaders and of "governments characterized by historic ignorance, avarice and irresponsibility" that engage in the "most consistent and grievous abuses of human rights that have occurred anywhere in the world since the dark ages" (Hancock 1989, pp. 183, 192–193, his emphasis).

Against this radically pessimistic perspective on the impact of development assistance, a major study, *Does Aid Work?*, conducted by Robert Cassen in the mid-1980s and updated in the mid-1990s, reaches a rather different and more nuanced conclusion (Cassen 1994, pp. 7, 224–225, his emphasis):

> In the broadest sense, this report finds that most aid does indeed "work." It succeeds in achieving its development objectives (where those are primary), contributing positively to the recipient countries' economic performance, and not substituting for activities which would have occurred anyway. That is not to say that aid works on every count. Its performance varies by country and by sector. On the criterion of relieving poverty, even the aid which achieves its objectives cannot be considered fully satisfactory.
>
> ... [Considering] official aid for long-term development, not ... emergency relief or the work of private voluntary organizations ... and only the developmental purposes of aid, not any other motives the donors might have ... *the majority of aid is successful in terms of its own objectives.* Over a wide range of countries and sectors, aid has made positive and valuable contributions. The report also refutes some of the common criticisms of aid — that it cannot reach the poor, or that it conflicts with development of the private sector.
>
> This does not mean that all is well with aid. A significant proportion does not succeed. The question is, how is this to be judged? Suppose it were known that x percent of aid did fail, how would this compare with other kinds of investment — in the private sector in industrial countries or in the public sector? Considering the difficult circumstances in which aid operates, one might conclude that the record compared well with the average for complex human endeavors.

The perceived ineffectiveness of international development cooperation has been considered an important contributing factor in donor fatigue, which is reflected in the diminishing public support for government spending on foreign aid (Smillie 1995; ICVA 1996) and in the reduction in ODA flows. Considering the wide diversity of motivations for development assistance, the multiplicity of delivery channels, and the different objectives of various programs, it is not surprising that when aid is viewed from a particular perspective — reducing poverty, empowering women, containing ethnic conflicts, helping refugees, building local capacity in the recipient country, or promoting donor-country exports, among others — specific projects and programs can be seen to fall short of expectations. As Cassen (1994) stressed, it is important to evaluate development-assistance undertakings in terms of their own specific objectives, which often differ from the goals that critics believe aid programs ought to pursue.

After reviewing a large amount of quantitative evidence, a report prepared at the World Bank (Dollar and Pritchett 1998) concludes that "aid works. Financial assistance leads to more rapid growth, poverty reduction, and gains in social indicators in developing countries with sound policies and institutions." However, rather than focusing on the amount of aid, the authors argued that good domestic policies and institutions are a necessary condition for aid to have a positive impact. According to their calculations, improvements in governance and policies of the same order of magnitude as those experienced throughout the developing world during the last decade may lift an additional 100 million people a year out of poverty. For this reason, they highlighted the intangible benefits of development assistance, which include dissemination of ideas, education of future leaders, and stimulation of policy debate within civil society, and emphasized the importance of building a broad base of institutions to ensure the delivery of public services.

In a major reversal of trends in thinking of the 1960s and 1970s in favour of multilateral channels for development cooperation, during the late 1980s and the 1990s multilateral development-cooperation agencies — in particular the World Bank group, IMF, and United Nations — have been questioned from many quarters. Most analysts would agree with Reginald Green's statement that "there is a consensus that global economic institutions function poorly" (Green 1995, p. 66). For example, as the World Bank expanded its scope of action into policy-based lending to support policy reforms in borrowing countries (through structural-adjustment loans) the distinctions between the roles of the World Bank and IMF (the two Bretton Woods sisters) became blurred in the 1980s. As a consequence, some critics of international organizations in general raised the question whether the World Bank and the IMF should be merged or even abolished. But this suggestion has not been taken seriously in most international policy-making circles (Bandow and Vasquez 1995).

The IMF and World Bank have also been attacked for of their adherence to what are perceived as a rather rigid set of policy prescriptions, the so-called

Washington Consensus (Williamson 1990), imposed on borrowers as a condition for access to resources. According to one of the pioneers of development thinking, Hans Singer, "nowhere in the Articles of Agreement of the IMF (nor of the World Bank for that matter) is there any mandate to evolve or prescribe proper development policies to its member countries, let alone to develop the specific school of prescriptions now known as the 'Washington Consensus' " (Singer 1995, p. 7). Criticism reached a high point in 1994, when the Bretton Woods institutions celebrated their 50th anniversary.[12] Environmental groups and grass-roots activists disrupted their Annual Meetings with demonstrations and chanted the slogan "fifty years is enough."

The World Bank study on aid (Dollar and Pritchett 1998) underscores the importance of good policies and institutions as a condition for aid to have a positive impact and argues that "what is good policy is not something that is subjectively decided in Washington. Rather, lessons about good policy emerge from the experiences of developing countries. What we mean by good management is — objectively — what has led to growth and poverty reduction in the developing world" (Dollar and Pritchett 1998, p. 47). However, considering the frequent changes in the policy advice provided by the World Bank over the last decades and the changing nature of the evidence to support what are considered good policies, the claim to "objectivity" has to be taken with a grain of salt.

However, even though the World Bank report highlights the importance of sound economic management and credible policy reforms and the need for developing countries to be to a large extent masters of their own fate, it fails to acknowledge that conceptions of good policy and sound economic management have varied over the last several decades. Moreover, international financial institutions like the World Bank have imposed a wide variety of policy reforms as conditions for access to their resources and have often pressured developing countries into adopting what the institutions consider appropriate policies at a given time, only to change their views with regard to the adequacy of such policies at a later time. *Rethinking Aid: What Works, What Doesn't and Why* (Dollar and

---

[12] The 50th anniversary of the Bretton Woods institutions and that of the United Nations (celebrated in 1994 and 1995, respectively) led to a flurry of proposals and suggestions for major reforms in the system of international institutions. See, among others, Urquhart and Childers (1990), Paarlberg and Lipton (1991), Adams (1994), Griesgraber (1994), International Institute for Labour Studies (IILS 1994), Kennen (1994), Patel (1994), Commission on Global Governance (CGG 1995), Griesgraber and Gunter (1995), and Stewart (1995). See also the various reports produced as part of the project Rethinking Bretton Woods, carried out at the Center for Concern in Washington, DC, under the coordination of JoMarie Griesgraber.

Pritchett 1998) does not sufficiently acknowledge the responsibility of international financial institutions in the design and implementation of failed policies in developing countries, especially in sub-Saharan Africa (Leandro et al. 1999).

Another reason for serious criticism of the World Bank in recent years has been that the bank apparently tolerates corruption in countries where it operates. In the case of Indonesia, for instance, it has been reported that 20 to 30% of Indonesian government funds earmarked for development are diverted to bureaucrats and politicians (Simpson 1998). Although World Bank staff have not been directly implicated in these activities, many appear to have been ignorant of local practices and habits and for this reason rather susceptible to deception (World Bank 1997a).

In the late 1970s, after the collapse of the fixed exchange-rate regime, and especially during the 1980s, as a result of the debt crisis, the new roles that the IMF began to play transformed this institution into "both a police officer of economic policy and a mediator between debtors and creditors" (Minton-Beddoes 1995, p. 127). The IMF interventions to address the Mexican peso crisis of 1994–95 and the East Asian crisis of 1997–98 have been severely criticized from many different quarters, as going well beyond the appropriate role for this institution (Kapur 1998). According to Martin Feldstein, "the IMF's recent emphasis on imposing major structural and institutional reforms as opposed to focusing on balance-of-payments adjustments will have adverse consequences in both the short term and the more distant future" (Feldstein 1998, p. 20). This is particularly worrisome in the case of South Korea, where the country needed resources to stave off a temporary liquidity crisis and the IMF demanded policy reforms that Japan and the United States had previously urged but that the Korean government had balked at (Feldstein 1998).

The 50-year-old United Nations system has also come under increasing pressure to reform and keep up with the times. Although there is general agreement that an international forum is needed to maintain peace, handle crises and conflicts, deal with various problems of a global nature, and foster sustainable human development, the effectiveness of the various United Nations organizations (the United Nations Secretariat, independent agencies, committees, councils, and affiliated bodies) has been seriously questioned. One major point of criticism is that the United Nations system has grown excessively and in a disorderly fashion, to the point that some observers have suggested that "by pruning obsolescent, inefficient, redundant, and corrupt branches, the UN [United Nations] could cut its budgetary costs in half" (Rotberg 1996). However, even if major gains in efficiency were to be achieved, the growing global and international agendas will certainly require additional resources for the United Nations system to adequately carry out its mandates (Méndez 1995).

During the Reagan administration, the United States government became a most severe critic of the United Nations for a variety of reasons, many of them of an ideological and political nature, but several others related to the inefficient and wasteful nature of many United Nations bodies. This "UN-bashing" mood persisted through the 1990s, primarily in the US Congress, which has repeatedly refused to appropriate resources to cover assessed contributions to the regular budget of the United Nations, provide funds for peacekeeping operations, or finance development-cooperation programs. The United States has been using its arrears to the United Nations budget, which in the mid-1990s exceeded $1.5 billion, as a stick to pressure for drastic organizational and procedural reforms and major cuts in the administrative budget. By mid-1998, arrears reached such a level that the United States was threatened with the loss of its vote in the United Nations General Assembly.

New demands for development cooperation

As discussed in the preceding chapters, the last two decades have witnessed profound changes in the context for development efforts, as well as in conceptions of development and how to bring it about. Whereas economic issues dominated the early years of the development-cooperation experiment, issues such as environmental sustainability, gender equality, the informal sector, and poverty reduction were incorporated into the design and implementation of development-cooperation programs during the second half of the 1980s, particularly after the debt crisis subsided (DAC 1989). Notwithstanding the decline in resources for development assistance, several political and noneconomic issues were added to an already overcrowded international development agenda during the 1990s. These included good governance, varieties of market economies, culture and religion, and conflict prevention. Curiously enough, even though disparities in the capacity to generate and use knowledge have become the most prominent feature of the emerging fractured global order, building scientific and technological capabilities in developing countries is not considered a priority issue in the international development-cooperation community.

Respect for human rights, democratization, popular participation, demilitarization, transparency in decision-making, and, in general, themes related to the idea of good governance are now routinely discussed in development-cooperation forums. This has prompted calls for the more active involvement of bilateral and multilateral institutions in promoting good governance. Some critics, particularly from the NGO community, have argued that human rights, democracy, and related criteria should be incorporated as formal conditions on access to loans, grants, and other forms of international assistance.

Bilateral aid agencies and multilateral financial institutions have been gradually developing their own views on the more political aspects of governance. The DAC (1996, 1997b) has addressed topics such as the role of civil society, human rights, legal systems, and democratic decentralization, and the World Bank has moved beyond its pioneering report on development and governance (World Bank 1992a), which covered aspects such as transparency in government decision-making, reduction of military expenditures, elimination of corruption, and improvements in the administration of justice. Although concerns have been raised that these issues exceed the apolitical mandate of most multilateral financial institutions and push them into potentially dangerous areas, they are likely to remain on the international development agenda for the foreseeable future. Pressures for greater political conditionality are likely to increase, particularly on concessional assistance in a resource-constrained environment. Indeed, the articles of agreement of the EBRD, which was established in the early 1990s to provide financing to the countries of Eastern Europe and the former Soviet Union, stipulate that borrowers must have democratic political systems.

The demise of the former Soviet Union and the collapse of centrally planned economies have left the scene free for a more sober appreciation of the variety of really existing market economies, particularly in the industrialized nations (Albert 1991; Hampden-Turner and Trompenaars 1993; Redding 1997). Within the general framework of capitalism, developing countries face strategic choices regarding the type of market economy they want to have and the roles to be played by the state, the market, and civil society in the conduct of economic and social affairs. Among the many issues open to debate on the varieties of capitalism, it is possible to identify the degree to which governments should provide guidance on the development of the productive system, the specific institutional arrangements to mobilize savings and allocate investment resources, the nature and scope of mechanisms to regulate the markets, and the channels through which civil society participates in economic-policy debates and decisions.

A study on the East Asian experience with economic growth and development carried out by the World Bank with Japanese funding during the early 1990s (World Bank 1993) provides an indication of the interest in exploring alternatives to what was perceived as the dominant "Anglo-Saxon" perspective on economic development prevailing in that institution. Issues such as the role of directed and subsidized credit figured as a prominent concern of a Japanese member of the

Board of Directors of the World Bank, as such policies played a major role in the industrialization of Japan and other East Asian countries. These questions were also raised in the *World Development Report 1997*, which focused on the role of the state in a changing world (World Bank 1997d), and in the debates on the appropriateness of the economic policies advocated through the Washington Consensus. As the competition between different varieties of capitalism intensifies in the coming years, multilateral financial institutions and development-cooperation agencies will need to develop a more pluralistic view of strategies for economic development.

The growing importance of cultural factors, ethnic allegiances, spiritual concerns, religion, and ethical issues has made it necessary for development-cooperation institutions to be more sensitive to these values issues, which have largely been ignored in the design and implementation of development-cooperation programs during the last several decades. For example, when approaching the questions of poverty, social safety nets, and gender equality in Islamic societies, it is necessary to take into consideration religious and cultural traditions. The Latin American Catholic Church has criticized neoliberal structural-adjustment programs as morally and ethically reprehensible, primarily because of what it perceives as their negative impacts on the poor. Also, it may be difficult to adopt the Western approach to the rule of law in societies that have no clear demarcation of roles between church and state.

Conflict prevention, conflict resolution, and postwar reconstruction provide a good illustration of the complexity of the new demands on bilateral aid agencies and multilateral financial organizations and support the adoption of a well-defined division of labour between the multiplicity of organizations that need to be involved to prevent deadly conflicts. Appendix 1 describes the main features of conflict prevention and the roles that the various international organizations can play. The high degree of uncertainty associated with conflict prevention makes it a rather inappropriate and risky undertaking for international financial institutions. Considering the dual financial-mobilization and development-promotion mandates of multilateral development banks, they need to be reasonably confident that their interventions, particularly when lending operations are involved, will have positive results and generate income streams that enable borrowers to repay these loans. Conflict prevention involves tasks that are better suited to United Nations bodies, bilateral aid agencies, regional political entities, and NGOs, combined with the diplomatic initiatives of influential countries and the possible use of military force.

Rising to the challenge? Responses and initiatives

The ODA squeeze, the questioning of aid and multilateral institutions, and the new demands placed on international cooperation for development have prompted a flurry of responses from the international development community during the 1990s. A few examples will illustrate the ways governments and various organizations engaged in development finance and international cooperation have reacted to the new circumstances.

Developed-country governments are beginning to perceive the need for a comprehensive approach to the reform of international development cooperation. Discussions aiming at a "new partnership for development" took place at the 1996 Lyons Summit of the leaders of the Group of Seven highly industrialized countries and the Russian Federation (the "G-8"), where they were joined by the top officials of the United Nations, IMF, World Bank, and WTO. The declaration that emerged from that summit emphasized the importance of quality over quantity in development cooperation, held that development aid should be based on solidarity and effective burden-sharing among all actors, placed the chief responsibility for development on developing countries, and stated that development should be sustainable, equitable, and environmentally friendly and create jobs. These views were reaffirmed at the 1997 Denver G-8 Summit, where a new initiative for aid to sub-Saharan Africa was also announced (SELA 1997).

During the early and mid-1990s, multilateral financial institutions, bilateral assistance agencies, and independent development-cooperation organizations undertook many initiatives that have been changing the way development cooperation works. Most of these organizations have experienced major reorganizations, changes in their product lines, significant budget cuts, staff reductions, and substantive modifications in their procedures. A large proportion of these initiatives have emerged as reactions to crisis situations, and this has made it difficult to plan and carry them out in a careful and well-thought-out manner. As a consequence, there have been many advances and retreats, and some institutions have experienced severe organizational shocks in fairly short periods. For example, the World Bank had two major reorganizations and four significant modifications in its organizational structure between 1987 and 1996, some of which reversed changes introduced 1 or 2 years earlier.

The Mexican peso crisis of 1994–95, the East Asian crisis of 1997–98, and the collapse of the Russian stock market in mid-1998 taxed the response capacities of international financial institutions to the limit. In the first case, a joint effort of the IMF, World Bank, IDB, and the US Treasury raised more than $40 billion to prevent the collapse of the Mexican economy. In the second case, a $120-billion rescue package for several East Asian countries was put together rather hastily, draining the resources of a broad range of multilateral institutions and bilateral agencies (the rather reluctant participation of private banks in the financial rescue efforts was secured at a later stage). In the third case, it is yet to be seen what quantity of resources will have to be mobilized to stabilize Russian finances. Concerns have been expressed about the possible recurrence of similar crises, particularly because it cannot be expected that international financial institutions will be able to periodically mobilize resources on such a massive scale to maintain the stability of the international financial system.

World Bank

As early as a decade ago, the World Bank launched its Strategic Agenda exercise, which anticipated the need for radical adjustments in World Bank operations, product line, and organizational structure, changes that would only come several years later in the mid-1990s (World Bank 1989). In March of 1997, the World Bank group approved a $250 million, 2-year Strategic Compact aimed at producing fundamental changes in the way this institution operates. According to the World Bank,

> The development business is undergoing dramatic change: surging private capital flows and declining support for official aid; greatly diversified sources of advice and technical assistance; and recognition of a broader development paradigm — with greater emphasis on local capacity and social, environmental and governance dimensions.
>
> At the same time, a powerful technological revolution is facilitating access to knowledge, a crucial factor of development. It is also having profound effects on how all organizations do business: more competitive, faster, flatter in their structures; more networked and eager to partner; and more learning-oriented, with knowledge recognized as a key driver of effectiveness.
>
> (World Bank 1997c, p. ii)

Admitting that, in many respects, it had failed to keep up with these trends, the World Bank acknowledged that

> close to one third of Bank-supported projects have unsatisfactory outcomes ... demand for the Bank's standard loan product is flat and its financial tools have aged ... there is a lack of professional expertise in key areas ... the Bank's development experience is not systematically catalogued or retained, and clients complain about the Bank's slowness

and standardized approach, while many potential partners have often been critics ... or perceived as competitors.

(World Bank 1997c, p. ii)

In response to these shortcomings, four key elements were identified in the Strategic Compact: refueling current business activities, primarily by easing budget pressures to protect the level and quality of client services; refocusing the development agenda on issues of social and environmental sustainability, as well as on the changing roles of the private and public sectors; retooling the World Bank's knowledge base so as to collect, synthesize, and disseminate best-practice knowledge and make it more accessible; and revamping institutional capabilities by realigning the institution's information systems, reformulating financial management, investing more in staff training, and relocating functions, authority, and staff to the field.

The World Bank is now putting into practice the ambitious agenda of the Strategic Compact, but it will take a few years to assess whether it succeeds in repositioning the World Bank in a vastly changed context for international development cooperation. It offered several new products in 1997, including lending instruments such as the Adaptable Program Loans and the Learning and Innovation Loans, together with measures to catalyze private investments in infrastructure (information about investment opportunities, creation of an Infrastructure Advisory Services Unit, cooperation with business associations, training and education). The World Bank has also expanded the range of guarantees it provides to subsovereign (provincial and municipal) governments and has begun to offer partial risk guarantees to lenders backing major investment projects and guarantees to support private-enclave projects, with both of these types of guarantee intended for poor countries eligible for IDA concessional loans (BWI 1997).

In addition, the World Bank has been quite eager to improve its relations with civil-society organizations, particularly with NGOs that have often been the most severe critics of the institution. It has appointed NGO liaison officers in practically all its field offices, and according to its 1996 annual report, "the Bank is strongly committed to going beyond traditional cooperation with member governments to include participation in decisionmaking by NGOs, community groups, cooperatives, women's organizations, the poor and the disadvantaged, as well as the private sector" (World Bank 1996a, p. 74). A new Development Grants Facility has been established to consolidate the administration of a variety of grants provided by the World Bank. At about $125 million a year, this new facility places the World Bank among the largest institutions making grants to developing countries. Besides the grant programs that have been in effect for quite a long time (for example, Consultative Group on International Agricultural Research, Research and Training in Tropical Diseases, Global Water Partnership (GWP), International Program for the Improvement of Educational Outcomes), it has initiated new grant programs during the early and mid-1990s, including the Post-Conflict Program, the Information for Development Program, the Institutional Development Fund, and a microfinance program (Alexander 1998).

Regional development banks

Practically all the regional development banks experienced significant changes during the 1990s. The IDB doubled its capital base and became a more important source of financial resources for Latin America than the World Bank, both in absolute and in net-transfer terms. The IDB underwent a lengthy, often acrimonious, and highly disruptive reorganization process during the first half of the 1990s. Moreover, scepticism regarding staff capacity to provide adjustment loans made the IDB Board of Directors request management to follow the lead of the World Bank in sector-adjustment lending during the late 1980s and early 1990s. The IDB has also entered into new areas, such as the provision of technical assistance and lending to improve the functioning of the judiciaries and of congresses in Latin American countries and has committed itself to doubling its lending for social development and, in particular, education.

The AfDB experienced severe financial difficulties and undertook a major reorganization during the first half of the 1990s but is very far from challenging the World Bank's leadership in this region. The AsDB encountered problems and controversy in the negotiations to increase its capital base, primarily because of differences between shareholders regarding the role it should play in the Asian region and differing views on issues such as lending to the public and private sectors, concessional lending to India and China, and the provision of loans to Viet Nam. With the potential addition of new members from Central Asia, with its role in defusing the East Asian financial crisis of 1997–98, and with a possible major capital increase, the number, complexity, and scope of AsDB operations may expand significantly in the coming years.

After experiencing significant start-up difficulties and being mired in controversies, the ERDB is gradually becoming a more important player in the Eastern European countries and the former Soviet Union, and it doubled its capital base in early 1996. In addition, several subregional development banks have been playing a minor but important financing role in a few sectors in some countries (for example, the Islamic Development Bank, the European Investment Bank, the Central American Integration Bank, the Andean Finance Corporation).

Institutional relationships between the World Bank and the regional development banks have been marked by cooperation, rivalry, and competition (Culpeper 1993; Kapur and Webb 1994; Rwegasira and Kifle 1994). To improve coordination and advance toward an appropriate division of labour between these institutions, a Task Force on Multilateral Development Banks was established in 1994 by the Development Committee of the World Bank and the IMF, with the mandate to undertake, for the first time, an assessment of the capabilities and coordination among the World Bank and the regional development banks. The Task Force report (Development Committee 1996) calls for intensified coordination at the country level, at that of the chief executives, and at that of the shareholders. It also recommended a set of shared goals: to mobilize international savings and concessional assistance for sustainable development, to ensure access of lower-income countries to special resources linked to policy reforms, to support the transition of formerly centrally administered economies to market systems, and to assist in the reconstruction of devastated economies and provide economic support for a lasting peace.

United Nations Development Programme

The United Nations system embarked in a laborious restructuring process in the early 1990s, and it is likely to continue to make organizational, financial, and operational changes in the transition to the 21st century. The Secretary-General's report, *Agenda for Development* (United Nations 1994), outlined a new set of United Nations policies to reposition it in the international development arena and gave overall responsibility for coordinating all development-related activities to the Administrator of the UNDP. However, this agency faced resource constraints during the early 1990s, as its erstwhile major supporter, the United States, reduced its contributions to the core budget, and several other donors followed suit. As a result, the UNDP's core budget has declined steadily for more than a decade, even though this was compensated for in large measure through donor contributions to the noncore budget and revenues earned from the provision of services to other international agencies and developing- and developed-country governments.

A major strategic-planning exercise launched in 1993 by Gustav Speth, the newly appointed Administrator of the agency, sought to define new directions for the UNDP. It began with the premise that

> We are at a crossroads in Official Development Assistance (ODA). Three
> generalizations can be offered regarding ODA. First, it is needed now
> more than ever and must be expanded to meet increasing needs and
> opportunities. Second, it must be thoroughly reformed to learn from past

mistakes and to escape fully the Cold War's legacy. And third, ODA even if reformed will still not provide an adequate response to inequitable economic growth and social injustice.

The crossroads of ODA is very much the crossroads of UNDP. Although we are at the end of an era of development experience ... . We have a UNDP that has begun to reposition itself to help meet the challenges of global transformation.

(Speth 1995, p. 5)

One of the main problems with the UNDP was "its lack of clear mission and focus," which was a consequence of being pulled "too many ways by too many forces," as a result of which it

tried to do too much, its resources were spread too thin, and its overstretched staff became less effective. Weak substantive capacity was exacerbated by carrying out too many "mailbox" or processing functions. There has been uneven leadership at headquarters and in the field. Moreover, UNDP's coordinating assignment is not fully accepted within the U.N. [United Nations] system as a whole — nor yet fully realized by UNDP. All of this adds to the difficulty of measuring results and having a clear sense of what UNDP is accountable for.

(UNDP 1995a, p. 13)

UNDP's strategic framework outlined a series of programmatic and organizational changes to improve the delivery of technical and financial assistance (UNDP 1993, 1994a, 1995a, b). The strategic framework aimed at repositioning the agency in a new context for development cooperation. It emphasized the concept of partnership, which involves extensive consultations with other development-cooperation actors, such as national authorities, the World Bank, other United Nations agencies, and key donor partners. Forging new partnerships for development has also involved civil society as UNDP has moved toward strengthening its involvement with NGOs, the private sector, and civil-society organizations. It also articulated the need for a differentiation of development-cooperation schemes on a country-by-country basis, a long-standing practice of UNDP, an agency that takes pride in its field presence, its close relations with developing-country governments, and the fact that it has 85% of its staff in program countries. In a significant move to advance its strategic framework, in June 1995, the Executive Board of the UNDP modified its rigid 25-year-old scheme for allocating resources to individual countries through the Indicative Planning Figure, which had severely limited the capacity of managers to direct resources where they could be most effective.

However, the highly political and uncertain context of the United Nations system and the recurrent financial upheavals of the agency make it very difficult to put into practice the measures advocated in the strategic framework. In addition, the World Bank — which has considerably larger and more stable financial resources than UNDP — is aggressively moving to strengthen its field presence everywhere, diversify the range of its services, and improve relations with governments, the private sector, and NGOs in the countries where it operates. In all likelihood, during the next few years, the UNDP will have to continue redefining its strategy in response to the changing circumstances, particularly to the challenge posed by the expanding presence of the multilateral development banks at field level.

Similar considerations apply to the specialized United Nations agencies, such as the Food and Agriculture Organization, the World Health Organization, and the United Nations Industrial Development Organization, which are all facing stiff competition from the World Bank and the regional development banks. UNICEF began a restructuring process in the mid-1980s, focusing its mission more clearly and embarking on a public-outreach campaign, and this process has spared the agency many of the problems experienced by other United Nations bodies.

European Union

After a lengthy review of priorities, practice, and experience in late 1995, the member states of the European Union and 70 developing countries comprising the African, Caribbean and Pacific (ACP) group signed the second financial protocol of the fourth Lomé Convention, which for two decades has been the main mechanism for development cooperation between European countries and their former colonies and territories. These difficult negotiations reflected a greatly changed global situation, incompatibilities between the Lomé Convention and the WTO, major political shifts in Europe and many ACP countries, and the changing concerns of donors regarding development cooperation.

In June 1996, after the signing of the second financial protocol (for the last 5 years of the 20th century), the European Center for Development and Policy Management (ECDPM) convened a major international conference on the current situation and future prospects of the Lomé Convention. Considering the member countries' variety of the economic, social, humanitarian, political, commercial, and cultural interests, it is not surprising it was difficult to find a common ground:

> it became clear in the meeting that common economic interests have declined since the 1970s. The common interests between the EU

[European Union] and members of the ACP are now less clear than they
were 20 years ago when the agreements were first signed. And, there are
some who suggest that the shared interests of the group of ACP countries,
beyond the Lomé connection to Europe, are also rather tenuous. ... The
tone of the debates on the Lomé Convention was summarized by one
observer as: "past imperfect, present tense, future uncertain."

(ECDPM 1996)

Nevertheless, most ACP participants at this event asserted that common interests
do exist and should be the base for a new understanding between the ACP and the
European Union. These common interests focus primarily on moral and human-
security concerns, which from a European perspective may seem too weak to
provide a basis for a new Lomé Convention.

According to ECDPM, the 1998 talks on the Lomé Convention took place
in a context of decreasing interest in ACP–European Union cooperation. This
situation was markedly different from the optimistic mood of good will in the
mid-1970s, when this development-cooperation scheme was launched. In the
1990s, development aid budgets were reduced; the European Union's geographical
interests were distinctly unfavorable to ACP countries; strong pressure was exerted
on Lomé-created commercial preferences; and mutual ties were increasingly
eroded between Europe and ACP countries (ECDPM 1996). Therefore, if the
special ties between Europe and the developing countries in its former colonial
sphere of influence are to be maintained — and the desirability of this may be
subject to question, in view of an overcrowded European Union agenda, which
includes enlargement, reform of its agricultural policy, launching of the Euro,
among other items — it will be necessary to develop a new rationale for maintaining the privileged relations between Europe and the ACP countries. In particular,
it will be indispensable to harmonize the preferential trade provisions of the Lomé
Convention with the agreements reached by the WTO, which rule out such trade
preferences.

Despite these changes, an interesting development in recent European
Union–ACP talks is the degree to which nonstate actors have pushed for greater
space in future European Union–ACP cooperation. The previous Lomé IV agreement had set the stage for "decentralized cooperation," a pluralist approach to
development cooperation that is yet to be fully operationalized. Decentralized
cooperation involves a participatory, bottom-up approach to development, in which
collaboration is promoted between diverse actors. This approach ultimately seeks
the decentralization of governments and donor agencies. Although decentralized
cooperation has had a mixed track record, there may be a promising future for it

as traditional development-cooperation approaches are superseded. Among the trends identified as push factors for the gradual entry of decentralized cooperation into the mainstream are the search for public–private synergies, the increasingly significant dynamic of development at the local level, changes under way in donor agencies, and the decentralization processes that many ACP governments are undergoing (Bossuy 1998).

In addition, as advanced in its Agenda 2000 report released in July 1997, the European Union is in the process of reforming its Common Agricultural Policy (CAP). Commitments to decrease subsidies and special trade preferences under the GATT Uruguay Round; budget constraints, which highlight the large amounts spent by the European Union in agricultural support; and the prospects for the enlargement of the European Union to include Eastern European countries that have large agricultural sectors all require CAP reforms that are likely to have important implications for developing nations. The negative impact of liberalizing measures will be felt most strongly among the countries benefiting from the preferences established by the Lomé Convention, even though developing countries as a whole are likely to benefit from the changes to be introduced in CAP (IDS 1998).

The DAC and bilateral agencies

As the umbrella organization for bilateral development aid agencies, the OECD's DAC has embarked on several exercises during the 1990s to review and adapt bilateral cooperation to the imperatives of a period of global change. In a major report on the subject, it stated that "the time is ripe to reflect on the lessons of development cooperation over the past 50 years and put forward strategies for the first part of the next century" (DAC 1996, p. 12). This report followed a ministerial pronouncement issued in May 1995, *Development Partnerships in the New Global Context* (DAC 1995b), which stated several strategic orientations to guide the actions of bilateral aid agencies. Chief among these are the ideas that development cooperation is a key investment in the future, that combatting poverty is the central challenge of development assistance, that cooperation should be aimed at strengthening capacities in developing countries, and that additional resources are required to revitalize development cooperation.

The DAC has sought to define long-term goals for development cooperation in the transition to the 21st century, focusing on improving the quality of life for all through development that is sustainable along the economic, social, and environmental dimensions. Some of these long-term goals, most of which have 2015 as a time horizon, are reducing the proportion of people living in extreme poverty in developing countries by at least one-half, achieving universal primary education in all countries, eliminating gender disparity in primary and secondary education, reducing the death rate for infants and children under the age of 5 by two-thirds, making primary health care and reproductive health services available to all individuals of appropriate ages, and ensuring that current trends in the loss of environmental resources are reverted (DAC 1996). The approach advocated by the DAC is to view development cooperation as an essential complementary factor in achieving development, and the DAC argued that development efforts have only been successful in countries where people and institutions have made sustained efforts to help themselves (DAC 1996).

In addition, as pointed out in the preceding section, the OECD's DAC has given high priority to the problems arising from regional and ethnically motivated violent conflicts. Based on the premise that "helping strengthen the capacity of a society to manage conflict without violence must be seen as a foundation for sustainable development," DAC has drawn detailed policy guidelines on how to deal with these situations and incorporate conflict prevention into the framework of development assistance (DAC 1997a).

To indicate the extent to which some countries are reacting to the changing context for development cooperation, we shall mention the cases of Japan, the United Kingdom, and the United States.[13] The United States appears to be ready for an overhaul of its aid policies and practices, although it is rather unlikely to recover the preeminent role it played during the first three decades of the development-cooperation experiment. Judging from public pronouncements and declarations by high-level government officials, American foreign-development assistance is likely to experience significant changes in the next few years, but increasing the resources allocated to development cooperation does not appear to be one of these changes.

For example, in the wake of the East Asian financial crisis, legislation pending approval in the US Congress in early 1998 proposed the establishment of a US Advisory Commission, comprised of at least five former US Secretaries of Treasury, to report to Congress on the future role and responsibilities of the IMF. This commission would also report on the advisability of merging the IMF, the World Bank, and the WTO, particularly in view of the cross-conditionality practices prevailing in these three institutions (BWI 1998). Although it is most unlikely that such a merger will be formally proposed by the US government and

---

[13] For a review of recent changes in bilateral assistance, see DAC (1997b) and International Council of Volunteer Agencies (ICVA 1996).

taken seriously in international circles, when added to the UN bashing mood prevailing in Congress, the appointment of such an Advisory Commission does not bode well for increased US support for international development-cooperation institutions.

A new US policy on Africa unveiled in 1997, several months before President Clinton's 1998 visit to the region, may signal a change in emphasis from aid to trade as a means to support African development efforts. The initiative includes lowering trade barriers to promote exports from the region, providing debt relief for highly indebted poor countries that implement adjustment programs and maintain economic stability, and providing support for improving infrastructure in countries south of the Sahara. The idea is to transform relations between the United States and African countries away from what is perceived as a welfare-style, donor–recipient model to a more mature partnership based on trade and mutual interests (The Washington Post 1997).

USAID, a major bilateral player on the development-cooperation scene, is also set to change the way it operates. In early 1998, it made public its new Strategic Plan, which states clearly the philosophy of American aid in the following terms:

> Promoting sustainable development among developing and transitional countries contributes to U.S. national interests and is a necessary and critical component of America's role as a world leader. It helps reduce the threat of crisis and create the conditions for economic growth, the expansion of democracy and social justice, and a protected environment. Under these conditions, citizens in developing and transitional countries can focus on their own social and economic progress, which creates demand for U.S. goods and services and expands cooperative relationships between the United States and assisted countries.
>
> (USAID 1998, p. 1)

In addition to reaffirming USAID's mission to contribute to the United States' national interests, the Strategic Plan views sustainable development as including not only implementing "open, market-oriented economic policies and institutions" but also strengthening democracy and good governance, building human capacity through education and training, stabilizing the world population, protecting human health, and protecting the world's environment for long-term sustainability.

Most of the document presenting USAID's Strategic Plan is devoted to a detailed description of goals, objectives, and performance measures, which are all particularly worthy of notice, primarily because they provide an indication of the way the administration of this agency thinks about the process of development. Emphasis is placed on quantitative indicators of performance, which are to be reviewed annually and to provide the basis for resource allocation. However, many of the indicators — all linked to performance targets and goals, USAID objectives, and US national interests — have little to do with decisions or actions under the direct control of this agency's field missions or central operating units.

For example, according to the plan, the strategic goal to encourage "broad-based economic growth and agricultural development" is supposed to be evaluated by indicators such as average annual growth rate of GNP per capita (in constant prices), the difference between the average annual growth rate in agriculture and that in population, the percentage of the population living below the poverty line, and the annual average growth rates of direct foreign investment and trade in goods and services. More tellingly, advances toward the strategic goal of strengthening democracy and good governance are to be evaluated using indicators such as the number of countries classified by Freedom House as free, partly free, and not free and the Freedom House scores for political rights and civil liberties.

However, in addition to the obvious imperfections of these indicators as means of measuring progress toward the stated strategic goals, it is also clear that US assistance plays a very minor role in the development outcomes reflected in these indicators. It appears that USAID's Strategic Plan makes the mistake of considering aid a direct producer of development outcomes, rather than viewing it as an enabling or facilitating condition, whose role is to help produce the development outcomes. The use of such indicators to evaluate USAID performance and guide resource allocations on a yearly basis has generated a great deal of bureaucratic creativity, as well as considerable stress and administrative gridlock, as managers struggle to produce indicators that reflect short-term progress in specific projects, even though these usually refer to long-term development processes.

Japan became the largest provider of ODA during the first half of the 1990s. By 1995, total Japanese ODA reached nearly $14.5 billion, topping second-place France and third-placed Germany be nearly 70 and 90%, respectively. However, in 1996, Japanese aid was cut by 34.9% in current US dollars (24.7% in constant US dollars), and in June 1997 the Japanese government announced that the ODA budget would be reduced for each fiscal year of a 3-year intensive fiscal reform. Added to the depreciation of the yen, the cuts in development assistance would be even larger in US-dollar terms. Moreover, as demands derived from the East Asian financial crisis of 1997–98 absorb a significant proportion of Japanese aid funds, it is likely that other assistance programs will suffer major budget cuts (ICVA 1996; DAC 1997a).

Together with the long-drawn recession that Japan is experiencing and the internal political difficulties it faces, these developments in ODA make it rather unlikely that Japan will assume a leadership position in the field of international finance and development cooperation as we approach the 21st century. Efforts to improve the quality of aid, strengthen its capacity for policy dialogues, and provide intellectual guidance for developing countries will, in all probability, be shelved, at least for a few years. Other countries are also set to revamp their development-cooperation programs. For example, shortly after assuming power, the labour government in the United Kingdom created the Department for International Development, in May 1997, and by November 1997 the United Kingdom had issued its first White Paper on development assistance in more than two decades. Although British aid had been declining for a number of years, the White Paper, which focuses on the elimination of poverty as "the single greatest challenge which the world faces," states that the government would start to reverse the decline in United Kingdom development assistance, and reaffirms the country's commitment to the United Nations target of 0.7 of GNP for ODA (DID 1997).

Among bilateral development-cooperation agencies, Canada's International Development Research Centre (IDRC) has always occupied a special place. As the first and, for a rather long time, the only agency with the mission to support the development of scientific and technological capabilities in developing countries, since the early 1970s it evolved a style of operation — focused on research, emphasizing capacity-building, treating developing-country institutions as full partners — that anticipated many of the practices that have become common among other development-cooperation organizations. It also enjoyed widespread support abroad and at home, and in the late 1980s it appeared poised to continue on expanding at a steady pace. However, IDRC did not escape the budgetary difficulties that bedeviled all development-assistance agencies during the 1990s: by 1995–96, the Government of Canada grant to IDRC was nearly 40% below the levels projected 6 years earlier. This required major organizational, programmatic, and financial adjustments. As a response, in 1991, IDRC launched a new strategic plan and embarked in a major reorganization, well ahead of other bilateral agencies and multilateral institutions.

The 1991 plan reaffirmed IDRC's mission to empower through knowledge, as "predicated on the explicit relationship between knowledge and development, and in the conviction that empowerment through knowledge is the key element in the development of nations, peoples, communities, and individuals." Because research provides the means to acquire appropriate knowledge, the strategic plan stated that "IDRC is dedicated to creating, maintaining, and enhancing research capacity in developing regions, in response to needs that are determined by the people of those regions in the interest of equity and social justice" (IDRC 1991, p. 7).

A key element identified in the IDRC strategy is the role this institution can play as a "knowledge broker" (IDRC 1991, p. 25), to help developing countries acquire the knowledge they need to fully use their resources and to "meet their needs without damaging their neighbors' or their children's prospects of doing the same" (IDRC 1991, p. 33). The strategic-planning document examines the changing context for development, summarizes the comparative advantage of IDRC, establishes directions for future work, and provides guiding principles for the operation of the institution. During most of the early 1990s, IDRC has been undergoing a rather difficult transformation process, which culminated in 1996–97 with the approval of a new program framework and with a Canadian government grant that will, in all likelihood, not be subject to further cuts and may even grow gradually.

Concluding remarks

Development finance and international cooperation have undergone fundamental changes during the last decade, and the 50-year old institutional arrangements associated with the development-cooperation experiment are struggling to adapt to the new circumstances. It is interesting to compare the situations prevailing after the end of World War II, when development cooperation was launched, and after the end of the Cold War, when this experiment appears to be coming to an end — at least as we knew it. Although the economic standing of the United States at present does not even approach the dominant role it played in the aftermath of World War II, in both cases it emerged as the dominant power with the capacity to exercise global leadership in many fields, including development cooperation. As pointed out in Chapter 2, the Marshall Plan and the Point IV Program were the most visible expressions of the United States' enlightened leadership and commitment to international development 50 years ago.

However, the general mood prevailing at present in the United States, the richest country in the world, could not be more different with regard to development cooperation. In addition to slipping to fourth place in terms of the total amount ODA, by the mid-1990s, the United States reduced contributions to multilateral institutions, failed to honour commitments, and placed unacceptable conditions on the provision of the amounts delivered. Despite enjoying the longest period of sustained economic growth in half a century, reaching stock-market levels of activity unimaginable a decade ago and achieving its first budget surplus in three decades, in 1997 the United States did not seem ready or willing to lead a renewal of international cooperation for development.

Japan appeared to be poised to make a bid for international leadership in this field during the early 1990s. However, the protracted economic crisis it has suffered for nearly a decade, the aftereffects of the East Asian financial crisis of 1997–98, and the inability of its political leaders to chart a clear course for economic recovery have prompted a precipitous drop in the level of Japanese ODA and signaled a hasty retreat from the possibility of its exercising leadership in development cooperation. The European Union is looking inward to resolve its own problems, faces difficult negotiations with the ACP countries, and does not look ready to lead an effort to revitalize development cooperation. Even Sweden, once a stalwart supporter of development assistance, cut its aid budget in the mid-1990s and retreated from its 20-year commitment to raise its ODA to 1% of GNP, adopting instead the 0.7% target agreed to at the United Nations General Assembly in 1970 (ICVA 1996).

Perhaps the most clear indication of this changed mood is the approach taken by rich countries to the highly indebted poor countries. For example, Mozambique, one of the poorest countries in the world, which has just emerged from a decade and a half of violent conflict, is trying to stabilize its economy and to begin a laborious reconstruction process. However, its efforts are stymied by the crushing weight of a debt service that eats up nearly half of the government's revenues. Despite being identified by the World Bank as one of the first countries that might benefit from debt reduction within the framework of the HIPC initiative, Mozambique's negotiations with Paris Club creditors nearly collapsed in January 1998, primarily because the representatives of creditor governments could not agree on how to share the burden of the $350 million needed to fully finance the debt-reduction plan. This took place at the same time as multilateral and bilateral agencies managed to rapidly raise more than $120 billion to help the East Asian economies (Gordon and Gwin 1998).

CHAPTER 6

THE SHAPE OF THINGS TO COME

Development cooperation is undergoing an arduous transition. Decades-old habits of thought and practice are being discarded while new ones are still in the making. A large number of development-assistance organizations, most of them created in the three decades following World War II, are struggling to adapt to a vastly changed international context. After a brief review of the implications of the various changes, trends, and responses described in the preceding chapters, we examine the mix of enduring and new motivations for development finance and international cooperation, especially in light of the dominant role now played by private financial flows to developing countries. This is followed by observations on the arrangements for development cooperation that are likely to emerge in the first years of the 21st century. This chapter ends with some remarks on the need to redefine development and leadership in the transition to the 21st century.

Summary overview

The concept of development was articulated shortly after World War II and can be viewed as the latest reinterpretation of the idea of progress within the framework of the Baconian program (Chapter 1). After a period of widespread and well-founded doubts about the prospects for human progress in the first decades of the 20th century, the optimism that prevailed following the Allied victory in World War II, the success of the Marshall Plan, and the unprecedented period of world economic expansion of the next three decades brought a renewed faith in the possibility of human advancement. In the last half of the 20th century, the idea of development embodied the hopes and aspirations once associated with the notion of indefinite progress in the 19th century.

Implicit in the concept of development was the notion that purposeful interventions could lead poor countries to achieve in one generation the material standards of living that the industrialized West achieved in three or more generations and without the heavy social costs. The provision of financial and technical assistance by rich to poor countries was seen as a key instrument for reaching this goal, and this led to the development-cooperation experiment in the late 1940s.

Spurred in part by the Cold War, a great variety of development-assistance agencies and programs were established in the following decades. However, by the early 1990s, the international context had changed dramatically, and the development-cooperation experiment was coming to an end.

Ideas and conceptions of development have changed over time. Although this should warn us against adhering rigidly to a particular set of views on how to achieve it (Chapter 2), it does not justify an "everything-goes" attitude toward development strategies and policies. There is an essential tension between recognizing the uniqueness and diversity of development experiences, on the one hand, and the need to identify some basic principles to guide development efforts, on the other. This underscores the importance of articulating shared conceptual frameworks for understanding, reinterpreting, and learning from the various routes that societies have taken to improve their living standards. The diversity of development experiences suggests that flexibility, willingness to admit mistakes, and open mind-sets are essential for fully exploring the range of options available to developing countries.

The main implications of the trends and changes shaping the new international context for development finance and international cooperation (Chapter 3) are summarized in Table 5. New security concerns make it necessary to adapt institutional arrangements to a more complex, fluid, and fragmented international context. Financial and economic interdependence require increased cooperation and improvements in the capacity of actors on the international scene to cope with globalized, rapidly shifting, and unstable economic and financial settings. Persistent inequalities between and within nations make it imperative to reduce extreme disparities in living standards and to protect the most vulnerable social groups to maintain a reasonable degree of social cohesion.

Growing social demands, particularly in countries and regions unable to satisfy them, are creating additional international tensions and require new initiatives to reduce poverty and improve the provision of basic social services. The renewed importance of culture, religion, and ethics (largely ignored in the thoroughly secular decades of the development-cooperation experiment) has made it necessary to consider nonmaterial issues and values in debates about development. The new salience of democratic governance, together with the variety of its forms around the world, has raised the issue of how to establish a collective learning process to improve the prospects for democratic practices. Finally, the advent of the knowledge society, along with the abyss separating countries with the capacity

Table 5. Trends in the emerging fractured global order and their implications for international cooperation.

International security in a postbipolar world	**Main implication:** Need to modify institutional arrangements to adapt to a more complex, fluid, fragmented context, in which a greater diversity of actors with different objectives deal with new security threats • Include additional state and especially nonstate actors in international cooperation initiatives • Redefine intervention in the internal affairs of states to prevent violent conflicts and adequately deal with intrastate conflicts • Possibly expand roles and responsibilities of supranational bodies • Strengthen existing and create new mechanisms to promote, monitor, and follow up on international agreements and commitments • Launch new initiatives to deal with emerging threats to security (environmental disruptions, mass migrations, organized crime, terrorism, weapons proliferation, among others) • Establish international law-enforcement mechanisms to deal with transnational security threats
Economic and financial interdependence	**Main implication:** Need to improve the capacity of all actors on the international scene to adjust more rapidly and effectively to a globalized, constantly evolving, and often unstable economic and financial context • Promote the adoption of standards and guidelines to foster economic and financial stability and to coordinate national economic policies (financial regulation, trade liberalization, monetary and exchange-rate policies, etc.) • Move toward a more flexible, coherent network of international-cooperation institutions with clearly identified constituencies and a better division of labour between them • Establish flexible, possibly temporary, spaces for dialogue, debate, and agreement between transgovernmental, transcorporate, and transassociational networks • Explore systematically the varieties of market economies now in existence and the main lessons that can be derived from the ways they work
Persistent inequalities and economic uncertainty	**Main implication:** Need to address the inequalities both between and within nations and to improve the capacity of most vulnerable groups • Differentiate types of assistance by constituency and increase financial and technical cooperation with those groups that need it most and can benefit significantly • Complement development assistance initiatives with other policies that can have a great impact on the growth prospects of poor nations (for example, open markets of developed nations to products from poor countries) • Devise mechanisms and instruments (for example, guarantee schemes, internationally agreed incentives) to promote private investments in poor countries and regions • Establish and expand initiatives to assist small business, informal-sector enterprises, ethnic minorities, women, the elderly and other marginalized groups
Social conditions	**Main implication:** Need to agree on a set of minimum standards of social conditions to be guaranteed for all human beings and to explore new institutional arrangements at all levels (subnational, national, regional, international) conducive to reaching and putting into practice such an agreement • Devise social policies that take into account demographic considerations (age structures, expectations, and needs of different social groups) to achieve standards of living compatible with human dignity

(continued)

Table 5 continued.

- Promote the idea of joint social responsibility (the state, the private sector, and civil-society organizations) for the provision of basic social services to the population, especially the poor
- Engage civil-society organizations and business associations at local, national, regional, and international levels in initiatives to improve social conditions
- Devise initiatives and mechanisms to strengthen the social accountability of NGOs and the private sector
- Given the threat of extensive and persistent unemployment, explore new institutional mechanisms to provide basic goods and services to those who do not have access to jobs
- Incorporate social-impact considerations into the design of economic-development strategies and of development-assistance initiatives, rather than focusing on measures to compensate for the negative social impacts of economic policies
- Explore new financing mechanisms for social development (for example, trust funds to complement government expenditures on social services; debt relief and debt swaps for social purposes; reallocation and decentralization of public expenditures to allow citizen participation in decisions and monitoring of social expenditures)

(continued)

Culture, religion, and ethical concerns	**Main implication:** Need to design and establish institutions and mechanisms to construct bridges across cultures, religions, and ethnic groups - Promote consideration and respect of cultural characteristics (the affirmation of cultural identity should be viewed as an integral part of the development process) - Foster international dialogue — especially among representatives of religious institutions, ethnic minorities, and grass-roots organizations — on preventing violent forms of cultural assertion - Work with mass-media representatives to better understand, and find ways of dealing with, the tensions between the processes of globalization and the reaffirmation of cultural identity
Governance and democratic practices	**Main implication:** Need to establish collective learning process to improve governance structures at all levels while respecting diversity of conditions prevailing in developing regions - Agree on basic universal principles to guide the search for legitimate and more effective forms of democratic governance that respect human rights but also take into account different historical and cultural circumstances - Establish mechanisms at the regional and international levels to monitor agreements and commitments pertaining to democratic governance - Create spaces to foster dialogue, debate, and consensus among representatives of the public sector, private sector, and civil society and link these spaces to governmental decision-making at all levels - Explore and experiment with new governance structures and mechanisms at the international level to address global problems and development cooperation in particular - Strengthen accountability, openness, transparency, and the rule of law, at the international level, in industrialized and developing countries, private corporations, and civil-society organizations

(continued)

Table 5 concluded.

Knowledge explosion and knowledge divide	**Main implication:** Need to establish national and international-cooperation mechanisms to address the growing "knowledge divide" between nations that have the capacity to generate and make use of modern S&T and those that do not
	• Review and redefine concepts of development and progress from a knowledge perspective, focusing on the key contribution of S&T capabilities to standards of living
	• Make S&T capacity-building one of the key objectives of international development cooperation during the next several decades
	• Experiment with ways to make available on a more equitable basis the knowledge and financial resources necessary for poor countries to take advantage of S&T advances (with the participation of government agencies, private corporations, and academic institutions from developed nations)
	• Expand existing and create new institutional and financial mechanisms to support endogenous S&T capacity-building efforts in developing countries
	• Explore the "leapfrogging" potential of poor countries in specific fields of S&T, particularly in those linked to improvements in social conditions (health, education, nutrition, environmental protection)
	• Strengthen S&T education in developing countries and use technological advances to make education more accessible and improve its content

Note: NGO, nongovernmental organization; S&T, science and technology.

to generate and use modern science and technology and those without it, has created the urgent need to devise mechanisms to build bridges across the knowledge divide.

Several interpretations have been offered to account for these trends and changes, and the concept of a fractured global order has been proposed to characterize the new international context emerging at the close of the 20th century (Chapter 4). This inherently paradoxical order is the result of processes that are putting all of us in contact with each other throughout the planet but are at the same time creating profound divisions and cleavages between and within social groups. Three partially overlapping domains configure the fractured global order: the global, the networks, and the local. Development cooperation works primarily in the domain of the networks, and its main task is to help to bridge the fractures that are emerging and deepening in the global order. The rise of transgovernmental, transcorporate, and transassociational networks, together with the vastly increased and more complex interrelations between and within them, has made the context for development finance and international cooperation much more complex and difficult to deal with. As a consequence, the capacity to design and implement measures to keep the unfavourable consequences of globalization in check — and to exploit the opportunities offered by the fractured global order — will be an increasingly valuable asset for developing countries.

The ODA squeeze, the questioning of aid and its impact, and the new demands placed on the international-cooperation system are now stretching to the limit the response capacity of the organizations in the development-assistance community (Chapter 5). Their reaction has been marked by much confusion, reorganization, counterreorganization, and operational changes that are often modified before they can yield results.

All of this calls for a new perspective on the restructuring of international cooperation for development during the next decade. Uncertainty, instability, paradox, and ambiguity are configuring a turbulent field in which the transformation of development assistance is taking place (Emery and Trist 1965). In this situation, there is no time for leisurely academic research aimed at improving organizational performance. It becomes necessary to learn while doing and to engage in real-time policy-oriented inquiries. Organizational structures, procedures, and practices must be monitored, evaluated in light of results, and adjusted as new circumstances emerge. Strategic planning needs to be integrated into day-to-day management to reduce lags in adaptive behaviour, and the organization must become an inquiring and learning system.[14] Such an exercise must begin with a reexamination of the reasons for engaging in development finance and international cooperation, which should guide the process of "creative destruction" that renews institutional arrangements in the international development community.

Enduring and changing motivations for development finance and international cooperation

Motivations for private firms to invest in developing regions, for private foundations and individuals to support programs in developing countries, and for rich countries to provide financial and technical assistance to the poorer nations have changed over time. Although many of the reasons for engaging in these activities have endured over decades, new motivations have been added as a result of the transformations in the international context.

The main motivation for investing in developing countries, or, for that matter, for investing anywhere, has always been the desire to obtain the maximum possible returns over a specified period and subject to a determined level of risk.

---

[14] These concepts were advanced a long time ago by several pioneers in management science, many of whom were associated with the "Philadelphia School of Planning" that emerged at the Wharton School of the University of Pennsylvania in the late 1960s and the 1970s. See, among others, Emery and Trist (1965), Vickers (1965), Perlmutter (1965), Beer (1966, 1972), Friend and Jessop (1969), Ackoff (1970, 1981), Churchman (1971, 1979), Ozbekhan (1971), and Schon (1971). For more recent restatements of their ideas see, for example, Senge (1990), Schwartz (1991), Ackoff (1994), and Trist et al. (1997).

The globalization of financial markets has made the search for higher returns much more complex, and private investors now face a wide range of options for placing their investments worldwide. *Portfolio flows*, which move quickly from one market to another in response to slight changes in the perceptions of returns and risks, are now engaged in a global search for the highest possible profits. However, identifying the stocks, currencies, bonds, derivatives, and other financial instruments to allow investors to obtain the optimal reward–risk combination is a difficult task that requires highly specialized knowledge and information. Few investors have the capacity to analyze in detail the options available, and most rely on the information and analyses provided by rating agencies, consulting firms, and investment advisors. This has given the largest and most visible of these organizations (Moody, Standard & Poor, Duff & Phelps) a significant influence on the direction of investment flows. This influence is heightened by what has been called the "herd mentality" of the players in financial markets, which amplifies fluctuations and increases instability.

The contribution that portfolio flows can make to developing countries depends on the quality of their domestic macroeconomic policies, the soundness of their local financial institutions, and the stability of their economic and political system. Few developing countries have the capacity to absorb short-term flows in large amounts without experiencing macroeconomic problems (for example, local currency appreciation). As a result, the development impact of volatile and highly concentrated portfolio flows is likely to be rather small and temporary, except in a few developing nations where such flows might provide significant balance-of-payments support.

What is perceived as the excessive mobility of capital flows has been severely criticized by, among others, Jagdish Bhagwati, a staunch supporter of trade liberalization. Bhagwati has been particularly against lifting all restrictions on portfolio-capital flows, which he has distinguished from direct foreign investment and trade in goods and services. In his view, a combination of ideology and interests is driving the process of financial globalization beyond what would be reasonable and prudent. Bhagwati has argued that despite the evidence of the inherent risks of free capital flows, a "Wall Street–Treasury complex" (Bhagwati 1998, p. 7) — analogous to the military–industrial complex denounced by President Eisenhower in the 1950s — is operating behind the "self-serving assumption that the ideal world is indeed one of free capital flows, with the IMF and its bailouts at the apex in a role that guarantees its survival and enhances its status" (Bhagwati 1998, p. 12). Considering that emerging markets in developing and transition economies are where returns to portfolio flows can be rather high, the excessive mobility of capital flows creates special problems and risks for these countries.

Commercial banks lend to developing-country governments and firms at rates that cover the interest paid on deposits, administrative costs, a "risk premium," and profits. The risk premium is charged because of what banks perceive as a greater probability that developing-country borrowers may default on their loans. In addition, when lending to subnational governments, state enterprises, and private firms, commercial banks often require a central-government guarantee to ensure repayment. Private bank loans to developing countries have followed boom and bust cycles, which are best exemplified by the lending binge of the 1970s and early 1980s (primarily to recycle petrodollars), followed by the debt crisis the 1980s and another lending boom during the early 1990s.

During the 1970s, commercial banks raced past each other to lend to developing-country governments, often charging hefty risk premiums and frequently without examining the soundness of the projects and schemes to be financed. Beginning with Mexico in 1982, many borrowers defaulted on their loans and created serious problems for American, European, and Japanese commercial banks.[15] The "Baker plan" was launched in 1985 to deal with what was perceived as a liquidity crisis, and additional loans were provided by commercial banks, multilateral financial institutions, industrialized-country governments, and bilateral aid agencies to help developing countries restructure and honour their obligations. This considerably helped commercial banks, which were given time to strengthen their financial positions and absorb loses. This was followed in 1989 by the "Brady plan," which institutionalized the idea of burden-sharing between creditors and debtors by making banks take losses, reducing the total amount of debt, and establishing a rigid repayment schedule for the reduced obligations.

A few years later commercial bank lending to developing regions resumed in earnest. Many firms in East Asian countries obtained loans from private American, European, and Japanese banks, once again without close scrutiny of the uses to which they were put. As revealed after the 1997–98 financial crisis, many of these loans were not reported to government authorities; most were short term; and borrowers did not cover themselves against currency risks. Even though no government guarantees were provided for these loans, in countries like Indonesia, South Korea, and Thailand, their total volume required determined government

---

[15] At an international conference organized by the Department of Economics of the University of Pennsylvania in 1986, a senior commercial bank manager argued that developing-country governments had behaved "like children in a candy store" and borrowed unwisely during the 1970s and 1980s. My reply was that many commercial bank officials had behaved "like drug pushers in a school yard."

intervention and support from multilateral institutions and bilateral agencies in unprecedented amounts to avert financial and economic collapse.

Provided that loan terms are reasonable and aligned with the activities to be financed, commercial bank lending can help developing-country governments and firms with resources to finance investment projects, cover temporary income shortfalls, and provide working capital. But for this system to work, borrowers must be prudent and exercise restraint in their dealings with commercial bank lenders.

Because *direct foreign investment* seeks a continuous stream of profits over the long and medium term, firms are prompted to locate where they can reduce production and distribution costs for their products and services. Although low labour costs remain a main attraction for many corporations to place their production facilities in developing countries, many other factors also play a role. The desire to secure access to natural resources, such as hydrocarbons, minerals, and land, have been among the traditional motivations for firms to invest in developing regions, to which has been added the desire to secure access to genetic resources linked to biodiversity has been added during the last decade. Less stringent environmental regulations have also played a role in the location of some manufacturing activities, and the availability of highly skilled labour has now emerged as a main motivation for high-technology firms to place their production and service facilities in a few developing countries (for example, electronic manufacturing in East Asia, software production in India, and computer customer-service facilities in Costa Rica).

With the globalization of product and service markets and the rise of strategic alliances between international firms, strategic positioning for global competition has also emerged as a main motivation for firms to invest in developing countries. This is particularly the case in certain fast-growing sectors of the world economy (air travel, banking, energy, electronic goods), in which the leading corporations design their strategies at the global level. Developing countries with large populations, particularly those with relatively stable and growing economies, have become a place of choice and a highly contested ground for direct foreign investment.

This type of investment can make significant contributions to development through increases in production and exports, creation of jobs, and technology transfers. Moreover, pressures from international environmental and civil-rights organizations have influenced the conduct of transnational corporations to the extent that issues of corporate social responsibility have come to the fore in recent years. This may improve the behaviour of at least those large corporations that are vulnerable to consumer boycotts. New standards for social and environmental accountability, coupled with programs to foster corporate citizenship and strategic philanthropy, can enhance the contribution of direct foreign investment to development (DRI 1998). The potential benefits to be derived from foreign investments can be considerably enhanced by appropriate government policies to reduce their possible negative impacts on the environment and the possible abuse of local labour. However, because of the high mobility of international capital, many developing countries are competing with each other to attract foreign investment. Tax breaks and incentives are regularly offered to induce foreign investors to locate their plants and facilities, which reduces government revenues. Environmental and labour regulations are frequently waived or even dismantled, which has a negative impact on social conditions. In some cases, these inducements are complemented with offers to provide the physical infrastructure (roads, ports, energy, water supply) required to operate the foreign plants, which further strains public finances.

The increased mobility of international capital, which can easily migrate to where it is treated more favourably, and the willingness of governments to outbid each other with tax and other incentives to attract foreign investors are undermining the capacity of governments to generate public revenue. As a consequence, many governments are facing what Rodrik (1997, p. 6) called "the unappetizing option of increasing taxes disproportionately on labour income" to maintain a reasonable level of public expenditure compatible with preserving social cohesion.

The motivations of *grant-giving foundations, philanthropic organizations, and individuals* include altruism, international solidarity, religious proselytism, and the desire to obtain social recognition. These flows are directed primarily to humanitarian relief, the protection of human rights, health and family planning, education and nutrition programs for children, cultural activities, environmental conservation, and building local capacity in a variety of fields. Because they are free from the constraints faced by bilateral aid agencies, international financial institutions and private firms and foundations can support more adventurous programs and engage in experimental activities that official donors and private investors would find too risky or controversial. The amount of funds channeled through grants may not be very large, but they can play a key strategic role in exploring new directions and testing programs that are later adopted by other organizations. In addition, private corporations occasionally contribute to development programs through grants, primarily with the purpose of improving their public image.

As forms of institutionalized philanthropy, foundations have actually had a very long history and played important roles in ensuring the welfare of individuals in societies around the world. For instance, private philanthropy in 18th-century United States was responsible for large areas of education, medicine, culture, science, and others outside the scope of a small government. As the developing nations approach the 21st century within a context of economic liberalization and scarce ODA flows, a large space is opening up for foundations to once again play key roles in development. However, foundations have been a source of controversy throughout history as they have experienced periods of mismanagement, fallen behind the times, or been used for political purposes. Despite its being recognized that foundations may be the independent centres of initiative and pluralistic diversity needed by a democratic society, the major US foundations in the early 1970s were described as "lethargic and outmoded" (Nielsen 1972, p. 434) while controlling enormous resources.

Motivations for ODA have changed in parallel with the evolution of development thinking and of institutional arrangements for development cooperation. Cold War political interests and altruism were the main reasons for launching the development-cooperation experiment in the late 1940s, but over time a more varied range of motivations for development assistance began to emerge. As motivations changed, conditions for access to financial and technical assistance were redefined. Political loyalty to one of the two opposing camps in the East–West confrontation gave way to conditions of tied purchases of goods and services, access to markets, economic policies, institutional reforms, democratic practices, environmental conservation, and respect for human rights. Cross-conditionality between development assistance agencies and multilateral institutions increased significantly, and private banks often conditioned their loans to developing-country governments on the adoption of policy reforms advocated by the IMF or the World Bank.

Table 6 presents a summary of the main motivations for providing development assistance.[16] There has been a gradual progression from narrowly defined notions of donor political and economic self-interest — complemented by moral concerns and altruistic motives — to broader conceptions of the common interest and the stability of the international system. However, self-interest still prevails, and political and commercial objectives continue to influence the levels and

---

[16] The table has been adapted from reports on the prospects for ODA in the 1990s prepared by Susan Ulbaek and Izumi Ohno at the Strategic Planning Division of the World Bank in the late 1980s. See, in particular, Izumi Ohno's (1990) report *Donor's Aid Motives: Implications for Multilateral Concessional Aid.*

allocation of aid budgets, as can be seen in the USAID Strategic Plan (1998) and in Japanese aid to Latin America (Katada 1997).

Different motivations interact closely with each other, either as complements or trade-offs. In some cases, human-rights concerns may override the purely economic or political interests of donors, whereas in others the opposite may be true. Development financing may be made conditional on adopting political reforms, as exemplified by the loans provided by the EBRD, whose articles of agreement state the promotion of multiparty democracy is one of its objectives. Environmental and security preoccupations may also reinforce each other, as in the case of assistance to the countries of Eastern Europe and the former Soviet Union to upgrade their nuclear-power installations and dismantle their nuclear missiles. In general, increased interdependence and the process of globalization, added to the multiple fractures that characterize the emerging world order, have made the political, economic, and social stability of the international system a growing concern of donors.

Taking into account private flows, grants by foundations and individuals, and ODA, it is possible to see that the structure of financial flows to developing countries is now skewed in favour of highly concentrated and mobile private investments and not geared toward the long-term development-finance needs of developing countries. Moreover, the vastly increased mobility of international capital limits the capacity of most developing-country governments to tax capital flows and profits. This makes it difficult to maintain a level of public expenditures commensurate with the growth of social demands, especially in the poorest countries. In terms of the fractured global order, the logic of financial capitalism in the domain of the global, operating through transgovernmental and transcorporate entities in the domain of the networks, does not often coincide with the interests of developing societies in the domain of the local.

From this perspective, a possible additional motivation for ODA may be to compensate for the negative impact that financial globalization has on economic stability and social cohesion. However, the initiatives taken by the high-income industrialized nations in various international forums point clearly in another direction. In addition to giving rather weak support for ODA, developed-country governments are actively promoting international agreements on foreign investment that would further tilt the balance in favour of international capital and against developing countries. These initiatives are being pursued through the Multilateral Agreement on Investment at the OECD, which gathers the high-income economies that provide a home base for most international investors, and

Table 6. Motivations for ODA.

Strategic and security interests (which respond to geopolitical and military considerations of donor countries)
- National level — The geopolitical importance of specific developing countries is a factor
- Regional level — The interests of regional alliances or treaties are a consideration

Political interests (which focus on obtaining political support for foreign and domestic policies)
- Foreign constituencies — Support is given to former colonial territories and other areas with special historic and cultural ties to the donor country with a view to obtaining international political recognition and support
- Domestic constituencies — Support of immigrant lobbies and ethnic groups in the donor country is sought

Economic and commercial interests (which emphasize direct commercial and financial benefits to the donor country)
- Benefits for the donor — Aid can lead to export opportunities, employment, support of domestic producers (through food aid), security for investments in developing countries, access to resources (oil, strategic minerals), access to a pool of highly qualified potential migrants (through fellowships), and future demand for exports (created through technology transfers)

Economic interdependence (which stresses the role of aid in promoting developing-country growth that helps donor countries indirectly)
- Investment in the future — Higher world economic growth, increased trade flows, and expanded private investment benefit not only developing economies, but also donor countries (by providing opportunities for economic expansion and a larger market)

Emergence of global problems (which concern both donor and recipient nations)
- Environmental sustainability — Global warming, destruction of the ozone layer, loss of biodiversity, tropical deforestation, etc., affect developed countries directly
- World population growth and imbalances — These are now seen as global problems requiring financial and technical assistance from donors
- Health threats (AIDS, epidemics) — These are also seen as global problems requiring financial and technical assistance from donors
- Crime, drug traffic, and terrorism — These problems call for international cooperation and the support of donors

Altruism, ethical, humanitarian, and religious concerns (which highlight the moral obligation of donor countries to assist the poor in developing countries)
- Human suffering — Donors wish to alleviate human suffering and express solidarity with fellow human beings
- Disasters — Humanitarian and emergency relief helps countries cope with natural and people-caused disasters
- Religious proselytism — The desire to win converts to a particular faith may be a concern

Stability of the international system (which aims at securing a stable world order to foster the long-term interests of donor countries)
- Political stability — Aid is used to prevent and contain local and regional conflicts and to promote the spread of democracy through peacemaking and peacekeeping initiatives, monitoring and supervision of elections, support for democratic practices and institutions, etc.
- World economic stability — Donors promote policy reforms in developing countries and take measures to avoid major disruptions of international finance and trade (provide funding to help defuse the debt crisis, the Mexican peso collapse, the East Asian crisis)
- Social stability — To eliminate the need for international migrations, donors sponsor programs to reduce population growth, combat poverty, promote human rights, and improve the situation of women in the developing regions
- Responsibility — Aid shows that rich countries are willing to accept responsibility for assisting the less fortunate in a global society
- International agreements — Donors help developing countries improve their participation in international agreements to make them more equitable, stable, and effective

Source: Adapted from reports prepared by Susan Ulbaek (Ulbaek 1989) and Izumi Ohno at the Strategic Planning Division of the World Bank in the late 1980s. See, in particular, Ohno (1990).
Note: ODA, official development assistance.

through the Multilateral Investment Agreement at the WTO as a follow-up to the Uruguay Round negotiations on trade-related investment measures.

The main objective of these two initiatives, which are strongly opposed by most developing countries, is to establish international agreements that widen and strengthen the rights of foreign investors far beyond those they currently have in most developing countries and to severely curtail the rights of governments to regulate the entry, establishment, and operation of foreign companies and investors. For example, foreign firms would acquire the right to enter and establish themselves, without any restrictions and with 100% equity, in all sectors of the economy; would be given the same treatment as local firms; and would also be given additional rights, such as the right to full and unrestricted repatriation of profits. In essence, these agreements seek to lock-in at the global level, preferably in a binding way, the benefits obtained by foreign investors in those places that provide most favourable treatment to international capital. In view of the asymmetries between foreign firms and the vast majority of local enterprises, this could create difficulties for the development of a strong domestic private sector in many developing countries.

These attempts to give greater security to international capital and increase the rights of foreign investors have to be seen in relation to the growing disparities in living standards between and within nations, the rise of global crime and drug traffic, the emergence of new security threats, and the increase of ethnic violence, which have all been related to the deterioration of social conditions in many parts of the world, particularly in the developing regions. With a little bit of hyperbole it may be possible to say that in the process of making the world safe for capitalism, economic and financial globalization is making it unsafe for capitalists and for just about everybody else.

The shape of things to come: development-cooperation themes, organizations, and resources

The combination of enduring and emerging motivations for development finance and international cooperation ensure that these activities will continue, although in a much changed way, during the coming decades. However, development assistance will remain a peripheral concern for the rich countries, especially as they focus their attention on solving their own internal problems (unemployment, inequality, crime), coordinating their economic policies to maintain the stability of the international economic system, improving their competitiveness, and easing the transition of the former centrally planned economies toward democracy and the market.

The arguments advanced in this book allow one to anticipate the shape of things to come in the turbulent field of development finance and international cooperation. We venture some ideas on what will emerge when the development-cooperation experiment of the past five decades is superseded by new organizational arrangements and resource-mobilization mechanisms.

Themes

The wide variety of areas covered by the expanding field of international cooperation for development will cluster around several main themes, primarily as a result of the need to find common ground and identify shared interests among a large number of actors with diverse objectives. These clusters of themes will cut across organizational boundaries and become the focus for initiatives involving government agencies, international institutions, foundations, private firms, and civil-society organizations.

Among these main clusters of themes it is possible to identify the following:

- *Stabilizing the international financial and economic system* — This will require concerted action by governments, international institutions, and private financial institutions. A main theme in this cluster will be how to create the conditions to harmonize the interests of private investors and developing countries. Among other things, this requires designing national and international policy regimes to ensure that private financial flows contribute effectively to development objectives.

- *Addressing global and regional problems that affect several countries* — This will require increased collaboration between countries and adaptations in the way national sovereignty is exercised. Environmental deterioration and the sustainable use of natural resources figure prominently in this cluster, which also includes the issues of international migration, internationalization of organized crime, and the spread of drug traffic.

- *Providing humanitarian assistance and emergency relief to deal with natural and human-made disasters* — When violent conflicts within countries prompt the need for relief efforts, it will be necessary to intervene in the internal affairs of sovereign states and to modify the prevailing conceptions of national sovereignty.

- *Providing technical and financial assistance to promote economic growth and social improvement* — This has been the main focus of traditional forms of development cooperation. The specific themes to be addressed in this cluster include the provision of technical assistance in fields such as agriculture, industry, and energy, as well as education, health, family planning, and poverty reduction. The provision of balance-of-payments support is also included in this cluster.

- *Establishing and strengthening institutions in developing countries* — This includes capacity-building for government policy-making in the social and economic fields, institutional reforms, and strengthening democratic practices and institutions. These issues require long-term and flexible interventions carefully designed to involve and empower developing-country partners in the public and private sectors and in civil society.

- *Creating and consolidating scientific and technological capabilities in the developing regions* — This will become a major cluster of development-cooperation initiatives in the early years of the 21st century. In particular, support will grow for the establishment of local research facilities and the acquisition of technologies in the areas of information and communications, environmental sustainability, and biosciences and biotechnologies.

- *Preventing deadly conflict between and within states* — While conflict prevention has received increased attention in recent years, it will take some time before a broad and coherent set of initiatives is launched, primarily because of our inadequate understanding of the combination of factors that lead to violent conflicts and how to prevent the eruption of deadly violence.

- *Embarking in a collective effort to redefine "development" and "progress" as we enter into the post-Baconian age* — The widespread uneasiness that has become evident with the current conceptions of development, the challenges posed by different civilizational outlooks, and the new salience of value and spiritual concerns will make it necessary to launch a joint cross-cultural effort to explore these important questions in the early years of the 21st century.

These clusters of themes will bring together different combinations of government agencies in developed and developing countries, private corporations, academic institutions, NGOs, and other actors on the international development scene. Whereas some large multilateral institutions and bilateral aid agencies may have a stake in several of these clusters, most development-cooperation organizations will focus on just a few.

Organizations

Institutional inertias and the accumulated strains of incremental adaptations will prompt a major redesign of most international development organizations, some of which have already embarked in such an undertaking. In addition, attempts will be made to define a reasonable interinstitutional division of labour and to identify redundant and missing institutions. Although these attempts will be resisted by some senior officials in these organizations, the combined pressures of new demands and diminished resources will ultimately prevail and lead to a rationalization of organizational arrangements for development cooperation.

Development-cooperation organizations will improve their efficiency and become more open and transparent, and their impact will be closely monitored and evaluated. Tighter conditions will be placed on intermediaries of development assistance (particularly NGOs) and on recipients to ensure better accountability. Programs will become more focused; greater emphasis will be placed on decentralization and the delegation of responsibility; and entrepreneurship and the exercise of creative leadership will be rewarded. Information systems will acquire greater importance as ways to foster new styles of work and as means to retain organizational memory. Temporary programs and organizational structures, with clearly defined expiration dates, will gradually replace the permanent organizations that were the norm in the early decades of the development-cooperation experiment. The more effective development-assistance agencies will become learning organizations, but many will have to become first "unlearning organizations" to forget past practices and work habits. Those that fail to do this will either disappear or be reduced to irrelevance over the next two decades.

The development-cooperation organizations of the future will adopt the form of flexible networks focusing on specific themes. They will combine several institutions in coalitions, although thematic networks will also emerge as subsets of large organizations. A prototype thematic network would incorporate the following entities:

- *A Thematic Network Board* — This would comprise representatives of government agencies from developed and developing countries, multilateral and bilateral assistance institutions, private corporations, foundations, academic institutions, NGOs, and other entities with a stake in the specific theme of the network. All board members would have the same voting rights, and the task of the board would be to decide on specific programs to be pursued by subsets of network members. Each member of the Thematic Network would contribute an assessed amount (determined according to pre-established binding criteria) to cover the operating costs of the Network Secretariat.

- *A small Network Secretariat* — The only function of the Network Secretariat would be to help identify and launch programs of interest to subsets of Thematic Network members. It would comprise a few staff on fixed-term contracts, supplemented by consultants, and would work largely through electronic mail and other forms of telecommunications to minimize overhead. It would be largely financed by the assessed contributions from the Thematic Network members and would regularly submit proposals to the Network Board.

- *Several program subnetworks* — These would comprise only the members interested in each specific program. The launching of the program subnetwork would be decided by the Network Board, based on the proposals submitted by the Secretariat. The proposals would define the terms of reference for the program, its duration, and organizational and financing arrangements. Participation in the program subnetworks would be voluntary and restricted to the Thematic Network members. Participants in a Program Subnetwork would also have to agree on their financial contributions to the program and on their respective voting rights. An ad hoc Program Board would be established to supervise and evaluate the conduct of the program, and a Program Secretariat would be temporarily established to coordinate and execute program tasks. Both of these would be disbanded on the completion of the activities, and each program would have a clearly defined termination date to avoid its being extended indefinitely.

Several program subnetworks would be operating at any given time, and the Thematic Network Board would have responsibility for assessing the overall progress of the various programs and the performance of the Network Secretariat and its staff.

Several entities already exhibit some of the characteristics described for the thematic networks and subnetworks, and many of these entities have come into existence in recent years. The Consultative Group on International Agricultural Research was jointly established in 1971 by the World Bank, several bilateral agencies, and private foundations; and a number of international secretariats focusing on specific issues (for example, micronutrients, tropical diseases, AIDS prevention) have been created with the support of bilateral agencies, multilateral institutions, and foundations. However, these initiatives have had rather limited participation from the private sector and civil-society organizations, and some of these network-like organizations have inherited the limitations of their multilateral and bilateral supporters.

The UNDP may be gradually moving in the direction of supporting programs of interest to particular combinations of donors and recipients, which would resemble the thematic network programs described above. An indication of this shift is that, for the first time in its history, the UNDP's noncore resources (over which donors can exert more control) exceed core resources in its budget (allocated primarily according to criteria defined by the Governing Board, representing all UNDP members). The World Bank recently established five functional networks focusing on themes such as environmental sustainability, finance and private-sector development, human development, and poverty reduction. There is still much confusion about the way these networks will interact with the various regional and country teams, as well as with technical departments, but the World Bank's creation of these networks signals its intention to focus professional capacities more sharply and to work across regional and country boundaries in an effort to improve organizational learning.

Other initiatives have combined the private sector and multilateral institutions, such as the World Bank's Infodev program to support information-technology initiatives in developing countries; NGOs and regional development banks, such as the joint program between the Nature Conservancy and IDB to fund initiatives for sustainable development; academic institutions, government agencies, and the private sector, such as the CYTED (Programa Iberoamericano de Ciencia y Tecnología para el Desarrollo [Ibero-American program of science and technology for development]), launched to coordinate scientific and technological activities between Latin American, Portuguese, and Spanish institutions; and private corporations, semipublic institutions, and developing-country government agencies, such as the Shell Corporation joint program with the Smithsonian Institute to monitor the environmental impact of Shell's Peruvian operations. The point is that there are many experiences to draw lessons from in designing institutional arrangements more appropriate to the fractured global order.

Richard Sack has proposed the name "structured informality" (1998, p. 4) to characterize several institutional arrangements that approach the organizational ones outlined in this section. As Executive Secretary of the Association for the Development of Education in Africa (ADEA), he has emphasized the importance of moving beyond established institutional channels to improve lateral communications between professionals and policymakers, respond more rapidly to the demands of policymakers and other users of the services provided by ADEA, and operate flexibly. All of this has led to low transaction costs for the members of the ADEA network (primarily government agencies and bilateral donors, but also individual professionals and international institutions). ADEA functions with a steering committee, working groups, a bureau and caucus of ministers, and a secretariat. It is hosted at the International Institute for Educational Planning of the United Nations Educational, Scientific and Cultural Organization.

Sack noted that Club du Sahel (attached to the OECD Secretariat in Paris) has functioned as an informal coordination group for donor agencies working in the Sahel for more than two decades and that its model corresponds to structural informality. Another example is GWP (hosted at the Swedish International Development Agency), which is concerned with the management of freshwater resources in developing countries and has been referred to as a "reinforced network" and a "virtual organization, with a minimum of formal structure." Johan Holmberg, Executive Secretary of GWP, described the network as

> characterized by informality and flexibility to avoid spending much time and attention on the preparation of rules and regulations. Membership should be voluntary and open to all organizations interested in water resources management. Decision-making should be by consensus and avoid the political posturing that would quickly result from a formal voting system. There should be an emphasis on scientific excellence. GWP should have a decentralized structure and a philosophy of shared responsibility throughout the system.

(Holmberg 1998)

The process of organizational renewal in the international development-cooperation community could be considerably helped through the creation of an Independent International Commission on the Future of Development Finance and International Cooperation. This commission would have a broad mandate to review the operations of a wide range of public, private, and civil-society organizations at the national and international levels and to make suggestions on how to restructure institutional and financial arrangements for development cooperation. It should be made up of prominent members of the international community, developing- and developed-country governments, the private sector, academic institutions, and organizations of civil society and should produce its recommendations after about 2 years of work. Several important precedents have been set for such an initiative, most notably Lester Pearson's commission, which issued the 1969 report, *Partners in Development* (Pearson Report 1969). More recent examples are the Ford Foundation project on the United Nations and the Carnegie Corporation Commission on Preventing Deadly Conflict. However, these commissions have focused on narrower sets of issues, and they draw their membership primarily from governments and international agencies. In all probability, private foundations will take the lead in supporting an independent commission to help chart the course for institutional reforms in development finance and international cooperation.

Resources

Development-financing arrangements will be renewed over the next decade or two as the inadequacies of existing schemes become obvious and unbearable. The changes are likely to be gradual, and governmental aid budgets will continue to play a major role, particularly in some of the thematic clusters. At the same time, there will be a great deal of experimentation with new financing mechanisms, and some innovative schemes will be tried on a pilot scale.

The most successful of the institutional innovations in development finance of the last five decades has been the establishment of multilateral development banks. To finance their regular lending programs they issue bonds, borrow from private-capital markets on rather favourable terms, and then lend those resources, with a modest markup, to developing countries at rates below what private markets would charge them. The distinction between "paid-in" and "subscribed" (or "callable") capital allows multilateral development banks to play a very efficient intermediary role between private-capital markets and developing countries. Shareholders have only to pay in cash a fraction of their share of total subscribed capital but are committed to contributing the full amount in the unlikely event that massive defaults from borrowers threaten these institutions with bankruptcy.[17] This allows the multilateral banks to appear extremely conservative by maintaining a maximum of one-to-one gearing ratio between their subscribed capital and their obligations to bondholders, which considerably reduces the cost of borrowing (even though they have a much larger gearing ratio between paid-in capital and outstanding bond obligations). In effect, this constitutes an intergovernmental guarantee scheme that has worked very well for more than five decades, partly because the financial management of multilateral development banks is prudent and the preferred-creditor status of these institutions ensures prompt and preferential payment by their borrowers.

Multilateral development banks and other development-finance institutions are now exploring other types of guarantee schemes, particularly to reduce the risks to private investors in developing countries and transitional economies. Some of these involve bond issues, securitizing existing developing-country obligations, and the use of exotic financial instruments. There has also been much discussion of special funds to soften the financial conditions of loans to the poorer countries by reducing interest rates and extending grace and repayment periods. Some of these initiatives will prove successful and will be launched during the next several years, thus expanding the range of options for development finance. In addition, investment banks are joining forces with multilateral institutions to raise investment capital in some specific sectors, particularly for infrastructure. Private firms in the more advanced emerging economies that can attract private-capital flows will also expand their access to the stock markets of industrialized nations, usually with the help of private investment bankers.

Some kind of automatic resource-mobilization mechanism will be put in place during the next two or three decades, at least on a pilot basis. The balance between the large potential benefits and the small costs of such schemes is so favourable that the resistance to "international taxes" cannot hold up their implementation indefinitely. A great deal of work has been done on the feasibility of the Tobin Tax on international capital movements, and more recently it has been

---

[17] Paid-in capital represented 20% of the subscribed capital when the IBRD, the regular lending arm of the World Bank, was established in the 1940s. Subsequent capital increases, in which the paid-in component was lowered, brought the ratio of paid-in to subscribed capital to about 6.5% in the early 1990s. In the early 1950s, IBRD management concentrated its efforts on obtaining a triple-A rating for its bonds, thereby ensuring good access and favourable borrowing terms to tap international capital markets. This helped to legitimize the model of the multilateral development bank for development finance and paved the way for the creation of the regional development banks (Kapur and Webb 1994).

suggested that a "bit tax" be imposed on international electronic commercial and financial transactions.

Some type of "cybertax" on information transfer may actually become necessary as the volume of Internet commerce becomes large enough to threaten national tax bases. However, care must be taken to ensure that tax schemes do not slow down or discourage the growth of the Internet or put access to the information society out of the reach of many individuals. In fact, such tax revenues could "be directed towards improving access to the Internet, educating individuals to become acquainted with the Internet and providing additional needed bandwidth" (Soete and ter Weel 1998, p. 867).

Although these taxes are still a long way from becoming feasible options, they have stimulated a great deal of interest and many negative reactions from developing-country governments and firms. Rather than establishing a global tax system, such schemes are likely to be tried first on a limited basis, most likely through voluntary agreements between private firms, government agencies, international institutions, and civil-society organizations, at the regional level (Najman and D'Orville 1995). Along similar lines, it would be interesting to explore the possibility of creating an international "gene tax," which would be levied on the profits made by international agricultural and pharmaceutical firms through the sale of products with genes from developing-country organisms.

Initiatives involving tradable permits are also on the table. The most notable of these is the "Clean Development Mechanism" agreed to at the Kyoto Conference of Parties to the United Nations Convention on Climate Change, which will allow developing countries to sell their unused carbon dioxide emissions rights to countries and firms that exceed their allowances. The first operations under this mechanism were under negotiation in 1998, with Costa Rica planning to sell about $20 million in emission offsets to private investors. Debt swaps and debt forgiveness will also play an increasing role in development finance, especially for the poorer countries. In addition, the Roman Catholic Pope has proposed that poor countries' debts be forgiven as part of the Year 2000 Jubilee, and several religious organizations are actively lobbying their governments to support such an initiative.

There is also discussion of creating regional and national trust funds with donations from private corporations, developed- and developing-country governments, foundations, and wealthy individuals. A few regional trust funds with a focus on specific themes will operate at a modest level during the first two decades of the 21st century. To a certain extent, the experience of "Counterpart Trust Funds," several of which were established in Latin America during the

1980s and 1990s with resources from bilateral debt swaps, provide small-scale examples of how regional trust funds might operate.

Wealthy businesspeople and artists are also becoming involved in international philanthropy to a growing extent. In the age of megamergers that make a few individuals incredibly rich, their example may draw still other wealthy persons to become more engaged in financing international development. Ted Turner's $1-billion gift to the United Nations, George Soros' hundreds of millions of dollars in contributions to Eastern European NGOs and academic organizations, Elton John's donation of more than $100 million (from royalties of his record in Lady Diana's memory) for the removal of landmines, and the tens of millions of dollars raised by rock musicians in support of causes as varied as famine relief in Africa and AIDS prevention indicate that the role of private giving is likely to grow in the near future. In addition, Microsoft's Bill Gates, the world's richest man in 1999, set up two foundations in recent years to give away hundreds of millions of dollars annually. One of these institutions, the William H. Gates Foundation, stands as the United States' sixth wealthiest foundation, with $5.2 billion in assets (Fortune 1999). Finally, there have also been proposals to establish lotteries to raise funds for international development. One such scheme links airline travel to card games and a lottery to raise funds for sustainable-development initiatives in developing countries.

Although private-investment flows and developed-country budget allocations will continue to dominate the scene of development finance and international cooperation, new financial mechanisms involving combinations of private investment, multilateral and bilateral lending, grants from foundations and individuals, and income from trust funds will acquire a growing importance in the early years of the 21st century. Combined with new organizational arrangements and identification of clusters of themes, these new schemes for mobilizing financial resources will radically alter the shape of development finance and international cooperation in the near future.

Concluding remarks: an arduous transition

A former high-level United Nations official once referred to development assistance in the following terms:

> An important experience, without precedent in modern history, is coming to an end. It will have lasted much less than was expected. Born in the midst of contradictions, it dissipates in ambiguity. It means renouncing an ambitious but ill-conceived enterprise. Its original noble intentions

have been progressively submerged by other considerations which, inevitably, have led to mutual recrimination and disillusion.

(Tibor Mende 1972, cited in Jaworski, 1994, p. 28)

The official was Tibor Mende, and the year was 1972. He was reflecting on the failure of development assistance to live up to the high expectations it had raised and on the perceived danger of its becoming an instrument of a new form of colonialism. Neither these hopes nor these fears were fully realized, but the quote underscores that development assistance has long been kept under close scrutiny.

If the demise of the development-cooperation experiment was prematurely announced in the early 1970s, might not the same be happening in the late 1990s? Probably not. In the first place, the transition from the 1960s to the 1970s did indeed see an "end" of sorts that signaled the full emergence of multilateral channels for development assistance and substantive changes in bilateral aid. Second, the magnitude, scope, and intensity of changes accompanying the emergence of the fractured global order in the late 1980s and the 1990s are much greater than those at any time during the last half century. Although it may end, not with a bang but a whimper (and maybe lots of whining), there is little doubt that the development-cooperation experiment as we have known it during the last five decades is coming to an end.

And yet, as motivations endure for private firms to invest in the developing world, for foundations, private philanthropy, and religious groups to reach beyond their home bases, and for rich countries to help the poor nations, development cooperation will continue its arduous process of transformation and evolve in directions corresponding more closely to the spirit of our times. Its main objective will be to bridge the multiple fractures defining the emerging global order. Although there are critics who see development assistance as widening, rather than bridging, these fractures, most of those concerned with improving the situation of the poor agree that development finance and international cooperation can play a significant and important role in the future. Therefore, it is not surprising that many proposals have already been put forward during the last few years to renew development cooperation.[18]

---

[18] Among the proposals advanced to reform development cooperation during the 1990s are those of Feinberg and Boylan (1991), Carnegie Commission on Science, Technology and Government (CCSTG 1992), Jaworski (1994), Serageldin (1993), Griffin and McKinley (1994), Hewitt (1994), Futures (1995), UNDP (1995a), Valderrama (1995), Van de Walle and Johnston (1996), Dollar and Pritchett (1998), and Overseas Economic Cooperation Fund of Japan and the World Bank (OECF and World Bank 1998).

Grant-making organizations, particularly private foundations, have a special role to play in the renewal of international development cooperation. In contrast to international financial institutions, which have to be conservative to preserve their financial standing, and bilateral cooperation agencies, which are instruments of foreign policy, private foundations can take greater risks, engage more readily in experimental programs, choose their areas of interest more freely, support initiatives for longer periods without having to show immediate results, and operate flexibly, without overbearing administrative or political constraints. They are also free from the private-sector need to show direct financial returns in the short term. Private foundations and development-cooperation agencies with considerable autonomy, such as IDRC, have demonstrated throughout their history the capacity for leadership in areas considered too risky, politically charged, or complex for the larger financial and technical-cooperation institutions, and, in doing so, they have been a catalyst for major global efforts (for example, the Green Revolution, contraceptive research, tropical diseases, science and technology policy, conflict prevention).

The transition to the post-Baconian age is a momentous period of human history in which reality is being reconfigured for all of us. In diverse ways and at diverse speeds, most societies are beginning to recognize that humanity has embarked on an uncertain transition toward something that cannot be visualized clearly as yet. Advances in knowledge during the last four centuries, particularly during the last five decades, have created remarkable opportunities to improve standards of living in ways undreamt of by our ancestors. But we need to devise new ways to take advantage of these opportunities for the benefit of all humanity. At this special time in history, when we are embarking on the transition to a post-Baconian age, conceptual advances must proceed hand in hand with institutional experimentation. This suggests the need for carefully designed large-scale interventions, or "institutional experiments," involving public, private, civil-society, academic, and international organizations to address the problems emerging as a result of the fractured global order.

A concerted international effort is needed to explore the meaning of development as Bacon's program becomes exhausted and as we enter the post-Baconian age. Although there are prominent analysts who view cultural conflicts as inevitable and possibly violent, institutionalized dialogue between cultures and civilizations can help to peacefully redefine what we mean by development and progress and devise ways of achieving them. Such dialogue is also essential to determining the direction of the initial steps to the design of a new program to guide human efforts in the decades and maybe centuries to come.

Finally, it is clear that these new times require a new style of leadership, much more flexible and capable of adaptation than the one we had during most of Hobsbawm's Short Twentieth Century, especially during the Cold War. To cope with the uncertainties, unsettling features, and anxieties of the transition to the post-Baconian age, as well as to take advantage of the extraordinary opportunities it offers, we need leaders who empower others and guide with a light touch, who are prepared to restrain their ambition and advance collectively by sharing power, and who are men and women of vision and practical imagination. They will be like the people the late, eminent social scientist, Eric Trist, described so well in calling for "resourceful, resilient people who can tolerate a lot of surprise and ambiguity emotionally while continuing to work on complex issues intellectually" (OCQWL 1982).

DEVELOPMENT COOPERATION AND CONFLICT PREVENTION

During the last half century, the international community has developed a system of institutions that has been quite successful in preventing and limiting interstate conflict. Between 1945 and 1995, there were only four military conquests that have endured and two successful wars of secession, and, for the first time in history, small states have been able to live without fear of conquest from larger and more powerful ones. Forced to fit within the straightjacket imposed by the Cold War, the various mechanisms established at the international level — the United Nations and its Security Council, regional political organizations (Organization of American States, Organization of African Unity), political–military alliances (North Atlantic Treaty Organization, the Warsaw Pact, South East Asia Treaty Organization), regional economic-integration agreements (European Union, European Free Trade Organization), the Bretton Woods institutions, and so on — managed to keep a lid on internal conflicts that threatened to spill across borders and upset the precarious balance characteristic of the East–West confrontation.

To a significant extent, the principle of noninterference in the internal affairs of other states — which was adhered to, at least on paper, by both East and West — also helped to contain interstate conflicts during the Cold War. However, with the end of that world order, symbolized by the fall of the Berlin Wall and the disappearance of the Soviet Union, civil wars and other violent conflicts have become more visible. Interventions to maintain international peace and security, as well as humanitarian interventions — usually under the aegis of the United Nations — have become more frequent and acceptable to the international community (Damrosch 1993; Ramón Chornet 1995; Stremlau 1996).

The end of the Cold War removed a filter that coloured our perceptions of internal conflicts, as well as expanding our range of vision to register many confrontations that could not be seen in the shadow of the East–West struggle. The

---

NOTE: THIS SECTION IS LARGELY BASED ON SAGASTI (1998) AND STREMLAU AND SAGASTI (1998).

pervasiveness, durability, and complexity of many violent-conflict situations —
which often combine historical grievances, ethnic allegiances, political ambitions,
religious loyalties, social disparities, and economic deprivation — became plainly
visible after the fall of the Berlin Wall. The convergence of ethnic diversity and
economic disparities, together with the presence of unrepresentative and repressive
governments unwilling or unable to allow sufficient political space to accommodate fears and grievances, can be particularly dangerous and explosive (Reinicke
1996; Bardhan 1997; Sagasti 1998).

The huge costs of violent conflicts, measured both in human lives and in
financial resources (which in the cases of El Salvador, Nicaragua, and Somalia
reached billions of US dollars), point to the obvious fact that it is much better to
prevent than to have to resolve conflicts. The cost-effectiveness of conflict prevention becomes obvious when one considers that about $2 billion was spent in
military operations in Somalia, primarily by the United States, to channel less than
$100 million of effective emergency relief. However, it is very difficult for the
international community to deal with something that has not happened as yet and
to pay attention, allocate political capital, and provide financial resources to
development activities that just might prevent widespread violence and deadly
conflict. Although the outbreak of violent conflict can quickly mobilize international action, especially if it takes place in a sensitive region of the world, the
more diffuse and long-term tasks of conflict prevention are seldom able to enlist
widespread support from many nations. This is particularly the case at a time
when severe cutbacks are occurring in financial resources for development assistance and cooperation.

Nevertheless, the laborious tasks of conflict prevention have prompted
several attempts to better understand the nature of violent conflicts and what can
be done to avoid them. Mohammed Sahnoun, who was the Special Envoy to
Somalia of the United Nations Secretary-General during the early 1990s, has provided a summary of the origins of some recent conflicts, showing the diversity and
complexity of their causes, also hinting at the wide range of interventions needed
to maintain peace in the troubled regions of the world (Table A1). The OECD's
DAC (DAC 1997a) issued a set of guidelines for development cooperation to deal
with violent conflicts taking place within, rather than between states, which mostly
occur within developing countries. After providing a framework for analyzing
conflicts, the guidelines focus on questions such as coordination within the
international community, the transition from humanitarian relief to development
interventions, the support to postconflict-recovery efforts, and the importance of
good governance and regional approaches to conflict prevention.

Table A1. Origins of deadly conflicts.

Violent conflicts have their own specific causes, identities, and characteristics. Some broad categories of the origins of potential and current conflicts are as follows:

- A failed process of integration in the creation of a nation-state (several crises in Central Asia, Chad, most Sahel countries, Somalia, and Uganda during its 8 years of civil war) (The absence of a national unifying factor, such as a social class or enlightened leadership, slows down the process, producing dangerous setbacks that may lead to civil wars.)

- A colonial legacy or a difficult decolonization process, linked mostly with the drawing of borders by colonial powers (Cameroon and Nigeria, Ghana and Togo, India and Pakistan, Israel and Palestine, the independence of Armenia, Azerbaijan, Eritrea, and Georgia)

- Liberation movements or social revolts later infected by the Cold War virus to become protracted conflicts (Afghanistan, Angola, Cambodia, El Salvador, Mozambique, Nicaragua, and Viet Nam)

- Ethnic tensions that lead to violent conflicts (Burundi and Rwanda, Liberia, Sri Lanka, and the former Yugoslavia) (Strong differences and traditional enmity between ethnic groups are compounded by historical factors, inadequate policies, and bad economic management. Power has usually been monopolized by a specific ethnic group, sometimes even a minority, that refuses to relinquish power for various reasons, including fear of revenge.)

- Conflicts of religious character (Algeria, Bosnia, Cyprus, India, Lebanon, Northern Ireland, the Philippines, and Sudan)

- Conflicts based in socioeconomic or political tensions (Central America, the Congo, Peru, Suriname, and the rise of fundamentalism in the Middle East and North Africa)

- The classic way of aggression prompted by the *esprit de grandeur* (the Iraqi invasion of Kuwait and the Iraq–Iran war) (Although more rare today, based on the experience of two world wars the UN Charter focused primarily on these conflicts.)

These categories can overlap, but by clarifying the diverse identities of crises, it may be possible to concentrate efforts for preventive action and conflict resolution. It may also lead to the isolation of aggravating factors, such as arms exports, foreign interference, ambitious leaders, damaged administrative and other infrastructures, weakened traditional processes of conciliation, and an often inadequate response to a humanitarian tragedy.

Source: Adapted from Sahnoun (1994).

The Carnegie Commission on Preventing Deadly Conflict (CCPDC 1997) distinguished between "structural" and "operational" tasks in preventive action. The former address the underlying root causes of conflict and aim at creating an environment that protects fundamental human rights, allows citizens to secure a livelihood, and provides opportunities for growth and development. The latter focus on measures applicable in the face of an immediate crisis to prevent the eruption of violent conflict. Guilmette (1995) suggested that there are six phases in the evolution of conflict situations — malaise, incipient crisis, denied conflict, open conflict, war, and reconciliation and reconstruction — each of which requires a different approach and calls for specific kinds of action. From the perspective of development assistance, these phases can be grouped into four overlapping periods: development interventions, diplomatic activities followed by military action, humanitarian aid, and return to development activities.[19]

Figure A1 suggests that during Guilmette's first three phases, in which malaise turns into crisis and then into denied conflict, there is a relatively long period during which development interventions, which belong to the category of structural prevention tasks, can play a significant role. Operational prevention tasks, which aim at reducing the risk factors and avoiding the escalation of conflict into war, are more appropriate to the shorter phases of denied and open conflict. If the situation deteriorates into war and deadly violence, subsequent efforts are needed to resolve the conflict and embark on postwar reconciliation and reconstruction.

It is clear that at every stage of the conflict cycle, there are opportunities for international organizations in general and for development-cooperation agencies in particular to play important roles. This is clearest during the postconflict reconstruction phase. Once peace has been restored, either through military victory or a negotiated settlement, the surviving governmental authorities are typically eager for international assistance. Outside powers usually support the involvement of bilateral agencies and multilateral institutions to ensure the consolidation of peace and to avoid the temptation to resume violence.

The mistakes of the harsh settlement of World War I were not repeated in 1945, and the international financial institutions can claim a share of the credit for the hugely successful reconstruction of the Axis powers and their reintegration into the global economy as full democratic partners of the United States and its European allies. Therefore, it is not surprising that in the aftermath of the Cold War the UNDP, bilateral aid agencies, and multilateral development banks have been under increasing pressure to assist reconciliation and reconstruction in Africa, the Balkans, Latin America, Southeast Asia, and elsewhere.

In his first speech to the 1995 joint annual meetings of the World Bank and the International Monetary Fund, James Wolfensohn, the President of the World Bank, stated that his immediate priorities for the coming months included anticipating and being organized for "post-conflict economic development programs, when war is replaced by peace" (Wolfensohn 1995, p. 13). The World Bank has been deeply involved in postwar reconstruction since the mid-1980s and

---

[19] For other accounts of the violent-conflict cycle and the different types of interventions that may be appropriate at different stages, see Damrosch (1993), Ball and Halevy (1996), Colletta et al. (1996), Goodpaster (1996), and Sisk (1996).

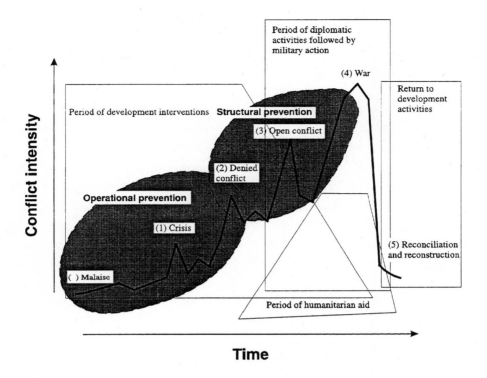

Figure A1. The evolution of violent conflict. Source: Adapted from Guilmette (1995).

begun to establish a comprehensive set of policies in this field (Holtzman 1995). The DAC (1997a, pp. 53–72) developed a series of recommendations for bilateral aid agencies, in which it argued that "the objective of post-conflict reconstruction is not to return to pre-crisis situations but to lay the foundations for peace and sustainable development." The range of suggested interventions cover questions such as restoring a working capacity for economic management, restoring internal security and the rule of law, fostering the reemergence of civil society, reintegrating uprooted populations, demobilization and social reintegration of former combatants, and clearing land mines.

However, during armed conflict, international development agencies must generally keep to the sidelines. In situations in which the United Nations has mandated sanctions, bilateral agencies and multilateral institutions may have an important role to play in helping to alleviate the economic disruption that these measures cause to neighbouring states or the traditional trading partners of the target state. Such assistance, when coordinated effectively with the United Nations, serves a humanitarian purpose while helping to strengthen the sanctions regime by reducing incentives to break sanctions and by signaling the international resolve to render them effective (Stremlau 1996).

Once the parties to a dispute indicate a willingness to enter into negotiations and a peace process gets under way, development assistance can contribute more directly to helping to resolve the crisis through conflict resolution and peace-building (Ball and Halevy 1996). To help in conflict resolution, international actors focus on identifying the common ground between the parties in the conflict, apply diplomatic pressures to reach a settlement, and offer technical assistance in specific areas under negotiation, such as the separation of forces. Following the cessation of hostilities, diplomacy, financial support, and technical assistance focus on strengthening political institutions, reforming internal and external security arrangements, and revitalizing the economy and the nation's social fabric. All of this should lead to the establishment of a government with sufficient domestic and international legitimacy to operate effectively and to put the peace agreements into practice.

During the peacebuilding phase, development-cooperation programs should aim at strengthening political institutions, consolidating external and internal security, and promoting economic and social revitalization. Ideally, all of this should facilitate the development of a new political culture by fostering tolerance, respect for the views of others, habits of compromise, and collaborative modes of behaviour. The design and delivery of such programs requires financial flexibility, contingency planning, sensitivity to local conditions, and a keen awareness of the possibilities and limitations of external interventions, attributes which have not been particularly characteristic of multilateral financial institutions and their staff. Considering that the World Bank and the regional development banks must play a crucial financial-intermediation role — which requires them to be highly attuned to the requirements and perceptions of international capital markets for their regular lending programs and to the reactions of taxpayers in donor countries for their concessional aid funds — it may be too much to expect them to also excel in the highly political tasks of conflict prevention. Similar considerations apply to bilateral assistance agencies, even though they can be more flexible and responsive when the national interest of one or more donor country may be at stake in resolving conflicts in particular developing regions.

The difficulties involved in postconflict transitions were clearly pointed out by Ball and Halevy:

> Because of the profound mistrust and animosity generated by civil wars,
> the extreme institutional weakness characteristic of post-conflict countries,
> and the destruction visited on society and the economy by armed conflict,

repairing the ravages of war is an arduous, complex and lengthy process. For countries moving simultaneously from highly exclusionary political systems to more open and participatory forms of government and from centralized economic systems to economies responsive to market forces, the process is even more complicated. It is unrealistic to expect that peace in these countries will be consolidated in less than a generation. What is more, it is by no means inevitable that, once set in motion, the peace process will succeed.

(Ball and Halevy 1996, pp. 65–66)

These considerations led Ball and Halevy to suggest that "donors should maintain the maximum flexibility in how they define the programs they will support. Based on its institutional comparative advantage, in discussion with the broadest possible range of local actors, and in close coordination with other members of the international development community, each donor should devise a long-term plan for building peace" (Ball and Halevy 1996, p. 66). For example, it is reasonable to argue that multilateral development banks should circumscribe their direct involvement in the postconflict transitions to the provision of technical and financial assistance for the rehabilitation of economic, social, and government infrastructure, allowing other institutions — United Nations agencies, regional bodies, bilateral aid agencies, NGOs — to assist in damage and needs assessment, building confidence, clearing mines, demobilization, resettlement, and other related activities of a more political nature.

Building peace is a fragile undertaking that may experience setbacks that reignite deadly violence. Grant-making institutions, such as the United Nations agencies, bilateral development-assistance agencies, private foundations, and some NGOs, can take greater risks and be flexible with the use of the resources at their disposal, but international financial institutions must be quite conservative to preserve the integrity of their financial-intermediation role. This argues for limiting the involvement of multilateral financial institutions to situations in which there is a relatively high degree of certainty that there will be no relapse into violent conflict and leaving involvement in more uncertain situations to organizations that can afford to take greater risks. In particular, a more appropriate interinstitutional division of labour would seek an enhanced role for the UNDP, as well as closer partnerships between this United Nations agency and the multilateral development banks (UNDP n.d.)

In advancing the cause of conflict prevention bilateral aid agencies and multilateral institutions will have to confront other politically sensitive issues that lie beyond the failed or failing state. For example, arms merchants, supported in many cases by governments that are also influential donors and members of the boards of international financial institutions, are taking advantage of the highly profitable arms trade to put modern weapons in the hands of parties involved in civil wars and violent ethnic conflicts throughout the world. Automatic rifles, mines, guided missiles, and grenades, among other weapons, are providing the means for indiscriminate killing in contexts in which self-restraint appears to have all but vanished.

A comprehensive approach to conflict prevention should also consider how to combine diplomatic initiatives with the support of local propeace organizations in the field and the eventual use of military force to defuse potential deadly conflicts. Moreover, it should incorporate issues such as the need to limit the spread of nuclear and other unconventional weapons, as well as to take into account the connections between drug traffic, organized crime, and illegal weapons trade, on the one hand, and the spread of deadly conflicts, on the other. The military dimension of conflict prevention has been clearly articulated in a report written by Gustav Daniker for the United Nations Institute for Disarmament Research:

> With all due respect for the benevolent activities of the Red Cross and its succour to war victims, for other humanitarian organizations and individual initiatives, it is time now to shift the emphasis of efforts for peace and the well-being of as many people as possible clearly towards *prevention*. The following future work sharing is conceivable: trouble spots have to be contained and crises have to be controlled — a matter for the bodies of collective security and a flexible, but sufficient apparatus of power that has to be placed at their disposal; wars and open conflicts have to be possibly prevented — a task for the political leadership of all nations concerned, of the U.N. [United Nations], of military alliances and regional groupings. If the worst comes to the worst, open aggression has to be countered by means of a skilful operational conduct, a well-controlled use of force and long-term strategic goals in such a way that a minimum loss of lives and material damage is caused — a matter for those who are responsible on the spot, i.e. the generals. If prevention has failed, the military intervention should at least be conducive to the restoration of a state of peace which is acceptable to all.
>
> (Daniker 1995, p. 124, his emphasis)

These considerations highlight the rather complex nature of conflict prevention, one of the several new demands placed on the system of institutions involved in international financing and development cooperation.

APPENDIX 2

ACRONYMS AND ABBREVIATIONS

ACP	African, Caribbean and Pacific countries
ADEA	Association for the Development of Education in Africa
AfDB	African Development Bank
AsDB	Asian Development Bank
AsDF	Asian Development Fund
CAP	Common Agricultural Policy [European Union]
DAC	Development Assistance Committee [OECD]
EBRD	European Bank for Reconstruction and Development
ECDPM	European Center for Development and Policy Management
EEC	European Economic Community
ESAF	Enhanced Structural Adjustment Facility [IMF]
GATT	General Agreement on Tariffs and Trade
GDP	gross domestic product
GNP	gross national product
GWP	Global Water Partnership
HIPC	Heavily Indebted Poor Countries trust fund [World Bank]
IBRB	International Bank for Reconstruction and Development [World Bank]
IDA	International Development Association
IDB	Inter-American Development Bank
IDRC	International Development Research Centre
IMF	International Monetary Fund
NGO	nongovernmental organization
ODA	official development assistance
OECD	Organisation for Economic Co-operation and Development
OPEC	Organization of Petroleum Exporting Countries
UNDP	United Nations Development Programme
UNICEF	United Nations Children's Fund
UNRISD	United Nations Research Institute for Social Development
USAID	United States Agency for International Development
WTO	World Trade Organization

REFERENCES

Ackoff, R. 1970. A concept of corporate planning. John Wiley & Sons, New York, NY, USA.

——— 1981. Creating the corporate future. John Wiley & Sons, New York, NY, USA.

——— 1994. The democratic corporation. John Wiley & Sons, New York, NY, USA.

Adams, P. 1994. The World Bank's finances: an international S&L crisis. The Cato Institute, Washington, DC, USA. Policy Analysis Series No. 215.

Albert, M. 1991. Capitalisme contre capitalisme. Éditions du Seuil, Paris, France.

Alexander, N. 1998. Accountable to whom? The World Bank and its strategic allies. Bread for the World Institute, Washington, DC, USA.

Alvarez, C. 1979. Homo faber: technology and culture in India, China and the West: 1500 to the present day. Allied Publishers, Bombay, India.

Amin, S. 1992. Empire of chaos. Monthly Review Press, New York, NY, USA.

Anderson, D. 1994. The drug money maze. Foreign Affairs 73(4), 94–108.

Annerstedt, J. 1993. Measuring science, technology and innovation. In Salomon, J-J.; Sagasti, F.; Sachs, C., ed., The uncertain quest: science, technology and development. United Nations University, Tokyo, Japan. pp. 96–125.

Arndt, H.W. 1987. Economic development: the history of an idea. University of Chicago Press, Chicago, IL, USA; London, UK.

Athanasiou, T. 1996. Divided planet: the ecology of rich and poor. Little, Brown and Company, New York, NY, USA.

Ball, N.; Halevy, T. 1996. Making peace work: the role of the international development community. Overseas Development Council, Washington, DC, USA.

Bandow, D.; Vasquez, I., ed. 1995. Perpetuating poverty: the World Bank, the IMF and the developing world. Cato Institute, Washington, DC, USA.

Bardhan, P. 1997. Method in the madness? A political-economy analysis of the ethnic conflicts in less developed countries. World Development, 25(9), 1381–1398.

Barney, G.O., ed. 1980. The Global 2000 report to the President. Government Printing Office, Washington, DC, USA.

Barney, G.O.; Blewett, J.; Barney, K.R. 1993. Global 2000 revisited: what shall we do? The Millennium Institute, Arlington, VA, USA.

Bauer, P.T. 1984. Reality and rhetoric. Harvard University Press, Cambridge, MA, USA.

Beckford, J.A., ed. 1986. New religious movements and rapid social change. Sage–United Nations Educational Scientific and Cultural Organization, London, UK.

Beer, S. 1966. Decision and control. John Wiley & Sons, London, UK.

———— 1972. Brain of the firm. Herder and Herder, New York, NY, USA.

Bezanson, K. 1999. The implications of the East Asian crisis for development effectiveness. Institute of Development Studies, Sussex, UK.

Bezanson, K.; Sagasti, F. 1995. The elusive search: development and progress in the transition to a new century. International Development Research Centre, Ottawa, ON, Canada.

Bhagwati, J. 1998. The capital myth. Foreign Affairs, 77(3), 7–16.

Bhalla, A. 1993. Technology choice and development. In Salomon, J-J.; Sagasti, F.; Sachs, C., ed., The uncertain quest: science, technology and development. United Nations University, Tokyo, Japan. pp. 412–445.

Blustein, P. 1997. Foreign aid that doesn't seem to persuade. The Washington Post, 22 May 1997.

Bossuy, J. 1998. Decentralised co-operation: a marginal enterprise, tomorrow conventional wisdom? Liaison South, 6, 2–5.

Brauman, R. 1995. L'action humanitaire. Flammarion, Paris, France.

Bressand, A.; Distler, C. 1995. La planète relationnelle. Flammarion, Paris, France.

Brown, L. 1984. State of the world: 1984. W.W. Norton, New York, NY, USA.

Brown, M. 1993. Ethnic conflict and international security. Princeton University Press, Princeton, NY, USA.

Brown, S. 1992. International relations in a changing global system: toward a theory of the world policy. Westview Press, Boulder, CO, USA.

Bruno. M. 1995. Foreword. *In* Global economic prospects and the developing countries. World Bank, Washington, DC, USA.

Bury, J.B. 1960. The idea of progress. Dover Press, New York, NY, USA.

Bushrui, S.; Auman, I.; Laszlo, E., ed. 1993. Transition to a global society. Oneworld Publications, Oxford, UK.

Business Week. 1998a. Global capitalism, R.I.P.? Business Week, 14 Sep 1998, pp. 40–42.

———— 1998b. Piece by piece, a plan? Business Week, 19 Oct 1998, pp. 38–40.

BWI (Bread for the World Institute). 1997. New products. News and Notices for World Bank Watchers, 19 (Dec.). http://www.bread.org/bfwi/bwp/news/19/2.html

———— 1998. More power to the IMF? News and Notices for World Bank Watchers, 20 (Apr), 1–18.

Cairncross, F. 1991. Costing the earth. The Economist Books, London, UK.

Carnegie Quarterly. 1993. Reducing the nuclear danger. Carnegie Quarterly (summer–fall).

———— 1996. Heading off a new nuclear nightmare: illicit trade in nuclear materials, technology, and know-how. Carnegie Quarterly (spring–summer).

Carnoy, M.; Castells, M.; Cohen, S.S.; Cardoso, F.H. 1993. The new global economy in the information age: reflections on our changing world. Pennsylvania State University Press, University Park, PA, USA.

Carothers, T. 1997. Democracy without illusions. Foreign Affairs, 76(1), 85–99.

Carson, R. 1962. Silent spring. Houghton Mifflin, Boston, MA, USA.

Carter, A.; Deutch, J.; Zelikow, P. 1998. Catastrophic terrorism. Foreign Affairs, 77(6), 80–94.

Cassen, R. 1994. Does aid work? Clarendon Press, Oxford, UK.

Castells, M. 1996. The rise of the network society. Blackwell Publishers Inc., Cambridge, MA, USA.

CCPDC (Carnegie Commission on Preventing Deadly Conflict). 1997. Preventing deadly conflict. Carnegie Corporation of New York, New York, NY, USA.

CCSTG (Carnegie Commission on Science, Technology and Government). 1992. Partnerships for global development: the clearing horizon. Carnegie Corporation, New York, NY, USA.

Cetron, M.; Davies, O. 1991. Crystal globe: the haves and the have-nots of the new world order. St. Martin's Press, London, UK.

CGG (Commission on Global Governance). 1995. Our global neighborhood. Oxford University Press, New York, NY, USA.

Churchman, C.W. 1971. The design of inquiring systems: basic concepts of systems and organizations. Basic Books, New York, NY, USA.

———— 1979. The systems approach and its enemies. Basic Books, New York, NY, USA.

Cleveland, H. 1993. Birth of a new world. Jossey Bass, San Francisco, CA, USA.

Colby, M. 1990. Environmental management in development: the evolution of paradigms. World Bank, Washington, DC, USA. Discussion Paper No. 80.

Colletta, N.J.; Kostner, M.; Wiederhofer, I. 1996. The transition from war to peace in sub-Saharan Africa. World Bank, Washington, DC, USA.

Connelly, M.; Kennedy, P. 1994. Must it be the rest against the west? The Atlantic Monthly, Dec 1994, pp. 61–91.

Cooper, R. 1993. Is there a new world order? *In* Sato, S.; Taylor, T., ed., Prospects for global order. Royal Institute of International Affairs, London, UK.

Coquery-Vidrovitch, C.; Hemery, D.; Piel, J., ed. 1988. Pour une histoire du développement. États, sociétés, développement. L'Harmattan, Paris, France.

Council of Europe. 1981. Technology and democracy: impacts of technological change on European society and civilization. *In* Collected papers of the Fifth Parliamentary and Scientific Conference held in Helsinki, 2–5 June 1981. Council of Europe, Strasbourg, France.

Cornia, G.; Jolly, R.; Stewart, F., ed., 1987. Adjustment with a human face. Oxford University Press, New York, NY, USA.

Cowen, M.P.; Shelton, R.W. 1996. Doctrines of development. Routledge, London, UK.

CPBN (Central Planning Bureau of the Netherlands). 1992. Scanning the future: a long-term scenario study of the world economy 1990–2115. SDU Publishers, The Hague, Netherlands.

Culpeper, R. 1993. The regional development banks. North–South Institute, Ottawa, ON, Canada.

DAC (Development Assistance Committee). 1989. Development cooperation in the 1990s. Organisation for Economic Co-operation and Development, Paris, France.

———— 1993. Development cooperation. Organisation for Economic Co-operation and Development, Paris, France.

———— 1994. Development cooperation. Organisation for Economic Co-operation and Development, Paris, France.

———— 1995a. Development cooperation. Organisation for Economic Co-operation and Development, Paris, France.

———— 1995b. Development partnerships in a new global context. Organisation for Economic Co-operation and Development, Paris, France. 4 May 1995.

———— 1996. Development cooperation. Organisation for Economic Co-operation and Development, Paris, France.

———— 1997a. DAC guidelines on conflict, peace and development co-operation. Organisation for Economic Co-operation and Development, Paris, France.

———— 1997b. Development cooperation. Organisation for Economic Co-operation and Development, Paris, France.

———— 1998. Development cooperation. Organisation for Economic Cooperation and Development, Paris, France.

Daedalus. 1989. A world to make: development in perspective. Daedalus, 118(1). Special issue.

Dahlman, C. 1994. The third industrial revolution: trends and implications for developing countries. Paper presented at the Foro Nacional International Conference on the New International Order, 13–14 Apr, Rio de Janeiro, Brazil.

Dahrendorf, R. 19803. Oportunidades vitales: notas para una teoría social y política. Espasa-Calpe, Madrid, Spain.

Damrosch, L.F., ed. 1993. Enforcing restraint: collective intervention in internal conflicts. Council on Foreign Relations, New York, NY, USA.

Daniker, G. 1995. The guardian soldier: on the nature and use of the armed forces. United Nations Institute for Disarmament Research, Geneva, Switzerland.

Dasgupta, P. 1993. An inquiry into well being and destitution. Clarendon Press, Oxford, UK.

Davidian, Z.N. 1994. Economic disparities among nations: a threat to survival in a globalized world. Oxford University Press, Oxford, UK.

De Almeida, M.O. 1972. Economic development and the preservation of the environment. *In* Development and environment. Mouton, Paris, France.

DID (Department for International Development, United Kingdom). 1997. Eliminating world poverty: a challenge for the 21st century. London, November 6, 1997.

Desai, M. 1995. Global governance. *In* Desai, M.; Redfern, P., ed., Global governance: ethics and economics of the world order. Pinter, London, UK. pp. 6–21.

Development Committee. 1996. Serving a changing world: report of the Task Force on Multilateral Development Banks. Washington, DC, USA.

Diamond, L. 1995. Promoting democracy in the 1990's: actors and instruments, issues and imperatives. Carnegie Commission on Preventing Deadly Conflict, Carnegie Corporation of New York, New York, NY, USA.

Diamond, L.; Plattner, M.F., ed., 1993. The global resurgence of democracy. Johns Hopkins University Press, Baltimore, MD, USA.

Dollar, D.; Pritchett, L. 1998. Rethinking aid: what works, what doesn't, and why. World Bank, Washington, DC, USA.

DRI (Development Research Insights). 1998. Private good = public gain? Has ethical pressure squared the circle? Development Research Insights, 28.

Drucker, P. 1968. The age of discontinuity. Harper and Row, New York, NY, USA.

———— 1993. Post-capitalist society. Harper Business, New York, NY, USA.

———— 1994. The age of social transformation. The Atlantic Monthly, Nov 1994, pp. 53–80.

Durning, A. 1992. How much is enough: the consumer society and the future of the earth. Worldwatch Institute, Washington, DC, USA.

Eatwell, J. 1996. International financial liberalization: the impact on world development. Office of Development Studies, United Nations Development Program, New York, NY, USA. Discussion Paper Series No. 12.

ECDPM (European Centre for Development Policy Management). 1996. The future of EU–ACP relations beyond the Lomé IV Convention. http:\\www.ecdpm.org; INTERNET. Cited Jun 1996.

Eggertsson, T. 1997. The old theory of economic policy and the new institutionalism. World Development, 25(8), pp. 1187–1203.

Emmerij, L. 1989. An introductory statement. *In* Emmerij, L., ed., One world or several? OECD Development Center, Organisation for Economic Co-operation and Development, Paris, France. pp. 25–29.

Emery, F.E.; Trist, E.L. 1965. The causal texture of organizational environments. Human Relations, 18, 21–32.

Fajnzylber, F. 1992. Technical progress, competitiveness and institutional change. *In* Bradford, C., ed., Strategic options for Latin America in the 1990's. Organisation for Economic Co-operation and Development, Paris, France. pp. 101–140.

Falk, R. 1995. On humane governance: toward a new global politics. Pennsylvania State University Press, University Park, PA, USA.

————— 1992. Explorations at the edge of time. Temple University Press, Philadelphia, PA, USA.

FAO (Food and Agriculture Organization). 1996. Food security assessment, FAO, Rome, Italy.

Farnham, A. 1994. Global — or just globaloney? Fortune, 17 Jun 1994, pp. 97–100.

Feinberg, R.E.; Boylan, E. 1991. Modular multilateralism: North–South economic relations in the 1990s. Overseas Development Council, Washington, DC, USA.

Feldstein, M. 1998. Refocusing the IMF, Foreign Affairs, 77(2), 20–33.

Fernández-Arias, E.; Montiel, P.J. 1996. The surge in capital inflows to developing countries: an analytical overview. The World Bank Economic Review, 10(1), 51–80.

Ferrer, A. 1996. Historia de la globalización. Fondo de Cultura Económica, Mexico D.F., Mexico.

Foreign Affairs. 1997. The Marshall Plan and its legacy. Foreign Affairs, 76(3), 157–221.

Fortune. 1999. How Bill Gates invests his money. Fortune, 15 Mar 1999, pp. 30–41.

Freeman, C.; Hagedoorn, J. 1992. Globalization of technology: Global Perspective 2010 and the tasks for science and technology. Science Policy Research Unit, University of Sussex, Brighton, UK.

Freeman, C.; Pérez, C. 1988. Structural cycles of adjustment, business cycles and investment behavior. In Dosi, G.; Freeman, C.; Nelson, R.; Silverberg, G.; Soete, L., ed., Technical change and economic theory. Frances Pinter, London, UK.

Friberg, M.; Hettne, B. 1988. Local mobilization and world system politics. International Social Science Journal, 40(3), 341–360.

Friend, J.K.; Jessop, W.N. 1969. Local government and strategic choice. Tavistock Publications, London, UK.

Futures. 1995. Futures 27(2). The United Nations at fifty: policy and financing alternatives. Special issue.

Giddens, A. 1990. The consequences of modernity. Polity Press, Cambridge, UK.

Goldsmith, E. 1996. The last word: family, communit, democracy. *In* Mander, J.; Goldsmith, E., ed., The case against the global economy and for a turn toward the local. Sierra Club Books, San Francisco, CA, USA.

Goodpaster, A.J. 1996. When diplomacy is not enough: managing multinational military interventions. Carnegie Commission on Preventing Deadly Conflict, Carnegie Corporation of New York, NY, USA.

Gordon, D.F.; Gwin, C. 1998. Poor country debt relief: taking the hiccups out of HIPC. ODC Viewpoint, Overseas Development Council, Washington, DC, USA.

Gordon, L. 1977. Foreword. *In* From Marshall Plan to global interdependence: new challenges for the industrialized nations. Organisation for Economic Co-operation and Development, Paris, France. pp. 5–11.

Goulet, D.; Hudson, M. 1971. The myth of aid: the hidden agenda of the development reports. International Documentation on the Contemporary Church–Orbis Books, New York, NY, USA.

Green, R. 1995. Reflections on attainable trajectories: reforming global economic institutions. *In* Griesgraber, J.M.; Gunter, B., ed., Promoting development. Pluto Press, London, UK. pp. 38–81.

Greider, W. 1997. One world ready or not: the manic logic of global capitalism. Simon & Schuster, New York, NY, USA.

Griesgraber, J.M. 1994. Rethinking Bretton Woods: towards equitable, sustainable and participatory development. Center of Concern, Washington, DC, USA.

Griesgraber, J.M.; Gunter, B., ed. 1995. Promoting development: effective global institutions for the twenty-first century. Pluto Press, London, UK.

Griffin, K.; McKinley, T. 1994. A new framework for development cooperation. United Nations Development Programme, Human Development Report Office, New York, NY, USA. Occasional Papers No. 11.

Groupe de Lisbonne. 1995. Limites à la compétitivité: pour un nouveau contrat mondial. Éditions La Découverte, Paris, France.

Guilmette, J.-H. 1995. Beyond emergency assistance: early warning, conflict prevention and decision-making. Canadian International Development Agency, Ottawa, ON, Canada.

Hagen, E.E. 1962. A framework for analyzing economic and political change. *In* Development of emergent countries: an agenda for research. The Brookings Institution, Washington, DC, USA. pp. 1–38.

Hampden-Turner, C.; Trompenaars, A. 1993. The seven cultures of capitalism. Currency–Doubleday, New York, NY, USA.

Hancock, G. 1989. Lords of poverty. The Atlantic Monthly Press, New York, NY, USA.

Hayter, T. 1971. Aid as imperialism. Pelican Books, London, UK.

Held, D., ed. 1993. Prospects for democracy. Stanford University Press, Stanford, CT, USA.

Helleiner, G.K. 1997. External conditionality, local ownership and development. University of Toronto, Toronto, ON, Canada. Mimeo, May.

Heller, A. 1981. Renaissance man. Schocken Books, New York, NY, USA.

Hensman, R. 1971. Rich against poor. Pelican Books, London, UK.

Hettne, B.; Wallensteen, P. 1978. Emerging trends in development theory. Swedish Agency for Research Cooperation with Development Countries, Stockholm, Sweden.

Hewitt, A. 1994. Crisis or transition in foreign aid. Overseas Development Institute, London, UK.

Hirschman, A. 1995. A propensy to self-subversion. *In* Rodwin, Ll.; Schön, D., ed., Rethinking the development experience: essays provoked by the work of Albert O. Hirschman. The Brookings Institution, Washington, DC, USA; The Lincoln Institute of Land Policy, Cambridge, MA, USA.

Hoagland, J. 1997. Why the Marshall Plan worked. The Washington Post, 8 Jun 1997.

Hobsbawm, E. 1994. The age of extremes: a history of the world, 1914–1991. Pantheon Books, New York, NY, USA.

Hogan, M.J., ed. 1992. The end of the Cold War: its meaning and implications. Cambridge University Press, Cambridge, UK.

Holm, H.-H.; Sorensen, G. 1995. Whose world order? Uneven globalization and the end of the cold war. Westview Press, Boulder, CO, USA.

Holmberg, J. 1998. Knowledge-intensive networks for development: the case of the Global Water Partnership. Human Systems Management, 17, 37–49.

Holt, P. 1997. Like welfare, foreign aid shouldn't go endlessly. The Christian Science Monitor, 5 Jun 1997. p. 7.

Holtzman, S. 1995. Post-conflict reconstruction. Social Policy and Resettlement Division, Environment Department, World Bank, Washington, DC, USA. Work in Progress Series.

Hopkins, T.K.; Wallerstein, I., ed. 1980. Processes of the world-system. Sage Publications, Beverly Hills, CA, USA.

———— 1996. The clash of civilizations and the remaking of world order. Simon & Schuster, New York, NY, USA.

Huntington, S.P. 1993. The clash of civilizations? Foreign Affairs, 72(3) 22–49.

———— 1996, The clash of civilizations and the remaking of world order. Simon & Schuster, New York, NY, USA.

———— 1999. The lonely superpower. Foreign Affairs, 78(2), 35–49.

ICVA (International Council of Volunteer Agencies). 1996. The reality of aid—1996. Earthscan Publications, London, USA.

IDRC (International Development Research Centre). 1991. Empowerment through knowledge: the strategy of the International Development Research Centre. IDRC, Ottawa, ON, Canada.

———— 1993a. Agenda 21: abstracts, reviews, commentaries. IDRC, Ottawa, ON, Canada.

———— 1993b. A guide to Agenda 21: issues, debates and Canadian initiatives. IDRC, Ottawa, ON, Canada.

IDS (Institute of Development Studies). 1998. CAP reforms: will developing countries benefit? IDS, Sussex, UK. Policy Briefing Issue No. 11, Feb.

IILS (International Institute for Labour Studies). 1994. The ILO and Bretton Woods: a common vision? IILS, Geneva, Switzerland.

Inglehart, R. 1990. Culture shift in advanced industrial society. Princeton University Press, Princeton, NJ, USA.

IPCC (International Panel of Climate Change). 1996. Climate change 1995: economic and social dimensions of climate change. Cambridge University Press, Cambridge, UK.

Jaguaribe, H. 1998. Mercosul e as alternativas para a ordem mundial. Paper presented at Seminario sobre Escenarios Mundiales, 18–19 Mar 1998, Centro de Estudios Estrategicos, Brasilia, Brazil.

Jaguaribe, H. 1994. A view from the Southern Cone. *In* Lowenthal, A.; Treverton, G., ed., Latin America in a new world. Westview Press, Boulder, CO, USA. pp. 53–64.

Jaki, S. 1974. Science and creation. Scottish Academic Press, Edinburgh, Scotland.

Jaworski, H. 1994. Hacia nuevas formas de relacion con el Sur del mundo. Servicio Central de Publicaciones del Gobierno Vasco, Vitoria-Gasteiz, Spain.

Jenkins, R. 1997. Special relationships. Foreign Affairs, 76(3), 157–221. Special Section on the Marshall Plan.

Johnston, D.; Sampson, C., ed. 1994. Religion: the missing dimension of statecraft. Oxford University Press, New York, NY, USA.

Jonas, H. 1984. The imperative of responsibility. University of Chicago Press, Chicago, IL, USA.

Jones, B. 1995. Sleepers, wake! Oxford University Press, Oxford, UK.

Julien, C. 1995. Breve radiographe d'une fracture sociale. Le Monde Diplomatique, Jun 1995.

Kaplan, R.D. 1996. The ends of the earth: a journey to the frontiers of anarchy. Vintage Books, New York, NY, USA.

———— 1997. Was democracy just a moment? The Atlantic Monthly, Dec 1997, 55–80.

Kapstein, E.B. 1994. Governing the global economy: international finance and the state. Harvard University Press, Cambridge, MA, USA.

Kapur, D. 1998. The IMF: a cure or a curse? Foreign Policy, 111, 114–129.

Kapur, D.; Webb, R. 1994. The evolution of the multilateral development banks. *In* Proceedings of the UNCTAD conference on the International Monetary and Financial System:

Developing Country Perspectives, Cartagena, Colombia, 18–20 April 1994. United Nations Conference on Trade and Development, New York, NY, USA.

Katada, S. 1997. Two aid hegemons: Japanese–US interaction and aid allocation to Latin America and the Caribbean. World Development, 25(6), 931–945.

Keller, W.; Nolan, J.E. 1997–98. The arms trade: business as usual? Foreign Policy, 109, 113–125.

Kennedy, P. 1993. Preparing for the twenty-first century. Random House Publishers, New York, NY, USA.

Kennen, P.B., ed. 1994. Managing the world economy: fifty years after Bretton Woods. Institute for International Economics, Washington, DC, USA.

Kincaid, D.A.; Portes, A., ed. 1994. Comparative national development: society and economy in the new global order. University of North Carolina Press, Chapel Hill, NC, USA.

Kirkpatrick, J. 1979. Dictatorships and double standards. Commentary, 68(5).

Korten, D.C. 1995. When corporations rule the world. Kumarian Press, Inc., West Hartford, CT, USA; Berret-Koehler Publishers, San Francisco, CA, USA.

Krugman, P. 1995. The fall and rise of development economics. In Rodwin, Ll.; Schön, D., ed., Rethinking the development experience: essays provoked by the work of Albert O. Hirschman. The Brookings Institution, Washington, DC, USA; The Lincoln Institute of Land Policy, Cambridge, MA, USA.

Lagos, R.; Muñoz, H. 1999. The Pinochet dilemma. Foreign Policy, 114, pp. 26–39.

Leandro, J.; Schaefer, H.; Frontini, G. 1999. Towards a more effective conditionality: an operational framework. World Development, 27(2), 285–299.

Lerner, D. 1962. The passing of the traditional society. The Free Press, Glencoe, IL, USA.

Lesourne, J. 1989. Development at a major turning point in time. In Emmerij, L., ed., One world or several? OECD Development Center, Organisation for Economic Co-operation and Development, Paris, France.

Lewis, J.; Kallab, V., ed. 1986. Development strategies reconsidered. Overseas Development Council, Washington, DC, USA.

Liepietz, A. 1992. Towards a new economic order: postfordism, ecology and democracy. Oxford University Press, New York, NY, USA.

Lind, M. 1995. To have and have not: notes on the progress of the american class war. Harper's Magazine, Jul 1995, pp. 35–47.

Linowes, D.F. 1990. Speech delivered to the White House Conference on Libraries and Information Services, Oct 1990.

Luttwak, E. 1998. Our prudent, incoherent China policy. Harper's Magazine, Jul 1998, pp. 19–23.

Machlup, F. 1980. Knowledge: its creation, distribution and economic significance. Vol. 1: Knowledge and knowledge production. Princeton University Press, Princeton, NJ, USA.

Machlup, F. 1962. The production and distribution of knowledge in the United States. Princeton University Press, Princeton, NJ, USA.

Macy, J. 1986. Dharma and development: religion as a resource in the Sarvodaya self-help movement. Kumarian Press, West Harford, CT, USA.

Maddison, A. 1995. Monitoring the world economy 1820–1992. OECD Development Centre, Organisation for Economic Co-operation and Development, Paris, France.

Mander, J.; Goldsmith, E., ed. 1996. The case against the global economy and for a turn toward the local. Sierra Club Books, San Francisco, CA, USA.

Marshall, G.C. 1947. Against hunger, poverty, desperation and chaos. Foreign Affairs, 76(3), 161. The Harvard Address in the Special Section on the Marshall Plan.

Mathews, J.T. 1989. Redefining security. Foreign Affairs, 68(2), 162–177.

———— 1997. Power shift. Foreign Affairs, 76(1), 50–66.

McClelland, D. 1962. The achieving society. D. Van Nostrand Co., Princeton, NJ, USA.

Meier, G.; Seers, D., ed. 1984. Pioneers in development. Oxford University Press, New York, NY, USA.

Meadows, D.H.; Meadows, D.L.; Randers, J.; Behrens, W.W. 1972. The limits to growth. Potomac Associates, Washington, DC, USA.

Mearsheimer, J. 1990. Why we will soon miss the Cold War. The Atlantic Monthly, Aug 1990, pp. 35–50.

Mende, T. 1972. De l'aide a la reconlonisation : les leçons d'un echec. Editions du Seuil, Paris, France.

Méndez, R. 1995. Paying for peace and development. Foreign Policy, 100, 18–32.

Miller, R., ed. 1992. Aid as peacemaker. Carleton University Press, Ottawa, ON, Canada.

Minton-Beddoes, Z. 1995. Why the IMF needs reform. Foreign Affairs, 74(3), 123–133.

Mkandawire, T.; Soludo, C. 1999. Our continent, our future: African perspectives on Structural Adjustment. International Development Research Centre, Ottawa, Canada.

Montoliu-Muñoz, M. 1990. New avenues for development thinking. Background paper for the Workshop on Development Thinking, 11 Jun 1990, Washington, DC, USA. Strategic Planning Division, World Bank, Washington, DC, USA.

Morrison, M. 1983. In praise of paradox. The Episcopalian, Jan.

Myers, N. 1989. Environment and security. Foreign Policy, 80, 23–41.

———— 1993. Ultimate security: the environmental basis of political stability. W.W. Norton, New York, NY, USA.

Najman, D.; d'Orville, H. 1995. Towards a new multiculturalism: innovative financing mechanisms for internationally agreed programmes. Independent Commission on Population and Quality Life, New York, NY, USA.

Nef, J. 1995. Human security and mutual vulnerability. International Development Research Centre, Ottawa, ON, Canada.

Nelson, R., ed. 1993. National innovation systems: a comparative analysis. Oxford University Press, Oxford, UK.

Nerfin, M. 1987. Neither prince nor merchant: citizen. Development Dialogue, 1987 (1), 170–195.

Nielsen, W. 1972. The big foundations. Columbia University Press, New York, NY, USA.

Nisbet, R. 1980. History of the idea of progress. Basic Books, New York, NY, USA.

Nolan, J.E., ed. 1994. Cooperation and security in the 21st century. The Brookings Institution, Washington, DC, USA.

North, D. 1990. Institutions, institutional change and economic performance. Cambridge University Press, New York, NY, USA.

Nussbaum, M.; Sen, A., ed. 1993. The quality of life. Clarendon Press, Oxford, UK.

Nye, J. 1994. Comment to Fred Bergstein's "Managing the World Economy of the Future." *In* Kennen, P., ed., Managing the world economy fifty years after Bretton Woods. Institute for International Economics, Washington, DC, USA. pp. 375–380.

O'Brien, C.C. 1994. On the eve of the millennium. House of Anansi Press, Concord, ON, Canada.

OCQW (Ontario Centre for the Quality of Working Life). 1982. A lecture given at the Ontario Centre for the Quality of Working Life, Oct.

Ohno, I. 1990. Donor's aid motives: implications for multilateral concessional aid. Strategic Planning Division, World Bank, Washington, DC, USA.

Ohlin, G. 1994. The negative net transfers of the World Bank. Proceedings of the INCTAD Conference on the International Monetary and Financial System: Developing Country Perspectives, Cartagena, Colombia, 18–20 April 1994. United Nations Conference on Trade and Development, New York, NY, USA.

Oman, C. 1994. Globalization and regionalization: the challenge for developing countries. OECD Development Centre, Organisation for Economic Co-operation and Development, Paris, France.

Oman, C.; Wignaraja, G. 1991. The postwar evolution of development thinking. Organisation for Economic Co-operation and Development, New York, NY, USA.

O'Neill, M.J. 1993. The roar of the crowd: how television and people power are changing the world. Simon and Schuster, New York, NY, USA.

Otsubo, S. 1996. Globalization: a new role for developing countries in an integrating world. World Bank, Washington, DC, USA. Policy Research Working Paper No. 1628.

ODC (Overseas Development Council). 1992. Humanitarian intervention in a new world order. ODC, Washington, DC, USA. Policy Focus Series, No.1.

OECF (Overseas Economic Cooperation Fund of Japan); World Bank. 1998. A new vision of development cooperation for the 21st century. Proceedings of a symposium held in Tokyo, Sep 1997. OECF, Tokyo, Japan.

Ozbekhan, H. 1971. Planning and human action. *In* Weiss, P.A., ed., Hierarchically organized systems in theory and practice. Hafner, New York, NY, USA.

Paarlberg, R.; Liption, M. 1991. Changing missions at the World Bank. World Policy Journal (summer), 475–497.

Patel, I.G. 1994. Global economic governance: some thoughts on our current discontents. Asian Development Bank Lecture, 28 Feb 1994. Asian Development Bank, Manila, Philippines.

Pearson Report. 1969. Partners in development. Report of the Commission of International Development (under the chairship of Lester Pearson). Praeger, New York, NY, USA.

Pérez, C. 1989. Technical change, competitive restructuring, and institutional reform in developing countries. Strategic Planning and Review, World Bank, Washington, DC, USA. Discussion paper No. 4, Dec.

Perlmutter, H.V. 1965. Towards a theory and practice of social architecture. Tavistock Publications, London, UK.

Peterson, P. 1999. Gray dawn: the global aging crisis. Foreign Affairs, 78(1), 42–55.

Picciotto, R. 1995. Putting institutional economics to work: from participation to governance. World Bank, Washington, DC, USA. World Bank Discussion Papers No. 304.
Plihon, D. 1995. Les mutations du systeme financier international. Cahiers Français, 269 (Jan–Feb), 11–17. La Economie Mondiale.

Putnam, R. 1993. Making democracy work. Princeton University Press, Princeton, NJ, USA.

Raffer, K. 1998. The Tobin tax: reviving a discussion. World Development, 26(3), 529–538.

Ramón Chornet, C. 1995. ¿Violencia necesaria?: la intervención humanitaria en derecho internacional. Editorial Trotta, Madrid, Spain.

Rath, A.; Herber-Copley, B. 1993. Green technologies for development: transfer trade and cooperation. International Development Research Centre, Ottawa, ON, Canada.

Redding, G. 1997. China's school of business. The Economist: World in 1998 Issue, pp. 92, 97.

Reid, E., ed. 1995. HIV and AIDS: the global inter-connection. Kumarian Press, West Harford, CT, USA.

Reinicke, W.H. 1996. Can international financial institutions prevent internal violence? The sources of ethno-national conflict in transitional societies. In Chayes, A.; Handler Chayes, A, ed., Preventing conflict in the post-communist world: mobilizing international and regional organizations. The Brookings Institution, Washington, DC, USA. pp. 281–338.

Righter, R. 1995. Utopia lost: the United Nations and world order. Twentieth Century Fund Press, New York, NY, USA.

Rodrik, D. 1997. Has globalization gone too far? Institute for International Economics, Washington, DC, USA.

Rosell, S., ed. 1993. Governing in an information society. Institute for Research on Public Policy, Montréal, PQ, Canada.

———— ed. 1994. Changing maps. Carleton University Press, Ottawa, ON, Canada.

Rostow, W.W. 1971. Politics and the stages of growth. Cambridge University Press, Cambridge, UK.

———— 1997. Lessons of the plan. Foreign Affairs, 76(3), 157–221. Special Section on the Marshall Plan.

Rothschild, E. 1995. Psychological modernity in historic perspective. In Rodwin, L.; Schon, D., ed., Rethinking the development experience. The Brookings Institution, Washington, DC, USA.

Rowbotham, S.; Mitter, S., ed. 1994. Dignity and daily bread: new forms of economic organizing among poor women in the Third World and the First. Routledge, London, UK.

Rodgers, G.; Gore, C.; Figuereido, J.B. 1995. Social exclusion: rhetoric, realities, responses. International Institute for Labour Studies, Geneva, Switzerland.

Rotberg, R. 1996. A fitness program for the UN. The Christian Science Monitor, 18 Dec 1996.

Rubin, E. 1997. An army of one's own. Harper's Magazine, Feb 1997, pp. 44–55.

Ryan, S.J. 1995. Culture, spirituality, and economic development. International Development Research Centre, Ottawa, ON, Canada.

Rwegasira, D.; Kifle, K. 1994. Regional development banks and the objectives of the Bretton Woods institutions. *In* Proceedings of the UNCTAD Conference on the International Monetary and Financial System: Developing Country Perspectives, Cartagena, Colombia, 18–20 April 1994. United Nations Conference on Trade and Development, New York, NY, USA.

Sachs, I. 1977. Pour une économie politique du developpement. Flammarion, Paris, France.

———— 1980. Statégies de l'écodéveloppement. Éditions Économie et Humanisme, Paris, France.

Sack, R. 1998. Strengthened partnerships through "structured informality." Association for the Development of Education in Africa Newsletter, 10(2), 4–5.

Sagasti, F.R. 1979. Towards endogenous science and technology for another development. Development Dialogue, 1979 (1), 13–23.

———— 1980. The two civilizations and the process of development. Prospects, 10(2), 123–139.

———— 1988. Reinterpreting the concept of development from a science and technology perspective. *In* Baark, E., ed., Man, nature and technology. Methuen, London, UK. pp. 37–55.

———— 1989a. The 1990s: decade of the emerging fractured global order. UNITAR Newsletter, 1(2), 7–10.

———— 1989b. International cooperation in a fractured global order. Impact of Science on Society, 155, 207–211.

———— 1990. International cooperation in a fractured global order. Futures, 22(4), 417–421.

——— 1994. Development cooperation in a fractured global order. FORO Nacional/Internacional–AGENDA: Perú, Lima, Peru.

——— 1995. Knowledge and development in a fractured global order. Futures, 27(6), 591–610.

——— 1997a. Development, knowledge, and the Baconian age. World Development, 25(10), 1561–1568.

——— 1997b. The twilight of the Baconian age. FORO Nacional/Internacional–AGENDA: Perú, Lima, Peru.

——— 1998. Development, exclusion and conflict prevention: beyond the "nothing left to lose" syndrome. Carnegie Commission on Preventing Deadly Conflict, Washington, DC, USA.

Sagasti, F.R.; Colby, M. 1993. Eco-development and perspectives on global change from developing countries. In Choucri, N., ed., Global accord: environmental challenges and international responses. MIT Press, Cambridge, MA, USA. pp. 175–203.

Sagasti, F.R.; Patrón, P.; Lynch, N.; Hernández, M. 1995. Democracia y buen gobierno. Apoyo–AGENDA: Perú, Lima, Peru.

Sahnoun, M. 1994. An environment for peace. IDRC Reports: Global Conflict and Path to Peace, 22(3), 4–6.

Sakamoto, Y., ed. 1994. Global transformation: challenges to the state system. United Nations University Press, Tokyo, Japan.

Salam, A. 1991. Science, technology and science education in the development of the South. The Third World Academy of Sciences, Trieste, Italy.

Sanford, J. 1997. Alternative ways to fund the International Development Association (IDA). World Development, 25(3), 297–310.

Santos, B. 1995. Toward a new common sense. Routledge, New York, NY, USA.

Sassen, S. 1999. Global financial centers. Foreign Affairs, 78(1), 75–87.

Saul, J.R. 1995. The unconscious civilization. House of Anansi Press Limited, Concord, ON, Canada.

Schmitz, G.; Gillies, D. 1992. The challenge of democratic development: sustaining democratization in developing societies. North–South Institute, Ottawa, ON, Canada.

Schon, D. 1971. Beyond the stable state. Temple Smith, London, UK.

Schwab, K.; Smadja, C. 1995. Power and policy: the new economic world order. *In* Ohmae, K., ed., The evolving global economy. Harvard Business Review Books, Boston, MA, USA. pp. 108–109.

Schwartz, P. 1991. The art of the long view. Currency–Doubleday, New York, NY, USA.

Sen, A. 1983. Development: which way now? The Economic Journal, Dec, 1983, pp. 745–762.

———— 1984. Resources, values and development. Basil Blackwell, Oxford, UK.

———— 1992. Inequality reexamined. Harvard University Press, Cambridge, MA, USA.

———— 1994. Population: delusion and reality. The New York Review of Books, 22 Sep 1994, pp. 62–71.

Senge, P.M. 1990. The art and practice of the learning organization. Doubleday, New York, NY, USA.

Serageldin, I. 1993. Development partners: aid and cooperation in the 1990s. Swedish International Development Agency, Stockholm, Sweden.

Serageldin, I.; Taboroff, J., ed. 1994. Culture and development in Africa. World Bank, Washington, DC, USA. Environmental Sustainable Development Proceedings Series No. 1.

Shrum, W.; Shenhav, Y. 1995. Science and technology in less developed countries. *In* Vasanoff, S.; et al. ed., Handbook of science and technology studies. Sage Publishers, Newbury Park, UK. pp. 633–635.

Simpson, G. 1998. World Bank memo depicts diverted funds, corruption in Jakarta. The Wall Street Journal, 19 Aug 1998.

Singer, H. 1995. Rethinking Bretton Woods from a historical perspective. *In* Griesgraber, J.M.; Gunter, B., ed., Promoting development. Pluto Press, London, UK. pp. 1–22.

Singer, M.; Wildavsky, A. 1993. The real world order: zones of peace zones of turmoil. Chatham House Publishers, Chatham, NJ, USA.

SELA (Sistema Económico Latinoamericano [Latin American Council]) 1997. The agenda of the industrialized countries and the international economic organizations. Paper presented at the XXIII Regular Meeting of the Latin American Council. SELA, Puerto España, Trinidad y Tobago. http://lanic.utexas.edu/project/sela/consejo

Sisk, T.D. 1996. Power sharing and international mediation in ethnic conflicts. United States Institute of Peace, Washington, DC, USA.

Slater, P.; Bennis, W. 1990. Democracy is inevitable. Harvard Business Review (Sep–Oct), 167–176.

Slater, R.O.; Schutz, B.M.; Dorr, S.R., ed. 1993. Global transformation and the Third World. Lynne Rienner Publishers, Boulder, CO, USA.

Slaughter, A.M. 1997. The real new world order. Foreign Affairs, 76(5), pp. 183–197.

———— 1999. The long arm of the law. Foreign Policy, 114, 34–35.

Smillie, I. 1995. The alms bazaar. International Development Research Centre, Ottawa, ON, Canada.

Smith, K; Berg, D. 1987. Paradoxes of group life. Jossey Bass, San Francisco, CA, USA.

Soete, L.; ter Weel, B. 1998. Cybertax. Futures, 30(9), 853–871.

Solomon, R. 1991. Partners in prosperity: the report of the Twentieth Century Fund Task Force on the International Coordination of National Economic Policies. Priority Press–The Brookings Institution, Washington, DC, USA. Background paper.

Sopko, J.F. 1996–97. The changing proliferation threat. Foreign Policy, 105, 16.

Soros, G. 1998–99. Capitalism's last chance? Foreign Policy, 113, 55–66.

South Centre. 1996. For a strong and democratic United Nations: a South perspective on UN reform. South Centre, Geneva, Switzerland.

Speth, J.G. 1994. Building a new UNDP: agenda for change. Address presented to the United Nations Development Programme Executive Board, United Nations Secretariat, New York, NY, USA, 17 Feb.

———— 1995. Administrator's introduction. In Building a new UNDP: a strategic planning framework. Office of Evaluation and Strategic Planning, United Nations Development Programme, New York, NY, USA. pp. 4–6.

Staley, E. 1954. The future of underdeveloped countries. Council of Foreign Relations, New York, NY, USA.

Stallings, B., ed. 1995. Global change, regional response. Cambridge University Press, Cambridge, UK.

Stavrianos, L.S. 1981. Global rift. William Morrow & Co., New York, NY, USA.

Sterling, C. 1994. Thieves' world: the threat of the new global network of organized crime. Simon and Schuster, New York, NY, USA.

Stern, E. 1991. Evolution and lessons of adjustment lending. *In* Thomas, V.; Chhibber, A.; Dailami, M.; de Meio, J., ed., Restructuring economies in distress: policy reform and the World Bank. Oxford University Press, Oxford, UK. p. 4.

Stewart, F. 1995. The governance and mandates of the international financial institutions. North–South Institute; IDRC, Ottawa, ON, Canada.

Stiglitz, J. 1995. Whither socialism? MIT Press, Cambridge, MA, USA.

Streeten, P. 1998. Globalization: threat or salvation? *In* Bhalla, A., ed., Globalization, growth and marginalization. International Development Research Centre, Ottawa, Canada. pp. 14–47.

Stremlau, J. 1989. Security for development in a post-bipolar world. Strategic Planning and Review Department, World Bank, Washington, DC, USA.

———— 1996. Sharpening international sanctions: toward a stronger role for the United Nations. Carnegie Corporation, New York, NY, USA.

Stremlau, J.; Sagasti, F. 1998. Preventing a deadly conflict: does the World Bank have a role? Carnegie Corporation of New York, New York, NY, USA.

Sunkel, O. 1995. Uneven globalization, economic reform, and democracy: a view from Latin America. *In* Holm, H.H.; Sorensen, G., ed., Whose world order? Uneven globalization and the end of the Cold War. Westview Press, Boulder, CO, USA. pp. 43–67.

Takahashi, K., ed. 1992. Reconstruction of a new global order: beyond crisis management. The Japanese Committee for a Post-Cold War Global System; Sasakawa Peace Foundation, Tokyo, Japan.

Tamames, R. 1991. Un nuevo orden mundial. Espasa-Calpe, Madrid, Spain.

Taylor, A.M.; Taylor, A.M. 1992. Poles apart. International Development Research Centre, Ottawa, ON, Canada.

The Christian Science Monitor. 1997. Liberty's ebb and flow. The Christian Science Monitor, 9 May 1997.

The Economist. 1994. War of the worlds: a survey of the global economy. The Economist, 1 Oct 1994.

———— 1996. All our tomorrows: a survey of the economics of ageing. The Economist, 17 Jan 1996.

———— 1997a. The future of warfare. The Economist, 8 Mar 1997, pp. 21–24.

———— 1997b. The Economist, 12 Apr 1997, p. 54. Editorial.

———— 1998. Capitals of capital: a survey of financial centers. The Economist, 9 May 1998. Special supplement.

The South Letter. 1998. The South Letter, 4(32).

The Washington Post. 1997. New trade policy for Africa unveiled. The Washington Post, 18 Jun 1997.

Trist, E.; Emery, F.; Murray, H., ed. 1997. The social engagement of social science. Vol. III: The socio-ecological perspective. University of Pennsylvania Press, Philadelphia, PA, USA.

Ulbaek, S. 1989. Changing motivations for development cooperation. World Bank, Washington, DC, USA. Internal document.

UNCED (United Nations Conference on Environment and Development). 1992. Agenda 21: programme of action for sustainable development. United Nations, New York, NY, USA.

UNCTAD (United Nations Conference on Trade and Development). 1996. World investment report 1996. UNCTD, New York, NY, USA.

UNDP (United Nations Development Programme). 1993. UNDP: a charter for change. Transition Team of UNDP Staff, United Nations, New York, NY, USA.

———— 1994a. Future of the United Nations Development Programme: initiatives for change. Report of the Administrator, Executive Board of the United Nations Development Programme and of the United Nations Population Fund. United Nations, New York, USA. Document DP/994/30, 23 May.

———— 1994b. Human development report 1994. United Nations, New York, NY, USA.

———— 1995a. Building a new UNDP: a strategic planning framework. Office of Evaluation and Strategic Planning, United Nations, New York, USA.

———— 1995b. Strategic management in UNDP. Office of Evaluation and Strategic Planning, United Nations, New York, USA.

———— 1996. Human development report 1996. United Nations, New York, NY, USA.

———— n.d. Beyond aid: questions and answers for a post-Cold War world. United Nations, New York, NY, USA.

UNESCO (United Nations Educational, Scientific and Cultural Organization). 1982. Different theories and practices of development. UNESCO, Paris, France.

United Nations. 1991. World population prospects. United Nations, New York, NY, USA.

———— 1993. Report on the world social situation — 1993. United Nations, New York, NY, USA.

———— 1994. Agenda for development. United Nations, New York, NY, USA.

UNRISD (United Nations Research Institute for Social Development). 1995. States of disarray: the social effects of globalization. United Nations, Geneva, Switzerland.

Urquhart, B.; Childers, E. 1990. A world in need of leadership: tomorrow's United Nations. Development Dialogue, 1990 (1–2).

USAID (United States Agency for International Development). 1998. USAID strategic plan. http:\\www.usaid.gov

Valderrama, M. 1995. Perú y América Latina en el nuevo panorama de la cooperación internacional. CEPES, Lima, Peru.

Van de Walle, N.; Johnston, T. 1996. Improving aid to Africa. Overseas Development Council, Washington, DC, USA.

Van Nieuwenhuijze, C.A.O., ed. 1972. Development: the western view. Institute of Social Studies, The Hague, Paris, France.

Vickers, G. 1965. The art of judging: a study of policy making. Basic books, New York, NY, USA.

Walker, R.B.J., ed. 1984. Culture, ideology, and world order. Westview Press, Boulder, CO, USA; London, UK.

Wallerstein, I. 1974. The modern world-system I. Academic Press, New York, NY, USA.

———— 1983. Historical capitalism and capitalist civilization. Verso, London, UK.

———— 1995. After liberalism. The New Press, New York, NY, USA.

WCED (World Commission on Environment and Development). 1987. Our common future. Oxford University Press, New York, NY, USA.

Weatherford, J. 1994. Savages and civilization: who will survive? Random House, New York, NY, USA.

Williamson, J. 1990. Latin American adjustment: how much has happened? Institute for International Economics, Washington, DC, USA.

Wolfensohn, J. 1995. World Bank Annual Meetings speech, 10 Oct. World Bank, Washington, DC, USA.

———— 1996. Address at a luncheon of the 1818 Society of World Bank Retirees. 7 Mar 1996. World Bank, Washington, DC, USA.

Work in Progress. 1998. Water for sustainable growth. Work in Progress, 15(2).

World Bank. 1989. Strategic agenda. Strategic Planning Division, World Bank, Washington, DC, USA.

———— 1991. World development report 1991: the challenge of development. World Bank, Washington, DC, USA.

———— 1992a. Development: the governance dimension. World Bank, Washington, DC, USA.

———— 1992b. World development report 1992: development and the environment. Oxford University Press, Oxford, UK.

———— 1993. The east asian miracle. Oxford University Press, New York, NY, USA.

———— 1995. World development report 1995: workers in an integrating world. Oxford University Press, Oxford, UK.

———— 1996a. Annual report 1996. World Bank, Washington, DC, USA.

———— 1996b. World debt tables 1996. World Bank, Washington, DC, USA.

———— 1996c. World development report 1996: from plan to market. World Bank, Washington, DC, USA.

———— 1997a. Internal World Bank report on corruption in Indonesia. World Bank, Washington, DC, USA, Aug.

———— 1997b. Private capital flows to developing countries. World Bank, Washington, DC, USA.

———— 1997c. The strategic compact: renewing the bank's effectiveness to fight poverty. World Bank, Washington, DC, USA.

———— 1997d. World development report 1997: the state in a changing world. Oxford University Press, Oxford, UK.

———— 1998. World development report 1998: knowledge and information for development. Oxford University Press, Oxford, UK.

Wright, R. 1986. Sacred rage: the wrath of militant Islam. Simon and Schuster, New York, NY, USA.

Zakaria, F. 1997. The rise of illiberal democracy. Foreign Affairs, 76(6), 22–43.

About the Authors

Francisco Sagasti is the director of the AGENDA: Perú program of activities at FORO Nacional/Internacional, an institution created to promote democratic governance and to foster dialogue and consensus on critical development issues. In addition to holding various academic, private-sector, and government-advisory positions in Peru and in other countries, he has been Chief of Strategic Planning and senior advisor at the World Bank; visiting professor at the Wharton School of Finance, University of Pennsylvania; and chair of the United Nations Advisory Committee on Science and Technology for Development. He holds a PhD from the University of Pennsylvania and engineering degrees from the National Engineering University in Lima, Peru. Dr Sagasti is the author or editor of 18 books and monographs, the latest of which are *The Uncertain Quest: Science, Technology and Development* (with Celine Sachs and Jean-Jacques Salomon) (Tokyo: United Nations University, 1993); *Democracy and Good Government* (with Pepi Patrón, Nicolás Lynch, and Max Hernández) (Lima: Apoyo–AGENDA: Perú, 1995); and *Preventing Deadly Conflict: Does the World Bank Have a Role?* (with John Stremlau) (New York: Carnegie Commission for the Prevention of Deadly Conflict, 1998). He is also the author of 150 academic papers and contributes frequently to newspapers and magazines in Lima, Peru.

Gonzalo Alcalde is a research associate at FORO Nacional/Internacional and has been involved in the AGENDA: Perú program of activities since 1995. He has also been an assistant analyst at Peru's Ministry of Economics and Finance. Mr Alcalde holds an MA from the Patterson School of Diplomacy and International Commerce at the University of Kentucky and has contributed to FORO Nacional/Internacional–AGENDA: Perú publications on social policy, poverty, and international cooperation.